Diversity Management in the UK

Routledge Research in Employment Relations

SERIES EDITORS: RICK DELBRIDGE AND EDMUND HEERY,
Cardiff Business School, UK.

1. Social Partnership at Work
Carola M Frege

2. Human Resource Management in the Hotel Industry
Kim Hoque

3. Redefining Public Sector Unionism
UNISON and the Future of Trade Unions
Edited by Mike Terry

4. Employee Ownership, Participation and Governance
A Study of ESOPs in the UK
Andrew Pendleton

5. Human Resource Management in Developing Countries
Pawan S Budhwar and Yaw A Debrah

6. Gender, Diversity and Trade Unions
International Perspectives
Edited by Fiona Colgan and Sue Ledwith

7. Inside the Factory of the Future
Work, Power and Authority in Microelectronics
Alan Macinlay and Phil Taylor

8. New Unions, New Workplaces
A Study of Union Resilience in the Restructured Workplace
Andy Danford, Mike Richardson and Martin Upchurch

9. Partnership and Modernisation in Employment Relations
Edited by Mark Stuart and Miguel Martinez Lucio

10. Partnership at Work
The quest for radical organizational change
William K. Roche and John F. Geary

11. European Works Councils
Pessimism of the intellect optimism of the will?
Edited by Ian Fitzgerald and John Stirling

12. Employment Relations in Non-Union Firms
Tony Dundon and Derek Rollinson

13. Management, Labour Process and Software Development
Reality bytes
Edited by Rowena Barrett

14. A Comparison of the Trade Union Merger Process in Britain and Germany
Joining Forces?
Jeremy Waddington, Marcus Kahmann and Jürgen Hoffmann

15. French Industrial Relations in the New World Economy
Nick Parsons

16. Union Recognition
Organising and bargaining outcomes
Edited by Gregor Gall

17. Towards a European Labour Identity
The Case of the European Work Council
Edited by Michael Whittall, Herman Knudsen and Fred Huijgen

18. Power at Work
How Employees Reproduce the
Corporate Machine
Darren McCabe

**19. Management in the Airline
Industry**
Geraint Harvey

20. Trade Unions in a Neoliberal World
British Trade Unions under New Labour
Gary Daniels and John McIlroy

21. Diversity Management in the UK
Organizational and Stakeholder
Experiences
Anne-marie Greene and Gill Kirton

Diversity Management in the UK

Organizational and Stakeholder Experiences

**Anne-marie Greene
and Gill Kirton**

Routledge
Taylor & Francis Group
LONDON AND NEW YORK

First published 2009
by Routledge
711 Third Avenue, New York, NY 10017

Simultaneously published in the UK
by Routledge
2 Park Square, Milton Park, Abingdon, Oxfordshire OX14 4RN

Routledge is an imprint of the Taylor and Francis Group, an informa business

First issued in paperback 2015

© 2009 Anne-marie Greene & Gill Kirton

Typeset in Sabon by IBT Global.

Library of Congress Cataloging-in-Publication Data
Greene, Anne Marie.
    Diversity management in the UK : organizational and stakeholder experiences / Anne-Marie Greene and Gill Kirton.
        p. cm. — (Routledge research in employment relations ; 21)
    Includes bibliographical references and index.
    1. Diversity in the workplace—Great Britain. 2. Diversity in the workplace.
I. Kirton, Gill. II. Title.
    HF5549.5.M5G74 2009
    658.3008'0941—dc22
                                                    2008047300

ISBN 978-0-415-43176-7 (hbk)
ISBN 978-1-138-87943-0 (pbk)
ISBN 978-0-203-86764-8 (ebk)

Contents

List of Tables   ix
Acknowledgements   xi

1   Introduction   1

2   Understanding Diversity Management   25

3   The Contexts of Diversity Management   45

4   Diversity Management in the Public Sector   65

5   Diversity Management in the Private Sector   90
    BY DEBORAH DEAN

6   Diversity Practitioner Perspectives   115

7   Line-Management Involvement in Diversity Management   138

8   Employee Experiences of Diversity Management   164
    BY CHRIS CREEGAN

9   Trade Union Experiences of Diversity   186

10 Experiencing Diversity Management: The Value of a
    Stakeholder Perspective   211

Notes   233
Bibliography   235
About the Authors and Contributors   251
Index   253

Tables

1.1	Stakeholder Participants at ServiceCo	17
1.2	Stakeholder Participants at PSO	18
1.3	Organizations Participating in the Research	20
1.4	Demographic Characteristics of Participants	21
2.1	Example Definitions of Diversity Management	32
2.2	Differences Between Principles of EO and DM	33
3.1	Equality Strands Covered by British Legislation	51
3.2	Employment Tribunal Statistics	52
3.3	Employment Tribunal Success/Compensation 2006–2007	53
4.1	Staff Breakdown by Gender November 2007	74
4.2	Staff Breakdown by Ethnic Origin April 2001	74
4.3	Staff Breakdown by Ethnic Origin November 2007	74
4.4	Staff with Disabilities November 2007	74
4.5	Benchmarks for Women by Band within PSO	79
4.6	Benchmarks for BME Staff by Band within PSO	79
5.1	Staff Breakdown by Gender	98
5.2	Staff Breakdown by Ethnicity	98
5.3	Staff Breakdown by Age	99
5.4	Staff Breakdown by Length of Service	99
6.1	Characteristics of Diversity Practitioners	118

Acknowledgements

The authors would like to thank all those stakeholder participants who gave up precious time to be involved in our research. We owe a particular debt to the key gatekeepers at ServiceCo and PSO who were instrumental in delivering access to their organizations. In addition, we would like to recognise the contribution made by Deborah Dean and Chris Creegan in working with us on the project. Finally, we acknowledge the funding provided by the European Social Fund (ESF) for the research project.

1 Introduction

THE CONTEXT FOR THE BOOK

Traditionally equal opportunities policies (EOPs) have been the main organizational tool used to tackle gender and race discrimination. However, over the last 10 years or so a diversity discourse, originating in the USA, has become more prominent in the UK. This recognizes broader dimensions of diversity including less visible bases of difference. Employers are exhorted to develop policy to harness workforce diversity towards business goals. From the diversity perspective, EOPs, with their emphasis on the social justice case for equality, are viewed as being less able to meet the social and economic challenges of the new millennium (Kandola and Fullerton 1998). Many advocates within the Human Resource Management (HRM) field suggest that diversity management (DM) is a more effective means of achieving equality for all. Moreover, it is clear from the global diversity literature that the diversity concept has taken hold in most of the industrialized world, including mainland Europe, Scandinavia, Australia, New Zealand and Canada.

However, although there are now a number of good practice guides and theoretical explorations, we argue that little is known about DM in *practice* in the UK. In particular, lack of knowledge about the processes and outcomes of DM means that there are significant areas of potential difficulty when implementing diversity policies and, more importantly, in achieving real diversity gains that contribute to business outcomes. An area of concern often cited by both academics and practitioners is that while senior commitment to diversity is often present, difficulties are found in implementing policies at local team and line management levels. However, once again, studies that look beyond the senior and policy-making level to the level of those at the 'coal face' who have to implement and who are affected by, the policies, are very thin on the ground.

This was the context of our successful bid to the European Social Fund (ESF), which funded our research project—*The Involvement of Stakeholders in Diversity Management: The way forward for equality policy and practice?*—which ran from 2003 to 2006. This project aimed to contribute to knowledge and understanding of DM in the UK by exploring equality and diversity policy and practice in a range of public and private sector organizations. A key objective was to investigate DM specifically at the level of organizational policy and practice, exploring the initiatives and measures, the processes involved in developing and implementing these, and views of the implementation and outcomes delivered. Moreover, for reasons which we discuss later in this chapter, we were particularly concerned to understand the role of what we termed 'stakeholder involvement' in DM—which groups and individuals within the organization were involved in developing and implementing organizational policy? This stakeholder perspective also meant including within the research the widest possible group of organizational members. However, our industrial relations perspective means that we placed special attention on gaining the views of non-management employees and trade union representatives, whose voices are often unheard in diversity debates.

In the context of an emerging debate about whether a global concept of diversity is possible or even desirable, the aim of this book is to chronicle the ways that UK organizations in the public and private sectors are responding to the diversity concept and the ways that different organizational stakeholders experience DM. A key part of this is a presentation of findings from our ESF research project. While some of these findings have already been the subject of journal publications (Greene et al 2007; Kirton and Greene 2006, 2007; Kirton et al 2006, 2007), this book provided us with the opportunity to present the research more broadly, providing space to offer the detail that really brings the qualitative data alive, and therefore we believe it provides a valuable medium for understanding DM in context.

THEORETICAL AND CONCEPTUAL FRAMEWORK

It is important to establish the theoretical and conceptual framework that underpinned the writing of the book, and the research that is presented in it, so as to provide a context for the approach we took to both the methods and data analysis and the structure of the book. This framework covers two main areas: first, our position with regard to the industrial relations field, and, second, our position with regard to equality and diversity.

Industrial Relations: Standing Outside the 'Malestream'

There is now a fairly established critique of the industrial relations field that attests to its gender blindness (see for example Forrest 1993; Dickens 1997; Wacjman 2000; Pocock 2000; Hansen 2002; Greene 2003; Kirton 2006; Healy et al 2006). It should be noted that while there have been changes over the last decade (Healy et al 2006), industrial relations arguably continues to be a field that is dominated by male researchers engaged in the study of men. Furthermore, these are often accounts about white men—industrial relations is also a field that is criticized for being blind to the effects of ethnicity (Holgate et al 2006; Bradley 1999). With direct relevance to the study of equality and diversity, therefore, it is easy to claim that the voices of those facing the most disadvantage in the labour market are often missing or ignored within mainstream (or what Forrest (1993) terms 'malestream') academic industrial relations. A number of factors explain this (see Danieli 2006 for a useful summary) but with relevance to our own research approach discussed later in this chapter, certain factors stand out as particularly significant. First, research on traditional male-dominated industries and occupations dominates the field; second, structures, systems and institutions are emphasized at the expense of social processes (both formal and informal); and third, there is an over-reliance on quantitative research methods.

Mainstream industrial relations research has focused on the institutional relationships between employers and trade unions with particular emphasis on collective bargaining. Thus research has been based in areas of work where trade union representation and collective bargaining coverage are high, namely on manufacturing and male manual worker regimes (Rubery and Fagan 1995; Forrest 1993). Wacjman (2000: 183) further discusses how what is classified as of interest in mainstream industrial relations has therefore reflected masculine priorities and privilege. It is clear that the areas of the labour market covered by trade unions continue to be those which are male dominated (Kersley et al 2006). Thus, huge numbers of women home-, tele-, domestic and self- employed workers are rendered invisible.

Industrial relations has also been criticized for the primacy placed on institutions and structures at the expense of social processes (Kelly 1998). Such a criticism has not immediately been connected to the neglect of discussion of different social groups. However, feminist critiques have certainly begun to link this to the absence of women in industrial relations research, notably when one begins to search for where women can be found in the conventional industrial relations account, based as it is on institutional relationships between employers and trade unions. More importantly than this, research based around formal institutional relationships is unlikely to uncover many women amongst employers or within trade unions (Cockburn 1983; Walby 1990; Ledwith and Colgan 1996; Kirton and Healy 1999), their hierarchies and power positions also being male dominated. Arguably, other oppressed, excluded and disadvantaged groups in the labour market, such as black and minority ethnic (BME), young and older workers, disabled and gay and lesbian workers will also tend to be absent from accounts focused on formal institutional relationships. In other words, because research has not in the main been concerned to uncover *social processes* of industrial relations, those social groups facing disadvantage in the labour market have been neglected.

This is also a methodological issue. Whitfield and Strauss (1998) trace the increasing use of quantitative methods in industrial relations research in the UK and North America. A quick glance through latest editions of industrial relations journals will attest to the continued predominance of quantitative research material. The emergence of the survey as the predominant paradigm is of concern because it is felt that the survey method is limited in uncovering processes behind structures and practices and emphasizes explanations focused on structures and environments rather than processes and actions (Kelly 1994). The focus of 'malestream' industrial relations on formal institutional relationships and structures will most often miss the voices of those non-dominant and least powerful stakeholders.

Given the discussion above, it is therefore not surprising that those subjects, processes and structures relevant to exploring equality and diversity issues in organizations are often seen as add-ons to mainstream industrial relations (as attested to by the fact that as Healy et al (2006: 290) state, they are often packaged as separate chapters or separate editions). Our interest in equality and diversity issues within organizations as industrial relations researchers is thus both automatic and deliberate. It is automatic in that given that we are interested in ensuring that non-dominant, less powerful voices are heard in our own industrial relations research, this leads to looking at issues relevant to DM (such as discrimination, equality, inequality, positive action and identity issues) as these are likely to affect marginalized groups. It is also deliberate, in that we would count ourselves amongst those industrial relations researchers for whom 'industrial relations is an ideological activity' (Healy et al 2006: 293) and therefore who have some kind of intention to achieve material and political outcomes from the research we engage in. Holgate et al (2006) call upon industrial relations researchers to reveal their positionality. To this end, we are not purely interested in DM as an academic exercise or a conceptual debate, but in trying to understand what DM in organizations means for those groups and individuals it is supposed to be benefiting and how it addresses and hopefully redresses disadvantage. Similarly we are not interested in critique of diversity for its own sake but the way in which such critique can play a part in improving understanding and policy- making so as to hopefully lead to improved outcomes—thus our aim is that our research might have some value beyond academic circles. For us, looking at women, BME and other disadvantaged workers requires investigation of DM issues at the organizational level.

PERSPECTIVES ON DIFFERENCE

Chapter 2 in this book provides a detailed analysis of the concept of DM, recognizing that it can be situated theoretically in a number of different ways. Prasad et al (2006: 2) place matters of difference and inclusion at the core of their understanding of the concept of diversity. However, as they argue, there is no consensus about what is to be included or what is considered different. For us, this is encapsulated by the sameness/difference dichotomy. This relates to questions about what counts as equality. Does equality mean treating people the same or differently? When we think conceptually about what diversity means, should we be playing down the differences which exist between people and thinking of employees as neutral individuals who contribute the same abilities, and who should receive the same access and be assessed in the same way regardless of social group membership? Alternatively, should we be acknowledging the importance of differences and valuing their very existence? And what differences should be included? Should we be looking at differences between individuals, or does it still make sense to talk about group differences between 'women', 'minority ethnic groups', 'older workers' or 'workers with disabilities' as comprising people who face similar problems and could benefit from similar solutions? We share the view of Prasad et al (2006: 6) that the most relevant (and arguably useful) focus should be on those that have faced systematic and historic disadvantage, which indicates that a focus on social groups in the workplace (i.e. women, BME, disabled, lesbian and gay, older and younger workers) continues to be relevant. This view 'explicitly acknowledg[es] the role played by past discrimination and oppression in producing socially marginalized groups' (ibid: 8).

This focus on discrimination, oppression and marginalization is particularly important because it emphasizes that the questions and debates relating to equality, diversity and difference, whilst having a renaissance more recently, have a much longer provenance. While questions of sameness and difference have taken a particular direction within more recent debates within the managerialist discourse of DM (which is discussed in more detail in Chapter 2), such questions certainly have a longer history within fields such as philosophy, and particularly in women's and gender studies. In this regard, the work of Iris Marion Young (1990) is particularly instructive, and it is useful to explore her conception of the 'politics of difference' in a little more detail because, as will become obvious in later discussion, it relates clearly to our own theoretical perspective on DM, which is firmly based around social groups.

Young's (1990) book, *Justice and the Politics of Difference*, establishes a position which challenges the sameness approach to equality that has arguably dominated the social policy arena since the 1970s in both the USA and the UK. This sameness approach can be seen to characterize most of the anti-discrimination legislation in these countries and across the EU even to the present day. Such an approach is underpinned by an 'assimilationist ideal' (Young 1990: 157), where the state and law should express rights in universal terms applied equally to all and where group-based differences, such as those based on race, ethnicity, sex and religion, should not make a difference to people's rights and opportunities. Essentially, the assimilationist ideal calls for group-based differences to be ignored and everyone to be treated as individuals.

However, Young's critique exposes the way in which the sameness or assimilationist ideal cannot gain equality for those groups facing disadvantage and discrimination in society and at work, and in fact helps support their oppression. First, to deny the importance of group differences is to deny the reality that society is clearly structured by social groups. This fits with later theorists such as Jenkins (1996: 6), looking at the ways in which individuals are involved in a continual process of categorization in their interactions with others on the basis of social identity. If it is recognized that social identity is integral to society, then clearly some groups are negatively affected by the social identities that people perceive them to possess. Social identity perspectives such as that outlined by Jenkins (1996) highlight that whatever group of workers we are looking at, it must be acknowledged that choices and life goals are defined by the opportunity structures that exist in society. Choices are enabled and constrained within the limits set by rules, norms and expectations, and people need material and social resources to challenge these social constraints.

Second, an important issue for Young is that this group difference should not be seen as something undesirable, but rather as emancipatory for those most disadvantaged in society (ibid: 163). Whilst there is recognition that the ideal of same treatment has brought significant improvements in the status of excluded groups, this sameness position of formal equality enshrined in law and social policy has not eliminated social differences in experiences and opportunities. The problem is that sameness approaches to equality tend to be based on distributive notions of social justice, such that what is required is more equal distribution of benefits, power, influence and so on. However, Young argues that such a position ignores social structures, institutional contexts, social relations and processes that actually determine those distributive patterns. For her, 'the concepts of domination and oppression, rather than the concept of distribution should be the starting point for a conception of social justice' (ibid: 16).

From this position, a rhetorical commitment to sameness makes it impossible to name and debate how group differences continue to structure privilege and oppression. In order to fit into this sameness ideal, members of excluded groups have to assimilate to fit the model of the dominant, privileged group. In addition, the sameness ideal allows privileged groups to ignore their own group specificity, so that their culture becomes the norm and anything else characterized as 'other'. Finally there is a danger that members of the excluded and oppressed groups begin to devalue their own experiences and interests. Young therefore finds it more empowering to affirm and acknowledge the group differences that already exist in social life, even when law and policy declare that all are equal. Therefore equality need not mean sameness.

Thus Young (ibid: 168) aims to reclaim the meaning of difference, so that it becomes something positive and desirable and something that should be positively embraced by the various social groups:

> By asserting a positive meaning for their own identity, oppressed groups seek to seize the power of naming difference itself, and explode the implicit definition of difference as deviance in relation to a norm, which freezes groups into a self-enclosed nature. Difference now comes to mean not otherness, exclusive opposition, but specificity, variation, heterogeneity. (ibid: 171)

Importantly, Young's conception of difference does not 'trap' individuals within certain social groups and a set of static characteristics. The politics of difference recognizes the heterogeneity within groups and the connections that can be made between them. Social groups are seen to reflect the ways that people identify themselves and others, which lead them to associate with some people more than others and to treat others as different. However groups are identified in relation to one another (ibid: 16). Indeed, according to her conception, groups can have overlapping experiences and are always similar in some respects and can potentially share attributes, experiences and goals. Membership of a group is not about a fixed set of attributes, but is a 'social process of interaction and differentiation' (ibid: 171), where certain affinities and their salience may shift for individuals at different times and in different contexts.

In terms of policy-making, then, Young argues for 'the justice of group-conscious social policies' (ibid: 173), recognizing that some of the disadvantages that people suffer can only be remedied by affirmative acknowledgement of the specificity of group difference. Moreover, using group-conscious policies is not just a means to an end of social equality, but that group-conscious policies are intrinsic to the whole idea of social (and we would add labour market) equality. The specific experiences, culture and social contributions of groups have to be publicly affirmed and recognized. Recognizing group difference need not mean more conflict in the public sphere or in the workplace; indeed, the recognition of differing group interests may in fact mitigate conflict emerging from resentment, misunderstanding and lack of voice.

This extended treatment of Young's analysis is important, because it is clear that there are alternatives to an arguably individualistic understanding of difference, such as has become appropriated by the managerialist discourse of DM (and which is discussed in detail in Chapter 2). Debates about difference and diversity and their relationship to equality have not begun, nor should end with managerial discourses of DM. Our understanding of difference and the policy interventions that should flow from this understanding are firmly based around the importance of social groups, and therefore this frames our analysis of and position on DM as a discourse and practice.

Perspectives on Diversity Management

So how should we study DM? What theoretical framework is most appropriate? Konrad et al (2006) provide a good review of some of the options, with Part One of their edited collection tracing a number of conceptual approaches and perspectives to DM, including psychological, HRM, critical discourse, post-structuralist and post-colonial. Our intention below is to provide a brief outline of each of these perspectives—in essence paths that we could have chosen for our research, but as will be discussed, none of these perspectives appear quite right for our purposes, although key issues emerge from each that should be taken up within our own critical industrial relations research approach.

The psychological perspective is concerned primarily with understanding the content and impact of individual stereotypes, and how people form impressions of others. Psychological theories have then been produced to try and explain the impact that these stereotypes have on the experience and outcomes of different groups in the workplace (Kulik and Bainbridge 2006). Generally, this is based on the level of the individual (for example cognition and perceptions), with little focus on social processes and interactions. Thus, while one can see how broader understanding about the way stereotypes work will inform our analysis, the psychological approach is less useful to us in trying to gain understanding of policy-making and the politics of implementation in organizations. In particular the organizational context is rarely the direct focus of research (ibid: 42), and much psychological research (particularly if it is experimental, laboratory-based research) is not good at reflecting the complexity of organizational decision making (ibid: 41).

The HRM perspective on DM (Kossek et al 2006) obviously has some immediate relevance to our research looking at the development and implementation of equality and diversity policy as this area is generally positioned as a key part of HR practice. This perspective aims to highlight the development and implementation of organizational initiatives that lead to a variety of DM outcomes. However, this perspective by itself is fairly uncritical, coming from a primary position which looks for the link between policy intervention and outcomes, particularly for organizational performance. For this reason, as we will discuss in Chapter 2, this perspective is therefore not sufficiently critical of the DM concept or of the business case for our purposes. In addition, it is concerned with the role of HR managers with less or little concern for the perspectives of different organizational stakeholders, especially non-management employees. Indeed, Pringle et al explicitly categorize this perspective as 'low in power awareness' (2006:

536) as it emphasizes the importance of maximizing organizational performance. However it should be noted that questions posed by this perspective, such as the relationship between different HRM interventions and the success of DM interventions (Kossek et al 2006: 69), would be useful to our analysis of DM policy in context.

Litvin (2006) provides a perspective on DM that comes from critical discourse analysis. In comparison to the HRM approach, this perspective is overtly critical, focusing as it does upon the relationship between language and power. In her chapter in the Konrad et al. volume, Litvin chooses the discourse of the business case for DM as her focus and deconstructs it in order to 'interrupt [its] taken-for-grantedness' (ibid: 75). One could imagine how this perspective could be used to analyze any element of DM discourse, with its use being in offering alternative understandings of the same thing, distinguishing overt and hidden meanings, and allowing some exploration of the often experienced gap between rhetoric and reality of policy in organizations. One can see how elements of this perspective will be useful to us in our analysis, for example in analyzing documentary data, and identifying the patterns of discourse used by the people in the organizations we studied. However, by itself, this perspective offers less understanding of the interactions between structure and individual agency (social processes) in the organization. In other words, we come from a position where DM is more than just discourse, and it is important to us to look at what the material effects of policy-making in organizations amount to.

Konrad et al's (2006) book also presents two further perspectives: post-colonial theory and the critical theory/post-structuralist perspective (Jones and Stablein 2006). Prasad (2006: 125) highlights the way in which post-colonial theory is useful to workplace DM researchers in understanding Western perceptions of 'otherness' and therefore understandings of difference in organizations, including of course the way in which these perceptions affect Western conceptions of DM in the first place (see Chapter 2 for more discussion of this). With its analysis of 'system of hierarchical binaries' (ibid: 134–5), post-colonial theory also directs us to look at the ways in which DM policy in organizations threatens white privilege and therefore may be resisted or set up to fail. Critical approaches to the study of DM in organizations explicitly acknowledge the 'complex web of economic, social and political forces that constitute the positions of the dominant and marginally diverse employees, managers, interested academics and associated workplace and research practice' (Jones and Stablein 2006: 149). In challenging the idea of grand narratives or of the explanatory power of structures (such as patriarchy or class etc), post-structuralism puts the focus on understanding at the individual level. This means that the meaning of concepts such as DM will vary depending on the perspective of the person concerned. Key debates revolve around identity ('the ways that people are represented as different or 'diverse' individuals or members of 'diverse' groups') and agency ('the capacity that people have to act, individually or collectively') (ibid: 160).

Both of these perspectives have elements useful to our own research, particularly the ways in which they support the need to understand the views of a range of organizational stakeholders and recognize the power dimensions of DM policy-making in organizations. However, both of these perspectives come from a position of theorizing largely in the abstract, whereas our research is situated firmly in the workplace context. As Jones and Stablein state, 'Theorists and practitioners of workplace diversity should draw on a range of theoretical frames consistent with their own explicit social and political agendas, and relevant to their local conditions' (ibid: 161). This situates our position firmly in the industrial relations field as the next section will elucidate.

Towards an Industrial Relations Perspective on Diversity Management

We would classify our research approach as a critical industrial relations perspective, but for the purposes of this particular research project, we found the term 'stakeholder perspective' salient for reasons we will go on to discuss. In line with an industrial relations approach, we are concerned primarily with the labour market, the employment relationship, and the strategies and actions of industrial relations actors, namely the nature of the interaction between employees, managers, trade unions (or other employee representative groups) and the State. Key to this is recognition of the mixture of conflict, co-operation and power that exists in the employment relationship. This view of the employment relationship appears to have general agreement in most industrial relations texts; focusing in on the contradictory nature of the 'structured antagonism' which managers and workers are locked into (for a summary, see Edwards 2003: 17). However, in beginning to reflect on what a stakeholder perspective means, unlike the HRM perspective discussed above, where the management view is prioritized, our research approach is essentially pluralistic, recognizing both the plurality and the legitimacy of a variety of stakeholder group interests in the workplace. This has important policy implications because a stakeholder perspective recognizes that different interest groups have a legitimate part to play in both the development and implementation of policy in organizations, and moreover that policy is likely to be more successful when those people affected by policies are involved in them, thus linking clearly to Young's (1990) analysis of the importance of social group difference for equality. This fits broadly with research that emphasizes the importance of employee involvement for the success of HR initiatives (for example, Gennard and Emmott 2003; Marchington et al 2001; Guest and Peccei 1998). Thus, we aim to capture the way in which DM is jointly regulated in the workplace.

A key part of our stakeholder perspective is thus an interest in joint regulation of the employment relationship in the context of the UK, which means involving trade unions. However, as yet, the ways in which trade unions have responded to the implementation of DM has gained only limited coverage in the academic and practitioner literature (Wrench 2004; Greene et al 2005; Kirton and Greene 2006). Part of this is to be explained by the wider theoretical debate about the concept of DM that is discussed in Chapter 2 of this book. In brief, we argue that the underpinning of the DM concept as it has emerged in the UK is generally unitarist and management-led and founded on a business case for equality, leaving little room for involvement of stakeholders such as trade unions or other employee representatives. This lack of understanding of the views of trade unions is significant for a number of reasons. First, although there has been a significant decline in trade union membership in the UK over the last 20 years, unionized settings still account for around half of UK workplaces (over 25 employees), just over one third are union members and 40 per cent had their pay set through collective bargaining (Kersley et al 2006). Second, Dickens (1999) compares the relative advantages of a legislative, business case or joint regulatory approach to equality. We feel that there is significant value in exploring the joint regulation of DM, and this therefore necessitates an exploration of trade union and non-management viewpoints. Third, there have been concerns in wider public policy forums about the alarming deterioration in conditions of work for those UK employees at lower levels of the organizational hierarchy (Taylor 2002). Additionally, there has been debate in academic arenas about the failure of current interventions to address the problems of inequality faced by those most disadvantaged (Webb 1997). A joint regulatory approach to equality policy-making is arguably more concerned about the 'sticky floor' than with the 'glass ceiling'; that is, with those employees at lower levels of organizations who are more likely to be trade union members. Indeed, survey evidence from the UK indicates that the presence of unions increases the likelihood of an organization having EO policies (Kersley et al 2006). To date, however, we know little about what DM initiatives look like in unionized settings, and what they might achieve for non-management employees at lower organizational levels, arguably those who face the greatest inequalities.

As mentioned briefly above, in the face of the ascendancy of the business case within equality/diversity rhetoric and policy in UK organisations, Dickens (1999) presented a case for what she called a 'three-pronged approach to equality action', detailing the existence of three mutually supporting strategies (business case, legal regulation and social (joint) regulation) for action on equality within organisations. The nature of the three strategies is worth explaining in a little more detail as we find that they are a recurring theme within analysis of our findings and will be referred to when we come to make some concluding remarks in Chapter 10. In Dickens' terms, the business case strategy relates specifically to the 'privatised approach' where EO (or we argue DM) is left to the individual organisation taking voluntary business case-driven action (see more discussion in Chapter 2). The strategy of legal regulation (see further discussion of the UK legislative context in Chapter 3) relates to the role of equality and anti-discrimination legislation in (i) setting and broadening employer equality agendas, (ii) shaping the climate in which employer decisions are made, (iii) providing universal standards and minima, and (iv) altering costs of discrimination and employer inaction (Dickens 1999: 12). Finally, the strategy of social regulation concerns the role of trade unions in jointly regulating the employment relationship and promoting equality action through equality bargaining (Dickens 1999: 14; see also discussion in Chapter 9). A social regulation strategy has the benefits of: (i) extending the employer determined equality agenda and making it less easy to abandon; (ii) extending the legislative agenda by offering collective outcomes for individual legal decisions and turning formal legal rights into substantive outcomes; and (iii) finally, through a 'voice mechanism', offering ways in which marginalised groups can themselves play a role in defining, developing and sustaining equality initiatives. Overall, Dickens' conclusion is that organizations should be utilizing all three strategies which together are argued to provide a sounder basis for supporting equality action than any of the three strategies alone.

The stakeholder perspective, as we utilize the term, whilst situated firmly in the industrial relations sphere, is also a critical one. Therefore, in line with the critical theory/post-structuralist and post-colonial approaches discussed above, our view is not of these stakeholders as neutral atomized individuals or groups. We are also concerned with identities, multiple perspectives, questions of agency and power. Given our desire to challenge the malestream of industrial relations, our approach recognizes that employees, managers and trade unionists have gender and ethnicity, while a whole number of other identities and influences (often overlapping and sometimes contradictory), both inside and outside the workplace, will affect their views and actions.

Furthermore, exploring stakeholder understandings of policy discourse and rhetoric within the organizations we research is key to this, arguably taking on board aspects of the post-structuralist and critical discourse analysis perspectives. Most industrial relations writers do not carry out discourse-based analysis, reflecting a commonly held view within the field that talk is less than action and therefore less worthy of study (Hamilton 2001). Kelly is among a minority of authors in the field who highlight the importance of discourse in framing employment relations issues and problems, stating that 'study of the day-to-day language, or discourses of industrial relations is therefore of major significance' (1998: 127). This is because, in terms of policy formulation, talk precedes action, and the talk of the actors defines the policy issues and the policy initiatives. Further, organizational policies are rarely 'once and for all' entities; rather they evolve and change over time often reflecting emergent ideas and discourses. Discourses are therefore powerful resources (Fairclough 2003) and can be used to 'denote a representation of norms for accepted thinking and thereby as a model for the interpretation and understanding of society' (De los Reyes 2000). Therefore, we cannot properly understand the policy measures that organizations utilize and the way that different stakeholders challenge them without appreciation of the discourses that are drawn upon to rationalize and justify their positions. Further, in describing and labelling things the way they do, organizational stakeholders seek to persuade others to accept or challenge policy and its measures, to change or reinforce certain attitudes or values (Hamilton 2001). From this perspective, discourse is not simply reflective of reality, but significant in constituting reality: it is a mode of action, as well as a mode of representation (Fairclough 1992).

However, identities and viewpoints do not stand separate to the institutional and societal structures that provide their context. Therefore, unlike the post-structuralist perspective, our approach emphasizes the importance of context for how DM plays out in organizations (see Greene, forthcoming, for a summary). There are now a number of writers who highlight the importance of contextualized approaches to DM (Janssens and Zanoni 2005; Benschop 2001; Kamenou and Fearfull 2006; Dass and Parker 1999). Part of this obviously relates to the wider political, legal and economic context, because different kinds of difference are likely to have greater salience in some places and certain moments (Prasad et al 2006: 3). More significant for our research is the micro level, the need to be aware of the affects of organizational context. Dass and Parker (1999) claim that an organization's DM approach will depend on the degree of pressure for DM action, the types of DM in question and managerial attitudes to a diverse workforce. Janssens and Zanoni (2005) identify the role of the customer and profile of customer service as a key determinant on the types of DM policy and approach that are implemented. For practitioners, an understanding that the approach and policy should be tailored to the specific organizational context should lead to a 'more contextually informed and organizationally realistic view of diversity management than is all too often suggested by the equality literature' (Foster and Harris 2005: 14). Thus, our research approach has to allow for in-depth consideration of the effects of social context.

Towards Appropriate Research Methods

Following from the discussion above, our research approach requires particular methods, ones which are able to explore the impact of context, as well as the capturing of multiple views and attitudes. Taking our position that the voicing of multiple stakeholders and a focus on social processes is central to industrial relations analysis, then this has implications for the ways in which research is carried out. This approach will naturally lead to research methodologies that utilize methods that are far more qualitative and ethnographically-informed (Greene 2001). We would share a view that such methods are particularly important for capturing the informal processes of industrial relations (Friedman and McDaniel 1998; Thompson and Ackroyd 1999). Use of such methods is however clearly going against the trend within industrial relations research (not least because of the popularity of quantitative and positivistic research designs with funding bodies), but also moves the field in new directions, for which many academics have been calling.

'Ethnographically-informed methods' seems to be a useful description to encapsulate the in-depth, qualitative nature of our methods, even though we did not use participant observation. Friedman and McDaniel (1998: 115–116) outline features that offer a broader definition of ethnography, within an industrial relations arena. First, direct and personal observation of people and situations are highlighted. Our main interest is in exploring more closely the dynamics of DM within the particular organizational context, looking at how people create and legitimate their worlds. Second, the 'voicing' of accounts is emphasized so that the perspectives, interpretations and experiences of the people studied are explored. These features lend themselves to the use of an in-depth interview which was the main method used in our research. These interviews were recorded and then fully transcribed so as to ensure that the direct voices of those interviewed could be utilized and analyzed and so that verbatim quotes could be presented.

Third, observations and analyses are made in the context of the people going about daily business and interacting with others. As already indicated, we did not undertake participant observation, but we did conduct observation at a number of diversity-related events. In addition, care was taken to be observant of a number of features when, for example, we conducted interviews or attended meetings. Thus, the perspectives and views of interviewees were situated firmly in their wider workplace contexts, building up 'thick description' (Geertz 1973) by overlaying different viewpoints, observations, rhetoric and factual information derived from a variety of sources. As is outlined below, we engaged in a variety of qualitative methods in the research, all with the purposes of building up a detailed picture of the context. This involved comparing and layering of information for a variety of sources; for example, interviews were compared with short answer survey responses, views of policies were compared with the text of policy documents themselves, management policy rhetoric was compared with non-management employee experiences of policy and so on.

Taking a stakeholder perspective had clear implications for who was involved in the research and what was studied. With regard to who was involved, as previously stated, we were keen to ensure that the widest group of stakeholders possible within the organizations were participants in our research, with a particular importance placed on gaining the views of those usually missed from DM research, including non-management employees (particularly women and BME employees) and trade union representatives. This was often the most difficult aspect of the research to organize. Second, the stakeholder perspective directed us to take particular consideration of the way in which policy and practice involved (or did not involve) multiple stakeholders and this formed a key part of our inquiry.

ESF PROJECT OUTLINE

As discussed above, the ESF research project aimed to explore the processes and views of outcomes of DM in practice in the UK, focusing in particular on different arrangements for stakeholder involvement. Thus, the formal objectives of the research involved: (i) a mapping of DM policy and initiatives within the organizations; (ii) an exploration of the experiences and perceptions of organizational stakeholders of DM policy and practice; and (iii) an investigation of the involvement of the stakeholders in policy formulation and implementation in order to identify the triggers to, rationale behind and conditions and circumstances of policies and practices.

The research was conducted from December 2003 till mid-2006 and utilized two main areas of fieldwork: case studies in two large organizations and interviews with DM practitioners in a variety of UK organizations. In summary, the following methods were used.

Case Studies

It should be noted that we had considerable difficulty gaining access to organizations, particularly in the private sector which testifies to the sensitive and controversial nature of equality and DM research. In the end, we gained access to two case study organizations, one a government department which we have given the pseudonym Public Sector Organization (PSO) and the other a private sector facilities management organization which we have given the pseudonym ServiceCo. These organizations provided interesting contexts in which to conduct the research for a number of reasons. First, we were pleased that we managed to gain access to an organization in both the public and private sector allowing some comparison. Second, the two organizations were at significantly different stages in DM policy-making. As would be expected in the UK public sector, PSO had a well-established DM policy developed over a significant number of years as an evolution of its EO policy, whereas ServiceCo was at the very early stages of developing its DM policy at the point at which we began research. Third, both organizations were unionized, providing contexts in which the joint regulation of DM was potentially possible.

Case study fieldwork involved the following main methods. One-to-one, semi-structured interviews were conducted with HR practitioners, equality and diversity specialists, senior managers, line-managers, trade union officials and representatives at each of the case studies. All interviews lasted between 1 and 2 hours and were recorded and fully transcribed. It should be noted that some key 'gatekeeper' participants (such as the Head of Employee Relations at ServiceCo) were interviewed a number of times over the period of the fieldwork, thus allowing some tracking of developments over time. In addition, we took advantage of being able to speak to key equality and diversity stakeholders where they existed; for example, we interviewed chairs of employee diversity groups at PSO.

Non-management employees were interviewed usually in groups of around six, rather than individually. This was due to access issues and difficulties in scheduling individual interviews. The focus group interviews were designed to be informal in order to facilitate open discussion amongst the participants, although time was necessarily constrained by work schedules. A member of the research team facilitated discussion by asking a small number of broad open-ended questions and took detailed notes of the discussion.

It should be noted that the question schedules for both the one-to-one and focus group interviews were broad and open, not directing respondents to talk about any particular diversity strand (for example, women's, BME, gay and lesbian issues). The precise nature of what was understood as diversity or equality issues within their organizations, and therefore any concentration on a particular diversity strand or policy initiative, was determined by the respondent themselves.

Members of the research team also sat in and observed at a number of diversity-related events including diversity training courses, conferences, specialist employee group meetings, and non-management employee involvement forums. Notes were taken by researchers sitting in at these meetings. Finally, a variety of documents were collected at each organization, including equality and diversity policy documents (complete and draft material), diversity campaign material, performance appraisal guidelines, demographic monitoring data, reviews and reports. These were analyzed alongside the primary research data.

ServiceCo Case Study

ServiceCo is a multi-sectoral, multi-national company formed from a mid-1990s merger between, and later acquisition of, large and long-established UK companies. Its project operations stretch across the UK and Europe, North America, the Middle East and North Africa. At the time of the research, ServiceCo had approximately 40,000 employees worldwide (13,000 in the UK) and annual revenue of £5 billion. In the UK,

ServiceCo has eight principal business sectors. The case study research concentrated on two of these sectors, Health and Transport.

The fieldwork in ServiceCo Health was undertaken in a large general hospital in the south of England which we call HealthSite. In 1999, ServiceCo signed its fourth health Private Finance Initiative (PFI) contract with HealthSite, where ServiceCo employed approximately 330 people. ServiceCo's work at HealthSite comprised Facilities Management, consisting of four services areas: Housekeeping, Estates, Portering and Catering. Industrial relations arrangements varied highly between ServiceCo's UK business sectors and the unions Amicus and TGWU (subsequently merged as Unite) and Unison were recognized at many Health-related workplaces. At HealthSite, ServiceCo recognized two unions, Unison and Amicus.

ServiceCo Transport involved both rail and road sectors, offering services from strategic planning and consultancy to rail testing and maintenance, building new roads and maintaining existing road infrastructure. Fieldwork in the rail sector was undertaken at a depot (RailSite) in the Midlands region of England, where ServiceCo was part of a consortium of organizations engaged in upgrading the West Coast Main Line. In the rail sector generally, ServiceCo recognized Amicus, TGWU and RMT. At RailSite, ServiceCo recognized Amicus. Fieldwork in the road sector was also undertaken at a depot (RoadSite) in the Midlands region, where ServiceCo was responsible for a highways maintenance and major projects contract for the local County Council. RoadSite was the main depot, where the TGWU was recognized and where approximately 75 staff members were based, including managerial, operative and administrative staff.

We were unable to acquire statistics on the density of union membership at ServiceCo, and only very vague indications from the Head of Employee Relations that the trade union representation across the organization tended to mirror wider trends in the Transport and Health sectors of the UK economy, which is 41 per cent and 43 per cent, respectively (DTI 2007).

The research at ServiceCo was carried out in 2004 and 2005 and involved a number of stakeholder participants as set out in Table 1.1.

Table 1.1 Stakeholder Participants at ServiceCo

Stakeholder Participant	*Number*
Head of Employee Relations (responsible for equality and diversity)	1
Senior Managers	7
Workplace trade union representatives	3
Line managers/supervisory staff	10
Two non-management employee focus groups	23
Total	44

We conducted observation of a national company-level Equality Training Seminar for senior/middle managers (largely Heads of Business and senior members of company-wide divisions); a Staff Forum (joint consultation vehicle) in HealthSite, involving management and non-management representatives; and two national company-level 'Great Debate' consultation meetings with a range of non-management and management staff from different business sectors. These meetings were interactive feedback sessions involving a randomly sampled 10 per cent of ServiceCo's employees. We also examined documentary evidence, including relevant policies, reports and monitoring data.

PSO Case Study

It is impossible to give details about PSO, in terms of size of the workforce or core activities, and be able at the same time to maintain the anonymity of the organization. The most that we are able to say is that PSO is one of the smaller government departments, and our fieldwork was conducted at its headquarters in London. As part of the Civil Service, PSO recognizes three trade unions—Public and Commercial Services (PCS) (representing a wide range of civil servants including those at lower grade levels), Prospect (representing professional occupations including engineers, scientists and managers) and First Division Association (FDA) (representing senior civil servants). We were unable to acquire official statistics for trade union density at PSO, but the PSO joint trade union side secretary informed us that approximate density was between 50 and 70 per cent depending on the region and area of business.

Semi-structured face-to-face and focus group interviews were carried out involving a number of stakeholder participants, as set out in Table 1.2.

Observation was conducted at a 2-day Valuing Diversity training course involving both management and non-management staff who had either self-selected to attend or had been asked by their line-manager to attend. In addition, we observed a a women's employee group meeting and a Conference on Diversity and Flexibility organized by the women's employee group.

Table 1.2   Stakeholder Participants at PSO

Stakeholder Participant	Number
Diversity Manager	1
National trade union representative	1
Workplace trade union representatives	7
Line-managers/supervisory staff	10
Four non-management employee focus groups	24
Chairs of employee groups (women's, race equality and LGBT)	3
Total	46

Documentary evidence, including relevant policies, reports and monitoring data, was examined. Finally, a short email survey of employee group members was conducted, involving 31 responses (Disability: 14; LGBT: 4; Race equality: 5; Women's: 8).

Interviews at both case studies covered three main areas: (i) the context of the equality and diversity policy and concepts in relation to the individual interviewee; (ii) job-related diversity/equality issues; and (iii) overall view of equality and diversity in the organization. Questions in (i) explored the respondent's general awareness and understanding of equality and diversity concepts and of these issues within their organization. Questions in (ii) looked at the individual managers' roles and incorporation of equality/diversity objectives and any equality issues facing them in their roles. Questions in (iii) covered perceptions of the equality/diversity culture and climate in the organization. Essentially the interviews were attempting to understand what DM means to and for the various stakeholders.

Interviews with DM practitioners

The aim of this second strand of the research project was to investigate the roles and perspectives of a range of practitioners involved in DM. A total of 64 individuals from 49 organizations participated in the research presented here. The organizations are listed alphabetically in Table 1.3 and consist of 15 public sector employers, 17 private sector employers, 2 voluntary sector employers, 11 unions and 4 non-governmental organizations.

It was a deliberate research strategy to have a mix of organizations in order to develop as round a picture as possible of developments in DM. Some organizations were approached because of existing contacts. The public sector employers were approached largely because of their reputation for being at the forefront of traditional equality policies. All of the public sector organizations we approached agreed to participate. Private sector employers were of particular interest because most DM research in the UK to date is located in the public sector, leaving a knowledge gap. However, they proved more difficult to recruit to the study. Most were identified through their membership of campaign organizations such as *Race for Opportunity* and *Opportunity Now*, which publish lists of members on their web sites. Membership of such organizations was taken to indicate a commitment to equality and diversity, and we also believed that they would be more likely to participate in the research. Thirty-five private sector employers were approached, 17 agreed to participate, while the remainder either declined or did not respond to repeated attempts to gain a response. Therefore, although the number of private sector organizations is greater than public sector, we would have liked to have seen more agree to participate. Given the stakeholder focus of the research

Table 1.3   Organizations Participating in the Research

Advisory, Conciliation and Arbitration Service (ACAS)
Amicus
Association of University Teachers (AUT)
B&Q
Barclaycard
Barclays Bank
Birmingham City Council
British Airways
British Conservation Trust Volunteers
Cambridgeshire Police Service
Cameron Woods Associates
Central Scotland Forest Trust
Centre for High Performance Development
Centrica
Commission for Racial Equality
Connect
Coventry City Council
Communication Workers Union (CWU)
Deloitte
Department of Health
Dumfries and Galloway Fire Service
General, Municipal and Boilermakers union (GMB)
Graphical, Paper and Media Union (GPMU)
The Guardian
Gwent Police Service
Hackney Council
HSBC
Inkfish
Inland Revenue
J P Morgan
Lehman Brothers
Metropolitan Police Service
Northampton Police Service
Public and Commercial Services Union (PCS)
Price Waterhouse Coopers
Prospect
PSO
Queen Mary, University of London
Race for Opportunity
ServiceCo
Tower Hamlets Council
Trades Union Congress
Unifi
Unison
University of Warwick
West Bromwich Building Society
Women's National Commission

project, it is relevant to note that 27 of the 34 private/public/voluntary sector organizations represented in the study have trade union presence/recognition.

The 64 individual participants consisted of:

(i) Organizational diversity specialists (23). These are defined as individuals whose job title contains 'diversity' or whose position in HR is largely dedicated to equality and diversity.
(ii) Organizational diversity champions (19). These are defined as individuals with operational line-management responsibilities who have volunteered to 'champion' diversity.
(iii) Trade union officers (16). These comprised 11 national trade union equality officers, representing individual trade unions and the TUC and 5 national negotiating officers (with equality and diversity experience) from one union.
(iv) Diversity consultants and campaigners (6). This included two diversity consultants and five representatives of relevant non-governmental organizations.

The demographic characteristics of participants are shown in Table 1.4, from which it can be seen (based on participating organizations) that from this research it appears that there are far more women than men involved professionally in DM and far more white than BME people.

The interviews with diversity practitioners took place during 2004–6 and were semi-structured, using a broad interview guide covering four main areas: practitioner's background and role, organizational thinking on diversity, stakeholder involvement and organizational policy and practice. The interview guide was designed with open questions in order to gather attitudinal data as well as concrete examples of DM initiatives and allow participants to tell us about their role and the activities of their organization from their perspective. We did not seek to investigate or verify the impact of policy initiatives. Interviews lasted between one and two hours, were recorded and were fully transcribed. In addition, key respondents were asked to provide

Table 1.4 Demographic Characteristics of Participants

	Diversity Specialists	Diversity Champions	Trade Union Officers	Diversity Consultants	Diversity Campaigners
Gender					
Female (44)	20	7	11	2	4
Male (20)	3	12	5	0	0
Ethnicity					
White (52)	17	17	14	2	2
Minority Ethnic (12)	6	2	2	0	2

examples of policy documents from their organizations which were analyzed along side their interviews. Finally, part of the project design also included two workshops with practitioners in the field, involving a mix of senior managers, trade union officers and academics, one completed at the beginning of the project and one at the end. This first workshop aimed to provide an opportunity for practitioners to influence the design and substance of the research, including what areas were investigated, as well as providing a space for discussion and networking. The second workshop provided a vehicle for dissemination, and with invitations offered to the case study organizations, allowed us an opportunity to check that participants felt that the account delivered seemed authentic. The workshop involved a mixture of plenary and small group sessions, both of which were recorded and fully transcribed.

OUTLINE OF THE BOOK

The book presents findings from our ESF project; however, each chapter also engages with relevant key themes from the existing literature, so that the empirical material is located within global conceptual and theoretical debates about DM and within the social, economic, legal and political contexts of the UK. In this way, each chapter is capable of being read separately, whilst also contributing to coherent themes across the book.

Following the introductory chapter, the next two chapters provide the background context for the later analysis within the more substantive chapters. Chapter 2 provides the theoretical and conceptual context for our discussion of DM in organizations, providing a critical analysis of key aspects of DM and identifying different directions that research has taken in the UK compared to the USA. This theoretical and conceptual context includes discussion of the shift from affirmative action to DM in the USA, the export of the DM concept to other countries and the subsequent shift from equal opportunities to DM in the UK. Drawing specifically on our stakeholder perspective, there is a critical analysis of the central tenets of DM and identification of key challenges, tensions and dilemmas of DM when considering multiple stakeholders. Specifically, the chapter considers how DM threatens to marginalize trade union involvement and to weaken employee voice. Chapter 3 provides an outline of the political, economic, social and legal contexts of the UK, drawing out the most significant features of the UK DM context in order to set the scene for the presentation of the empirical material. This provides essential background information, recognizing that organizational-level policy-making cannot be understood without reference to the key elements of the external context that impact upon an organization's functions, operation and policy-making.

Chapters 4 and 5 are also context-building chapters, but also include substantive empirical material. They are structured around the key divisions of the UK labour market, public and private sectors, and a literature review in each provides the broader sectoral context for consideration of our analysis of the two case studies carried out in each of these sectors. Chapter 4 considers developments and trends in public sector management in the UK, including 'new public management', and their effects on approaches to equality and diversity. This discussion frames the analysis of the PSO case study considering the internal and external pressures/triggers for diversity, perspectives of key organizational stakeholders, policy responses and views of their impact/effects. The extent to which the business case for DM has overshadowed the traditional public sector commitment to the social justice case for equality is explored. Chapter 5 follows in a similar vein but explores the uptake of DM in the private sector in the UK, based around analysis of the ServiceCo case study. The extent to which the business case for DM dominates in the private sector is reflected upon.

The next four chapters move specifically to look at the perspectives of each of the major organizational stakeholders. Chapter 6 begins by providing an overview of DM work in the UK, considering the structures that organizations establish in order to develop, support and implement equality and DM policy. Specifically it draws on the fieldwork involving DM practitioners, exploring what the shift to DM means for the roles and activities of those charged with responsibilities for development and implementation of initiatives. Chapter 7 moves to look at the management perspective on DM. As will be discussed in Chapter 2, the DM concept highlights the pivotal role of line-managers in embedding policy and in leading the cultural change that is considered necessary in order to achieve an organizational climate that values diversity. Therefore, while some analysis of perspectives of senior managers is considered, this chapter concentrates on exploring the perspectives and experiences of line-managers. It specifically draws on fieldwork involving managers in the two case studies.

Chapter 8 now moves to the non-management employee perspective. The chapter begins by tracing the way in which DM research and literature often tends to focus on middle management levels, or professionals at the 'glass ceiling' within organizations. However, we know relatively little about how DM policies are perceived by, and how they impact on non-managerial employees at lower levels within organizations. Our empirical research offered us the opportunity to focus in particular on those employees at 'the sticky floor', including those in minimum wage and casualized employment. The chapter draws on interview and observation data involving employee group members and other groups of employees from the two case study organizations. Finally, in line with our stakeholder approach, and our interest in the joint regulation of diversity, Chapter 9 looks at trade union perspectives. Trade unions have traditionally played a role in campaigning and bargaining for equality and have often been the vehicle for employee voice. DM is a potential threat to trade union involvement for a number of reasons that are examined in this chapter. Using existing literature, the chapter discusses trade union experiences of DM drawing on interview and observation data involving national trade union equality officers and branch/workplace trade union representatives at the two case study organizations.

Chapter 10 provides a conclusion to the book, summarising key themes and debates to emerge and the findings presented and critically appraises the value of a stakeholder perspective. We review the different stakeholder experiences of DM and highlight the tensions and dilemmas that these multiple experiences reveal. We discuss the prospects for DM to advance the equality project, arguing that DM is not simply something that can be 'done' to employees and that organizations can benefit from the active involvement of employees.

2 Understanding Diversity Management

INTRODUCTION

Diversity management (DM) has been described as a new organizational paradigm (Gilbert et al 1999). Visit the website of any major UK or North American private or public sector organization and we are confident that you will find a stated claim or at least stated intention to value, embrace or celebrate workforce diversity. Many organizations in the UK signal their commitment to diversity by joining national campaigns such as the Employers Forum on Age, the Employers Forum on Disability, Opportunity Now (gender equality organization), Race for Opportunity (race equality organization) or Stonewall (lesbian and gay campaign organization). Some proudly state how they have won awards for their diversity initiatives from these 'issue-focused' campaigns, but at the same time many organizations also clearly position their diversity policy within a broader, more inclusive agenda. That is, many organizations state that for them diversity is not 'simply' about gender, race/ethnicity, disability and so on, but about respect for individuals and their needs. Why are organizations so enthusiastic about diversity? It is striking that whilst a growing number of organizations' diversity statements will be found in the corporate social responsibility section of their website, most imply that workforce diversity is not only a moral issue, but critical to their success and future sustainability. Some go so far as to talk about 'leveraging' workforce diversity for the benefit of the business. In fact, the idea of diversity as critical to business success has permeated corporate images and advertising via slogans such as 'everyone is welcome at Tesco' (the largest UK retailer) or 'HSBC, the world's local bank'. Further, many organizations are proclaiming that their commitment to diversity starts at the very top of the organization, implying that it has not just come about as a reactive response to external pressures, such as anti-discrimination legislation, or internal staff grievances and complaints. In the 2000s, organizations typically see themselves as having voluntarily developed diversity policy.

Thus, a browse through major organizations' websites captures many of the key issues within the contemporary diversity debate that this book will explore. This chapter situates the empirical research presented in the book by stepping back to consider when and where the debate about diversity started. As we suggest, the language of diversity is now commonly used to talk about issues that once would have fallen under labels such as 'equal opportunities' (EO), 'equal employment opportunity' (EEO), 'affirmative action' (AA) and so on, depending on the country. Along with Cox (1994) and many other authors, we believe that the language used to talk about equality and diversity issues has important implications for theory, research, policy and practice. As indicated earlier, one significant implication is that diversity is now commonly presented as a core business issue. While the corporate adoption of what we call the 'diversity paradigm' is evident in 2008 within organizations throughout most of the industrialized world, this has not always been the case. In fact, the diversity discourse is a relatively recent phenomenon that took off in the USA around the mid- to late 1980s, arrived in the UK and other countries such as Australia and New Zealand around the mid-1990s and in mainland Europe a little later. Why is this? Why did the diversity discourse emerge? What are its conceptual and philosophical roots? What are its key dimensions? How can the popularity of the discourse be explained? To tackle these questions, this chapter first discusses the shift from 'EEO' and 'AA' to DM in the USA, moving on to examine the 'export' of the diversity discourse to other countries and the subsequent shift from 'EO'-type policy-making approaches to DM in the UK and other countries. If we are to understand the contemporary policy context, we need to be aware of the historical evolution of the concepts that underpin policy. We argue this because DM did not spring out of nowhere; rather, there are a whole set of social, economic, legal and political factors that gave rise to its ascendance as the preferred contemporary label for equality policy-making. At the same time, the validity and universality of the diversity discourse is contested by academics (Humphries and Grice 1995; Jones et al 2000). In exploring these factors, the chapter provides a critical analysis of key aspects of DM and identifies the different directions that research has taken in the UK compared to the US context. More specifically, in line with our research approach discussed in Chapter 1, it identifies key challenges from a stakeholder perspective, considering how DM threatens to marginalize trade union involvement in equality policy-making and to weaken employee voice.

FROM EEO AND AA TO DM—THE USA EXPERIENCE

There are a number of areas covered by EEO law in the USA, including discrimination on grounds of age, disability, sex and race, but it is AA that has provoked the most debate and attracted the most controversy. AA emerged in the 1960s in the wake of the Civil Rights Act of 1964 as a specific policy response, enshrined in law, primarily to endemic employment discrimination against African Americans within a historical context of slavery and racial segregation (although it should be noted that women were also included in AA). AA was intended to provide redress for past wrongs and was therefore seen as a vehicle for achieving social justice. The idea underpinning AA was that contemporary inequalities of outcome are a function of deep-rooted structures of inequality, reproduced from one generation to the next, rather than attributable to the specific acts of individuals operating in the current context. From this perspective as elaborated in Chapter 1, a simple principle of non-discrimination or even anti-discrimination legislation is insufficient to overcome the embedded and systemic disadvantage that minority groups face (Williams 2000; Young 1990). Reflecting this, AA required employers to take positive steps not only to end discrimination, but also to implement proactive programmes to hire, train and promote people from historically disadvantaged groups. Despite causing much academic, political and public debate about the rights and wrongs of AA, it is argued that by about 1970, few (less than 20 per cent of) American employers had made significant changes in employment practices or structures. From around 1972, the scope of AA was expanded by statute to include small firms, and enforcement was stepped up by enabling the Equal Employment Opportunity Commission (EEOC), as well as individuals, to sue employers for non-compliance. The effect was that, by the mid-1970s, significant numbers of employers had proactive AA measures designed to increase representation of women and black and minority ethnic (BME) people. Proactive in this context meant setting goals, but, contrary to popular belief, *not* quotas which the law did not allow.

By the early 1980s, AA was facing intense political opposition led by the newly elected President, Ronald Reagan, opposed to regulation in general and whose administration reduced AA enforcement, cutting funding such that monitoring of compliance was weakened (Kelly and Dobbin 1998). It is argued that negative perceptions of AA were based largely on incorrect use of the term 'quota' and omission of the word 'qualified' in much of the debate. That is, AA became widely associated with enforceable quotas and the hiring of unqualified people in order to boost the numbers, with obvious negative connotations, including the perception that hiring and performance standards were being lowered and the belief that AA stigmatized beneficiaries (Gilbert et al 1999). Most controversial of all the criticisms was the myth that people who had never personally experienced discrimination were benefiting from AA at the expense of white males; that is, AA was equated with reverse discrimination, widely regarded as morally wrong (Yakura 1996). In fact, AA measures were actually flexible goals, not quotas; goals do not demand hiring workers when there are no vacancies or hiring unqualified people (Gilbert et al 1999). However, AA did involve giving preferential treatment on the basis of group membership, and to this extent it challenged the democratic ideal of individual equality (Williams 2000). Negative attitudes based on these misconceptions and a general suspicion of the ideal of group equality entered the public and political mindset ensuring that AA received little support.

By the mid-1980s, official statistics indicate that fewer US employers had special recruiting or AA programmes for women and BME groups than in the mid-1970s (Kelly and Dobbin 1998). Kelly and Dobbin (1998) argue that in the face of the controversy surrounding AA and the diminishing political will to enforce it, EEO/AA specialists began to make new arguments for equality action. Essentially they turned to the 'business case', thus prefiguring the diversity discourse that by the late 1980s had firmly taken hold. Some of the elements of the 'new' diversity policies were virtually identical to EEO/AA measures, including anti-discrimination policies, recruitment procedures and even targeted training programmes. But the language used to talk about such measures had changed to become more business-friendly. An increased emphasis on the business case also fitted well with demographic changes that were at the same time altering labour and consumer markets. The now (in)famous *Workforce 2000* report (Johnston and Packer 1987) alerted USA employers to the (allegedly) dramatic changes that were occurring in the American workforce. In particular, the report highlighted that by 2000 white males would no longer be the dominant demographic group *entering* the USA labour market. This prompted widespread discussion in the media, business and academic forums of the greater need for organizations to recognize the importance of managing a diverse or multi-cultural workforce. *Workforce 2000* actually talked about the impact of workforce diversity in a broad sense, including the increasing labour market participation of women and the ageing workforce. But it was the vision of increased racial/ethnic diversity that attracted most attention by the media and other commentators. Many of the most alarming predictions and discussions were the consequence of the researchers' errors or readers' misinterpretations. For example, the report was often (mis)read as stating that by 2000 white males would no longer be the dominant demographic group *within* the USA labour market, rather than only relating to new entrants (Litvin 2006), implying a shortage of white males and therefore a need for organizations to recruit more widely. Overall, the widespread diffusion of the business case for diversity can be traced back to the *Workforce 2000* report; arguably it arrived at a critical moment in the history of EEO/AA and became a tool that EEO/AA specialists used in an attempt to refresh interest in and commitment to equality policies. In particular, anti-discrimination policies were re-theorized as responses to a competitive labour market and the business advantages of a diverse workforce (Kelly and Dobbin 1998).

Despite the fact that, as is discussed later, we see some elements of what is now defined as the diversity discourse within later formulations of and justifications for EEO/AA, the diversity discourse does not sit easily on top of the debates and controversies of AA (Yakura 1996), and (partly at least) for this reason, it is often presented as an entirely new policy approach.

Thus, for political reasons, to signal a departure from the controversy that riddled AA, human resource managers, diversity specialists (often former EEO/AA specialists) and line-managers alike tried to establish boundaries between DM and EEO/AA (Kelly and Dobbin 1998). In particular, it is stressed that DM is an internal voluntary policy approach, rather than imposed externally by law. Nevertheless, the debate about the extent to which DM is simply repackaged EEO/AA practices rages on in the USA. However, it is important to recognize that the most controversial AA measures are usually not included in DM (i.e. group-targeted recruitment and training programmes). We return to the discussion about the 'differences' between equality and diversity approaches later. Next we consider the influence of these debates on other industrialized countries, with a special focus on the UK.

DM GOES GLOBAL

As previously stated, by the mid-1990s, the diversity discourse had started to go global, and it continues its march across the world, although not without meeting controversy and challenge. Teicher and Spearitt (1996) chart the chequered emergence of DM in the Australian context that bears some similarity to the USA experience. They claim that DM was heralded as 'second generation' EEO, following a raft of anti-discrimination and AA legislation enacted in Australia in the 1970s and 1980s that had been found wanting (for different reasons) by both employers and equality activists. AA legislation in relation (only) to women was introduced in 1986, and, as with the USA, AA in Australia quickly and incorrectly became equated with quotas, causing it to become rapidly unpopular among employers, the general public and some beneficiaries (i.e. some women). Reporting mechanisms and sanctions for non-compliance were weak and its impact therefore limited. Within this context, it was foreign-owned (usually USA) companies that pioneered DM, but evidence suggests that some managers were skeptical at least initially about its transferability (Teicher and Spearitt 1996). Nevertheless, it is argued that DM has seen a surge of popularity in Australian managerial and public policy contexts, which can be attributed to government policy (particularly in the contested area of multiculturalism and racism) and to global firms with a head office-driven diversity agenda (Sinclair 2006). Arguably, the diversity discourse, with its abandonment of the principles of AA, its claim to include and value everyone for the benefit of the business, is a sweeter pill to swallow than a policy designed to challenge racism head-on.

The UK context for the emergence of the diversity discourse was somewhat different primarily because AA was and is not allowed by law. However, British law does allow for 'positive action' where members of a particular sex or race are under-represented in a particular workforce.

Under the rubric of positive action, employers can, but are not required to, train members of that sex/race to help equip them for such work, but it is unlawful to give preferential treatment at the point of selection in recruitment and promotion. Both older and more recent research confirms that UK employers, particularly in the private sector, dislike positive action and are disinclined to establish measures (Cockburn 1991; Walsh 2007). In practice, the two main pieces of early legislation (the Sex Discrimination Act 1975 and the Race Relations Act 1976) were really concerned with tackling discrimination, rather than promoting equality. Essentially the legislation did little more than require organizations to establish a principle of non-discrimination and provide an opportunity for redress for individual victims of discrimination. There was and continues to be no systematic monitoring of employers' compliance, and penalties for non-compliance were and are generally low (Johnson and Johnstone 2005).

These minimalist acts underpinned the dominant organizational approach to equality policy-making for at least two decades, meaning that employer policies were typically minimalist. From the late 1970s onwards, many larger employers developed EO policies according to a 'one size fits all' formula that included a set of prescriptions primarily relating to procedures for eliminating discrimination in recruitment and selection (Webb 1997). The early anti-discrimination acts and EO policies promised more than they delivered partly because employers seemed unwilling to go beyond the very minimalist requirements of the law. Yet despite being minimalist, EO policies still managed to provoke public and political controversy, with accusations that they unfairly advantaged certain groups and were a product of the 'loony left'. Cockburn (1991) argued that British equality legislation was the product of the era of welfare capitalism and that this ended with the election of the Conservative government in 1979. Like the Reagan administration in the USA, the Thatcher government of 1979–1993 was opposed to labour market regulation and therefore did nothing to promote compliance and enforcement of equality legislation.

Within this hostile political climate, by the late 1980s, UK academics, trade unions, equality activists and other commentators had begun to critique EO on the grounds that managers were able to ignore or subvert policy prescriptions, that subjectivity and bias still managed to creep into decision-making and that already marginalized groups were further stigmatized by positive action. Moreover, organizations were charged with paying mere 'lip service' to equality and with having EO policies that were no more than 'empty shells'. Thus, the kind of social and cultural transformation necessary to achieve greater equality of outcome seemed elusive (Cockburn 1989; Glover and Kirton 2006). Against a background of increasing disillusionment with EO policies, equality activists began to place increasing emphasis on the business case for equality in an attempt to provide a more compelling basis for employer action. Later, in 1997, the election of the Labour government provided a more equality-friendly context (for example, the Labour Party Manifesto of 1997 promised that a future Labour government would 'eliminate unjustifiable discrimination wherever it exists' (Johnson and Johnstone 2005)). However, the Labour government has also been keen not to alienate the business community and has therefore strenuously promoted the business case for diversity. Thus, employers meanwhile have been made progressively more aware by government campaigns of the increasing demographic diversity of the workforce and the implications of this for future recruitment.

Arguably, the changing social and economic context and changing political and public discourses of equality paved the way for the emergence in the UK of DM, just as they had earlier in the USA, albeit with some subtle (and some not-so-subtle) contextual differences (Glover and Kirton 2006). Rajvinder Kandola and Johanna Fullerton's book, *Managing the Mosaic: Diversity in Action*, first published in 1994 (second edition in 1998) by the then Institute for Personnel and Development (now Chartered Institute for Personnel and Development), can be credited with disseminating the diversity concept in the UK (Kandola and Fullerton 1994). Their stated hope was that the book would provide a 'starting-point for a re-evaluation of the work that has been done in the name of equal opportunities but also a chance to make a new start' (ibid: 2). At the time of the book's publication, most of the diversity literature was written by American academics, but more recently academics around the world have begun to engage with the diversity discourse. The evidence produced shows that the diversity discourse is having an impact on many organizations in many countries. In the context of the wider Europe, it is pointed out that, to date, the trajectory of DM is different from that in the USA because there was nothing like the USA experience with AA and therefore no parallel political movement against it (although the UK's experience with positive action described above distinguishes it somewhat from its European neighbours). Further, there has been nothing like the pressure for action on equality issues that has been witnessed in both the USA and the UK, where social movement organizations have long campaigned vociferously for equality along various dimensions, including race, gender, disability and sexuality. In addition, most European countries have not seen a group of dedicated professionals working specifically on these issues to parallel the experience of the USA, UK, Australia and New Zealand at least (Wrench 2001). Recent evidence from corporate websites across Europe shows that around 40 per cent of companies in seven selected European countries other than the UK use the term 'diversity', compared with over 80 per cent of UK companies (Point and Singh, 2003). Moreover, the focus of DM policies in European countries other than the UK is also more likely to be on issues to do with race and ethnicity, rather than a broader, more inclusive agenda. This is a consequence of perceived social problems or challenges surrounding migration, refugees, multi-culturalism and religious affiliation, all of which are hot topics in Europe (for example, De los Reyes 2000; Kamp and Hagedorn-Rasmussen 2004; Subeliani and Tsogas 2005) and to which different European countries have responded in different ways (see Kirton and Greene 2005). However, arguably in the mainland European context, the discourse of diversity has allowed these issues to be put on the employment and organizational policy agenda in some cases for the first time (Wrench 2004).

KEY ASPECTS OF DM

Even though it is generally recognized to different degrees by different authors that DM is related to EO-type approaches (i.e. it is not something entirely new), most authors distinguish at least theoretically between DM and EO. Whilst we acknowledge that in some organizations the DM policy might simply look like EO policy with a new name, we argue that it is important to mark out the conceptual differences between DM and EO in order to provide a schema against which to analyze and evaluate organizational policies. There are numerous definitions of DM in the literature, but they generally share several key features. Two examples, one from the USA and one from the UK, are given in Table 2.1, from which we highlight an emphasis on individual differences and the business case.

From the USA and UK literature, we also identify four central tenets of DM that distinguish it from an EO paradigm. First, we can say that as a process DM refers to 'the systematic and planned commitment on the part of organizations to recruit and retain employees with diverse backgrounds and abilities' (Bassett-Jones 2005: 169). As for the central

Table 2.1   Example Definitions of Diversity Management

US Definition	UK Definition
People are different from one another in many ways—in age, gender, education, values, physical ability, mental capacity, personality, experiences, culture and the way each approaches work. Gaining the diversity advantage means acknowledging, understanding and appreciating these differences and developing a workplace that enhances their value—by being flexible enough to meet needs and preferences—to create a motivating and rewarding environment. (Jamieson and O'Mara 1991: 3–4)	The basic concept of managing accepts that the workforce consists of visible and non-visible differences which will include factors such as sex, age, background, race, disability, personality and work style. It is founded on the premise that harnessing these differences will create a productive environment in which everybody feels valued, where their talents are being fully utilized and in which organizational goals are met.(Kandola and Fullerton 1994: 8)

Table 2.2 Differences Between Principles of EO and DM

Equal Opportunity	Diversity Management
Reliance on legal regulation and bureaucratic procedures to eliminate discrimination	Systemic, cultural transformation of the organization to promote the value of workforce diversity
Highlights discrimination and the penalties that organizations face under the law	Uses positive imagery and celebratory rhetoric
Efforts justified by reference to legal compulsion and the social justice case	Efforts justified by reference to the business case
Social group-based differences are the focus—e.g. gender, race/ethnicity, disability etc.	Individual differences are emphasized, including lifestyle, appearance, work style etc.

tenets, we can state that DM (i) advocates a systemic (or cultural) transformation of the organization, rather than a reliance on legal regulation and bureaucratic procedures; (ii) uses positive imagery and celebratory rhetoric, rather than highlighting discrimination and the penalties that organizations face under equality laws; (iii) efforts are justified by reference to the business case, rather than legal compulsion or the social justice case; and (iv) includes a broad range of individual and social group-based differences (Cox 1994; Kandola and Fullerton 1998; Kersten 2000). For clarification, the differences between EO and DM are also shown in Table 2.2.

It is important to stress that the differences between EO-type approaches and DM are more a question of emphasis than binary, and any attempt to distinguish the two is bound to be somewhat crude. For example, all industrialized countries have some kind of equality laws with which employers are required to comply. However, as suggested above, in most countries, such laws are either minimalist in nature or are so poorly enforced that in practice organizations have to do very little in order to comply or be seen to comply. Therefore, whilst the law cannot be ignored, in most (larger) organizations, compliance with legislation is taken as read, and within a DM paradigm, any additional, voluntary efforts are justified by reference to the business case. (The legal context of DM is discussed in more detail in Chapter 3.) It is also important to note that even if we can settle on the central tenets of DM, organizations do not approach policy and practice in a uniform way. In terms of thinking about what all this means for DM policy and practice, Liff's (1997) typology of DM approaches, despite being over a decade old, retains some usefulness as an analytical framework. This differentiates between four sets of underlying policy principles and aims that recognize to different degrees the legacy and imprint of traditional EO-type approaches with which most organizations are still likely to be working. The framework also fits well with debates about sameness and difference approaches to equality as discussed in Chapter 1. The two caveats are first that in practice organizations' policy aims might be multi-dimensional and complex and therefore not fit neatly into any of the approaches that Liff identifies; second that the diversity debate and policy and practice have moved on in the decade since Liff wrote her paper. We return to the latter point below.

The first approach Liff (1997) identifies is *dissolving differences*. Here differences between people are not seen as based on social group membership (such as gender or race), but are individually based. It follows that initiatives would seek to respond to individual rather than group needs—for example, individual career management policies. If someone has training needs, this should be addressed regardless of whether they are, for example, a man or a woman, or black or white. The point is for people to see themselves as individuals, rather than identify with similar others based on social group characteristics. Further, monitoring the workforce by characteristics such as gender, race and ethnicity would be seen to offer little of value or might even be counter-productive to a dissolving differences approach. Essentially, this approach ignores or downplays the wider social causes of inequality, including unequal access to training and education and does not see inequality as patterned by social group membership. This approach has echoes of EO insofar as the underlying aim is to treat people the same regardless of social group characteristics. The second approach is *valuing differences*. Here Liff (1997) refers to social group-based rather than individual differences, with policy recognition of the way in which, for example, gender or race can contribute to patterns of under-representation and inequality. Positive action initiatives would be included, for example, provision of training for employees from under-represented groups to help them succeed in the organization and to help overcome past group disadvantage. There would also be some adaptation of organizational policies in order, for example, to recognize different holidays and diets. The third approach is *accommodating differences*, where there is a commitment to creating policies that open up opportunities (such as flexible working patterns) to under-represented groups. This approach might be found where the most compelling business case for diversity relates to the changing demographic composition of the labour market—for example, a need to recruit more women. This approach is very similar to traditional EO-type policies, and whilst it goes some way to recognizing both individual and socially-based differences, it does not question the fundamental social or organizational structures of inequality. The final approach is *utilizing differences*, where social group-based differences are recognized and provide the basis for different treatment. This approach is not concerned with social justice, rather employee differences will be put to use for the benefit of the organization. This might be described as a 'special contribution' perspective which argues that different people (for example, women, BME people etc.) might be able to contribute to organizations in different ways with their different values, experiences, ways of thinking and so on (Billing and Sundin 2006). Liff suggests that policy initiatives designed to tap gender-based differences might include different career tracks for 'career' and 'family' women.

Writing in 1997 when the EO paradigm was still dominant, Liff believed that the dissolving and valuing differences approaches were the dominant strands in the diversity debate. We argue that theorizing, research and policy and practice have now shifted, and the main strands of the diversity debate at least in the UK-based literature, but probably beyond, now centre on valuing *individual* differences and utilizing these differences. To be clear, we do not necessarily regard this as progress, as will be made clear in the analysis of the empirical material presented in subsequent chapters. That said, organizations may still in some circumstances use diversity initiatives in an effort to dissolve or accommodate certain differences, but the primacy of these debates has receded. Part of the explanation lies in changing discourses of difference and changing responses to difference. Differences are now widely understood in the social sciences and in everyday life as multi-faceted, ambiguous and complex with forms of difference intersecting with others (Jenkins 2004). In theoretical and policy terms, this means that we cannot simply regard women, for example, as a unitary, homogeneous group even if we do see something similar in women's life patterns. We also need to consider differences between women, such as race, ethnicity, sexual orientation and religious faith, and the way that these differences may divide women's life experiences and thus require more sophisticated theorizing of women's concerns and interests as well as multi-faceted policy responses. In terms of institutional responses to differences in the UK context, the rhetorical approach at least is to value and affirm differences, rather than to attempt to assimilate or deny differences. This is evidenced by a range of social, welfare, employment and educational policies that emphasize the importance of recognizing, accepting and valuing differences. This is a sea change from the days when to be equal was to be the same. In relation to the labour market, this perspective on differences is promoted by the UK government:

> A diverse workforce can be more creative than one which has been recruited in the image of a particular manager. It may be able to establish new clients for the business, and to help to reach a wider market. (Cabinet Office 2001)

This takes us to a discussion of the business case for diversity, a key aspect of DM and one of the major theoretical, research and policy challenges.

The Business Case

As previously stated, traditional EO has been largely concerned with social justice, although business case arguments also formed part of the basis for policy (Colling and Dickens 2001). But what exactly is the business case for DM? Four main advantages to organizations are usually emphasized: (i) taking advantage of diversity in the labour market, (ii) maximizing employee potential, (iii) managing across borders and cultures, and (iv) creating business opportunities and enhancing creativity (Cornelius et al 2001). The first point—taking advantage of diversity in the labour market—highlights the changing demographic composition of the workforce such as the increased employment participation of women, the ageing workforce and larger numbers of minority ethnic workers. This argument is founded on the belief that only organizations that attract and retain a diversity of employees will be successful, particularly in tight labour markets. UK organizations seem to be particularly persuaded by this argument, and it is in fact one of only two 'proven' benefits according to Kandola and Fullerton (1998: 36). The second point—maximizing employee potential—argues that the harnessing of human capital possessed by diverse groups will improve organizational performance. Conversely, it is argued that unfair and discriminatory treatment creates low morale and disaffection leading to poor performance. Therefore, organizations need to actively manage diversity in order to extract the highest levels of performance from employees—but according to Kandola and Fullerton (ibid), this is a 'debatable benefit'. The third point—managing across borders and cultures—mainly concerns the globalization of world markets and the international labour market on which many organizations draw. Here the argument is that a diverse workforce can enhance an organization's ability to reach and satisfy a broader customer base—again, a 'debatable' benefit according to Kandola and Fullerton (ibid). The fourth point—creating business opportunities and enhancing opportunities—is about tapping the supposedly culturally specific experiences and insights that a diverse workforce possesses in order to move the organization forward. If, for example, we think about product development, is it possible that women are better placed to identify products that other women might buy or might Asian workers know more about the kinds of foods in which Asian customers might be interested? According to Kandola and Fullerton's categorization, this would at best be a debatable, but possibly only an indirect benefit of DM; in other words, difficult if not impossible to prove.

In practice, there is conflicting evidence on whether or not and which kind of organizations might benefit from workforce diversity. A similar discussion has taken place on whether equality is good for business. It has been argued that the business case for *equality* is 'partial and contingent' and does not have universal purchase (Dickens 1994). For example, some organizations compete on the basis of low cost; therefore, relatively expensive equality measures, such as work–life balance policies, might not be cost-effective. In addition, some organizations might actually benefit from an absence of equality insofar as discriminatory practices can contribute to the bottom line. For example, organizations can benefit from the utilization, but under-valuing of women's labour (Dickens 1994). After all, the gender pay gap means that women are cheaper to employ. Translating Dickens' arguments into the language of diversity, it is possible for organizations to benefit from having and utilizing a diverse workforce, but whether or not there will be benefits from *valuing* diversity depends very much on the type of organization and its business and employee relations strategies. An organization with a cost-minimization strategy might regard its low-paid workers as entirely dispensable and replaceable and be unwilling to invest in potentially costly DM initiatives, particularly when the benefits are most likely debatable at best. Kirton (2008) argues that the rhetoric of diversity could also be used to conceal organizational 'non-action' on discrimination and inequalities and to convey the impression that 'there's no problem here'. If everyone is different and has different needs, aspirations and so on, why does it matter if there are different outcomes? With this kind of neo-liberal thinking, unequal outcomes can easily be reconstructed as simply different. Thus, the celebratory metaphors of diversity can be used to deny the existence of injustice, inequalities, discrimination and exploitation (Kersten 2000).

Advocates of diversity (Ross and Schneider 1992; Kandola and Fullerton 1994; Schneider 2001) have tended to gloss over these issues, making broad-brush statements about the benefits of diversity that lack a contextualized analysis. There is no solid evidence that DM policies are any less partial and contingent than traditional EO. There are, however, suggestions that DM can deliver organizational benefits if initiatives are formulated in ways that are sensitive to the existing culture and practices and if some of the potential dilemmas and challenges are dealt with (Cornelius et al 2000; Sinclair 2000; Maxwell et al 2001). We now turn to the tensions, dilemmas and challenges of DM.

CHALLENGES OF DM

This section is concerned with the challenges of DM, in particular those posed by the business case—we look behind the rhetoric of the business case to unpack the tensions and conflicts. In addition, we address three challenges from a stakeholder perspective that were explored in the research that the book presents. First, is there space for trade union involvement within DM? Second, do employees benefit from DM? Third, do line-managers buy into DM?

Behind the Rhetoric of the Business Case

One fundamental criticism of the business case is that it need not necessarily lead to valuing people as individual human beings; employees might be 'valued' simply as factors of production, contributors to the bottom line

(Litvin 2006). To illustrate this point, Kirton (2008) gives the example of the multi-national corporation Wal-Mart. She argues that from the company's web site (www.walmartstores.com) it appears that it has devoted an impressive amount of resources to diversity. It states that, 'thanks to several diversity-focused initiatives, we are a leading USA employer of Hispanics, African Americans, women and seniors'. The company clearly states its affiliation to the business case when it says that one of its diversity goals is to have 'a workforce that's representative of our diverse customer base'. There is an 'Office of Diversity' which includes a 'Diversity Initiatives Department', a 'Human Resources and Diversity Insight Department' and a 'Diversity Relations Department', headed up by a senior vice president and chief diversity officer. Over the last few years, Wal-Mart has won various awards in the areas of diversity and inclusion. Yet in October 2005, *The Independent* newspaper in the UK reported in an article entitled *Fat? Over 40? Don't bother applying for a Wal-Mart job* that a 'secret memo' had revealed a plan by the company to make it harder for older, 'less healthy people' to get a job in its stores. The strategy was allegedly designed to reduce the company's health care costs. Wal-Mart has also been accused of taking advantage of the precarious situation of illegal immigrants in the USA to reduce its labour costs, employing them at sub-minimum wage levels with no benefits (Mir et al 2006). Kirton (ibid) argues that Wal-Mart is not alone in promoting a positive image of its diversity strategies and in using celebratory rhetoric to do so and yet apparently engaging in employment practices that point in a diametrically opposite direction. Another example offered by Kirton (ibid) is soft drinks group Coca-Cola. In 2000, the company paid out $192 million to settle charges of race discrimination made by 2,000 African American employees (*The Guardian*, 17th November 2000), despite having a range of diversity initiatives in place. Kirton (ibid) argues that these examples, and many others like them, demonstrate the way that diversity policies founded on the business case all too often lack real substance and genuine commitment to valuing diversity. Kirton (ibid) asks why so many organizations bother even to pay 'lip service' to diversity when it is clear that doing so costs them money (in terms of the cost of training, communication, literature and any concrete initiatives)? From an institutional perspective, it could be argued that the adoption of diversity statements and policies lends the organization legitimacy in the eyes of stakeholders and that such legitimacy is necessary for survival and prosperity. At a time when diversity is sweeping the developed world, there are powerful normative and isomorphic forces pushing organizations to jump on the 'diversity bandwagon'.

From a policy perspective, one of the reasons for the gap between the 'rhetoric and reality' of DM is that most organizations put forward generic business case arguments (such as those summarized earlier). It is rare to see a specific business case tailored to the particular organization, its sector, markets and customers. This is intuitively erroneous. From a study of service sector companies, Janssens and Zanoni (2005) are among a number of authors who make a convincing case for contextualized understandings of and approaches to DM. They find that organizations understand diversity in relation to the way that particular social group differences affect the organization of service delivery. In some organizations, while it might be necessary to hire a diverse workforce, differences might be seen as a potential problem hindering, rather than assisting, effective service delivery. In others, the customer might be the central actor in defining which dimensions of diversity are relevant and therefore valued by the organization (for example, hospitals with diverse patients). In yet other organizations, the customer might be remote and invisible (such as call centres), and DM might be more concerned with internal employee relations matters (Janssens and Zanoni 2005). This contextual variation will inevitably impact on the way that diversity is 'managed' and the 'types' of diversity that are sought and valued. There is also of course an inherently exploitative and opportunistic dimension to constructing employees simply as organizational resources, which can only underscore the contingent (and therefore fragile) nature of business case justifications for diversity initiatives.

Furthermore, when the business case is the prime rationale for diversity initiatives, then DM initiatives have to be justified in financial terms (Sinclair, 2006). Academics have been accused of not providing practitioners with a method to 'numerically assess' DM within their organizations (Gilbert et al 1999: 72). A preoccupation with measuring the contribution of workforce diversity and DM initiatives to organizational success is particularly notable in the USA literature (see Ng and Tung 1998; Gilbert and Ivancevich 2000; Wheeler 2003). However, even though studies call for 'hard measures' (Gilbert and Ivancevich 2000), they have not really properly answered how practitioners are to isolate the effects of other variables (such as the state of the economy or labour supply) on organizational performance and how they are to actually prove some of the more debateable claims—for example, the diversity contribution to innovation and creativity (see Ashton 2003). The difficulties of evaluating diversity and of showing return on investment have been identified as major barriers to diversity initiatives (Wentling 2004). This discussion of the problems of the business case brings us to the specific areas that we are interested in from a stakeholder perspective.

Is There Space for Union Involvement in DM?

Recent history tells us that employers will not always voluntarily improve their policies and practices, terms and conditions. 'Bottom-up' pressure for equality exerted through trade unions has in the past proved just as important as the 'top-down' commitment of senior management (Colling and Dickens 1998; Dickens 1999). Dickens et al (1988: 65) highlighted this in their research into 'equality bargaining' in the UK in the 1980s, arguing that a 'review of discriminatory terms and practice is more likely to occur where there is some form of joint regulation than where issues are unilaterally determined by employers'. We would question whether there is any reason to believe that the climate for equality has changed so that 'grassroots' activism is no longer necessary to push for progress. On the contrary, in fact, there is recent evidence that workplaces with recognized trade unions are still more likely to have developed formal equality policies than non-unionized firms and that unionized workforces generally still experience less pronounced inequalities than non-unionized ones (Colling and Dickens 2001; Walsh 2007).

With UK organizations now typically using a discourse that has shifted away from traditional EO towards DM, there is some concern that unions will have less influence on the policy agenda (Greene et al 2005; Kirton and Greene 2006). Will the ultimate consequence be that unionized workplaces lose their status as more equal ones? From a trade union perspective, there are three main problems with DM. The first problem is the underpinning economic rationale for DM. It is argued that this inherently stands in contradiction with the employee rights-based approach that trade unions take. Although it goes without saying that unions have an interest in the long-term financial health of organizations, their primary concern is employee interests. So although the unions will often promote the business case for diversity, where the business case might call for poorer treatment and conditions or lower pay, for example, it is the employee perspective that unions must necessarily uphold. The second problem is the focus on the individual within the DM paradigm. Trade unions are collective organizations and, as such, they rely on collective identification—people perceiving that they have something in common with similar others. EO focuses on patterned, social group-based discrimination and disadvantage and potentially at least raises people's awareness of a collective dimension to their individual circumstances. On a practical level, unions see collective agreements as the vehicle for reducing inequalities, rather than individualized management techniques recommended within the DM paradigm. The third problem is that DM is positioned as a top-down managerial activity. As suggested above, it is the vision and commitment of top management that is seen as critical to the success of DM initiatives, rather than the involvement of other stakeholders such as trade unions. When employee involvement does feature in DM, it is usually in individualized forms such as suggestion schemes or attitude surveys (Kirton and Greene 2006). These problems combine, theoretically at least, to direct DM policy efforts away from the trade union aim of social justice, dilute the union focus on group-based forms of discrimination and disadvantage and marginalize the role of trade unions in bargaining for equality. However, it is necessary to add a note of caution here. This is a summary of the theoretical problems that DM holds for trade unions, particularly in the UK context. In practice, the picture is more mixed both in the UK and other countries and contingent on the economic, social, political and industrial relations context. For example, in Denmark, the unions have used the diversity discourse to pursue involvement in addressing the previously neglected policy issue of race and ethnic inequalities, thus indicating some positive benefit from a discourse of diversity as opposed to equality (Greene et al 2005). Generally unions are pragmatic organizations accustomed to using whatever practical and discursive tools at their disposal in order to pursue their goals. These issues are discussed in more detail in subsequent chapters.

Do Employees Benefit from DM?

It is particularly noticeable that within both the theoretical and policy debates about the benefits of DM, non-management employee perspectives are often absent, and it is taken for granted that if organizations have much to gain from workforce diversity, then by extension employees will benefit from DM initiatives. Therefore, one of the issues that stands out for us concerns whether and how non-management employees benefit from DM, as opposed to from more traditional EO approaches. Jones (2004) sees DM as a 'discourse of exploitation' rather than the new paradigm for equality policy-making. We see three major dilemmas of DM that suggest that non-management employees are unlikely to be the main beneficiaries of DM initiatives. First, as suggested above, the business case for diversity cannot meet the interests of all. For example, in practice, whilst in the name of the business case some equality and diversity issues are vigorously tackled, others will be neglected if no strong business reason for action can be identified. This has been raised as a concern in relation to the difficulties of constructing a business case for employing disabled people (Woodhams and Danieli 2000). In fact, in much of the DM literature and in organizational policies, there is an implicit, if not explicit focus on gender and race, rather than on broader diversity issues, meaning that issues such as disability, sexual orientation and age can disappear from the research and policy agenda, contrary to the DM claim to be more inclusive than EO. Further, if organizations utilize employee differences simply to improve business performance, some employees might feel exploited and unfairly treated, rather than valued. Second, DM policies usually place the emphasis on the individual employee. This can mean that group-targeted 'special measures' or positive action initiatives, such as development programmes for BME people or women, fall out of favour. In many organizations, it is these very measures that have increased the proportion of previously under-represented groups in the management hierarchy. Thus, a focus on the individual might prove insufficient to reverse historic under-representation. Furthermore, taken to an extreme, how can a business case be made on the basis of individual differences (Woodhams and Danieli 2000)? Third, as we discuss in subsequent chapters, DM policies emphasize senior level commitment over 'grassroots' involvement. Although it is widely accepted that the most senior people in the organization certainly need to publicly support DM policy, the more challenging project is ensuring that all organizational members 'buy into' diversity and operationalize that commitment into everyday behaviour and practices. It is also necessary for employees to be involved in order to identify their experiences and needs. One way to do this, as some organizations recognize, is to find ways of involving different groups of employees via, for example, trade unions and employee networks.

In terms of the culture of organizations, one of the issues that the celebratory rhetoric of diversity conceals is the possible resistance of majority group members when organizations become more diverse and the effect that this can have on minority group members. A substantial segment of the USA diversity literature focuses on the effects of workforce diversity on work groups and teams, exploring the conflicts and tensions that can surface (particularly within racially mixed work groups) and their effects on morale and performance (Jehn et al 1999; Pelled et al 1999; Bacharach et al 2005; Brief et al 2005). These are thought to be important considerations because conflict management takes up employees' time as well as managers' and reduces the ability of the work group to retain good employees. In addition, it is argued that supportive peer relations foster trust, empathy and reciprocity, thus facilitating information and knowledge exchange that is vital to personal and organizational development (Bacharach et al 2005). At the present time, empirical research presents a mixed picture. For example, some studies show that social group (especially race) diversity impacts negatively upon work relations (Jehn et al 1999; Pelled et al 1999), while others find that it has a positive effect (Ng and Tung 1998).

Kossek et al's (2003) study of the diversity strategy of a USA university shows that gradually increasing the employment of previously under-represented women and 'minorities' does not necessarily lead to an improved climate in terms of perceptions of fairness of resource allocation or good mixing in social interaction. Similarly, from their research, Brief et al (2005) state that people in more racially diverse organizations report lower quality work relationships than those in less racially diverse organizations. However, Kochan et al (2003) conclude that, although racial and gender diversity does not have the positive effect on performance proposed by optimists, neither does it necessarily have a negative effect. Indeed, they state that there was some 'promising evidence' that under certain conditions 'racial diversity may even enhance performance' (ibid: 17). The extent to which these findings apply beyond the USA context is difficult to determine. Although racial conflict is by no means a uniquely American phenomenon, it is particularly acute in the USA and is rooted in the country's history of slavery and racial segregation (see, for example, Bacharach et al 2005).

Do Line-Managers Buy into DM?

One significant criticism of the traditional EO approach is that it was largely seen as a specialist, peripheral activity that had little to do with line-managers. In contrast, within DM, there is a very clear role for line-managers (Kandola and Fullerton 1994, 1998), an aspect we explore in-depth in Chapter 7. It is argued that DM is likely to be most effective when there is pro-active line-management involvement (Cornelius et al 2000). Therefore, a significant challenge is how to obtain line-management buy-in and embed diversity into everyday managerial practice.

Given that many organizations now devolve authority for a range of staffing decisions to line-managers, they are critical to the success of DM, particularly to the culture change at the heart of policy implementation. Many organizations are grappling with how to make DM a 'core competency' so that managers have to demonstrate how they build diversity into their own performance (Schneider 2001). While in theory DM represents an opportunity for interested and committed managers to get involved in equality and diversity, in practice there is evidence of line-managers' reluctance to give priority to diversity issues (Cornelius et al 2000; Maxwell et al 2001). The freedom to manage and to exercise discretion that comes with devolution can also provide an opportunity for line-managers to ignore the equality and diversity agenda (Cunningham 2000). However, it is important not to vilify line-managers as it is also clear that they face many conflicting priorities and that these difficulties might lead them to opt out of actively 'managing diversity'. However, for some line-managers, it might not be a question of lack of time or commitment, rather that they might genuinely be at a loss to understand exactly what it is they are supposed to do to demonstrate that they value diversity (Foster and Harris 2005). In addition, some line-managers might believe that the DM policy is simply senior management rhetoric, a passing fad, and therefore they might not take it seriously (Maxwell et al 2001).

Another question impacting on the role of line-managers is whether diverse teams are easier or more difficult to manage than relatively homogeneous ones. If the latter is the case, the diversity efforts are almost bound to meet management resistance. Again, there is conflicting evidence in both the USA and UK literature (see, for example, Iles 1995; Kossek et al 2003). Even proponents of diversity recognize that the likelihood that diversity will promote team creativity and innovation and improve problem-solving and decision-making is debatable (Kandola and Fullerton 1994). As stated above, some research has highlighted the way that diversity in work teams can (or be widely held to) lead to divisions, conflicts and poor interpersonal relations, potentially contributing to poor performance. This might result in line-managers having a preference for homogeneous work groups in order to avoid the extra time and effort they might believe is necessary to manage diverse ones. While they might appreciate the possible long-term benefits of a diverse workforce, in the meantime there might be costs involved, such as selection/retention processes and co-operation processes. Thus, managers might face a dilemma of choosing between short-term costs and long-term benefits (Schneider and Northcraft 1999).

CONCLUSION

The criticism of DM in the more critical academic literature has centred on the 'upbeat naivety' (Prasad et al 1997) contained in most definitions and statements. The idea that DM can move the equality project forward in ways that benefit everyone is widely thought to be nothing more than wishful thinking (Lorbiecki and Jack 2000). Even the very idea that diversity is 'do-able' (that it can be managed and harnessed for organizational ends) is false according to some commentators (Prasad et al 1997).

Most models of DM prescribe culture change as necessary for the success of initiatives. This stands in contrast with traditional EO which depended more on bureaucratic methods—formal rules and procedures—an approach that has been criticized for failing to guarantee fair and equal outcomes or even treatment (Jewson and Mason 1986). In some areas such as the UK public sector, culture change has been part of a wider package of initiatives that have included DM elements under the umbrella of 'modernizing government' and 'New Public Management' designed to rid bureaucracy of its inefficiencies (Cunningham 2000). However, there is rarely any indepth analysis of exactly how culture change can be achieved. There is often an assumption that organizational culture is something that can be easily manipulated by senior management to achieve business goals, and the complexities of managing something as intangible as culture are downplayed. One of the supposed benefits of DM is that it is inclusive and does not exclude anyone, 'even white, middle-class males' (Kandola and Fullerton 1994: 9). This is meant to avoid the problems of backlash associated with the EO emphasis on particular groups and on special measures to assist them. In theory, this should then create a more positive climate for diversity. However, if DM successfully achieves its aim of attracting and retaining a diverse workforce (at all levels), then this will inevitably involve loss of privilege for some groups, who will find the competition for rewards such as bonuses and promotions intensified (Cockburn 1991; Sinclair 2000). This is bound to attract a degree of anger and resistance, and confronting these reactions is arguably part of the process of DM (Miller and Rowney 1999), but a difficult and challenging one. The views and experiences of multiple organizational stakeholders on these issues are presented in subsequent chapters drawing on our original UK-based research. In exploring multiple viewpoints on the policy and practice of DM, we hope to contribute to the creation of a more textured picture of whether the realities of DM are living up to the rhetoric.

3 The Contexts of Diversity Management

INTRODUCTION

The purpose of this chapter is to consider the political, economic, social and legal contexts within which organizations develop and implement diversity management (DM) policies. These broad contexts are important for understanding the book's empirical research. Considerable change has occurred over the last 30 years or so, and the evolving context poses many challenges for organizations and policy-makers in the equality and diversity field. This chapter briefly outlines the USA context and focuses more specifically on the UK. This is of course no coincidence. As shown in Chapter 1, the USA is the birthplace of DM, and the UK, where DM has been widely adopted as a policy paradigm, is the location of the book's empirical research. But more than this, the USA and the UK share much in common as liberal societies with laissez faire economies and relatively unregulated labour markets, providing a relatively unrestricted environment for the emergence of new social patterns and novel ways of organizing work (Hakim 2000). Indeed, in relation to the specific topic of this book—DM—it is argued that the 'conservative, right-wing agenda of the 1980s and early 1990s in the UK and USA provided a political environment in which a deregulated, voluntarist, diversity approach could flourish' (Noon and Ogbonna 2001: 4). In order to set the context for the empirical research presented in subsequent chapters, this chapter provides a summary overview, rather than in-depth analysis, of what we see as critical contextual issues for our research. It is also beyond the scope of this chapter to offer any detailed explanation of the different employment patterns outlined (see Glover and Kirton 2006 and Kirton and Greene 2005a for more on this aspect). The fundamental premise of the chapter is that the organizational-level policy-making that our research explores cannot be understood without reference to the key elements of the external contexts impacting upon organizations' functions, operations and policy-making. There is so much that could be said about the context, but in line with our research approach as outlined in Chapter 1, the contents of this chapter reflect the fact that the book is written from an industrial relations perspective, and we are therefore interested in the labour market, the employment relationship and the strategies and actions of key actors, including the state, employers and trade unions.

CHANGING ECONOMY AND LABOUR MARKET

In a context of globalization, industrialized countries have experienced a shift from a manufacturing to a service economy to the extent that the majority of jobs in the UK and USA are now in the service sector. The consequence has been a polarization of employment opportunities with an increase in professional and management jobs or 'knowledge work' as it is often called, but also in low-skill, low-paid part-time or temporary jobs, the latter two categories being a particular feature of the UK economy. The overall incidence of these forms of 'non-standard' work (part-time and temporary) has seen an increase in the last decade in the UK (McOrmond 2004). Aiding and abetting the spread of non-standard work, new information and communication technologies (ICTs) have blurred the boundaries of work and non-work in both time and space for many categories of worker, including professional and management and lower level service sector workers. Thus, another central feature of the so-called 'new economy' is the intensification of work (Glover and Kirton 2006).

Related to this new economic context, flexibility has become one of the major employment policy debates of the present period. Recent evidence indicates that the standard model of work—Monday to Friday, nine to five—may no longer be standard (McOrmond 2004). The '24/7' culture that we are witnessing involves so many of us in working long unsocial hours, including evening and weekend working either in the workplace or at home, that this may now be the norm, rather than the exception. Who benefits from these changes in working patterns? They might signal attempts by individuals to achieve work–life balance and also attempts by employers to respond to market demand, suggesting that everyone wins. But, stepping back for a moment from the contemporary win–win rhetoric, the extent to which non-standard working arrangements are new is questioned. In fact a substantial minority of the population—especially women and black and minority ethnic (BME) workers—has a longstanding tradition of shift, temporary and part-time work. Thus, an apparent willingness to engage in flexible, non-standard working patterns might be theorized as a historical (rather than a new) response by marginalized workers to a hostile employment context (McOrmond 2004).

On the one hand, there is now an argument made that increasing employment flexibility creates opportunities for previously under-represented or marginalized groups (especially women) to participate in the labour market (Purcell 2000). On the other hand, this kind of economic change has significant consequences not only for the demographic composition of the labour market, but also for employment inequalities. For example, Purcell

(2000) argues that, although women's employment has increased as a result of the expansion of the service sector, the quality of jobs offered to them has deteriorated considerably with a knock-on impact on women's pay, life-time earnings and pensions. Therefore, whether flexibility offers a route to greater overall equality is highly debatable (see also Dickens 1999).

The changing demographic composition of labour markets is one of the key policy issues facing the state, employers and trade unions, which is of course not unrelated to the flexibility debate. As discussed in Chapter 2, it was the *Workforce 2000* report that highlighted the increasing demographic complexity of the US labour market and triggered the intense and long-lasting debate about how employers should respond. Despite the fact that the report highlighted three main issues—increasing participation of women, increasing ethnic diversity and ageing workforce—the most extreme reactions related to the prospect of increasing ethnic diversity. However, overall, in industrialized countries, one of the most significant social and economic changes of the post-war period has been the exponential increase in women's employment participation. Marriage and motherhood both have far less of an impact on women's employment participation rates than formerly. In both the UK and USA, nearly half (approximately 46 per cent) of people in the labour market are now women. Around 70 per cent of British women and 60 per cent of American women are economically active (EOC 2004; Bureau of Labor Statistics 2007). However, women's pattern of employment participation in the USA is different from that seen in the UK. Although American women have a lower rate of participation, they have a much stronger tendency to work full-time over the life course, so that their employment pattern resembles that of American men (Bureau of Labor Statistics 2007). Around 20 per cent of American women work part-time, whereas about 44 per cent of women in the UK do so. In both countries, motherhood still has some impact: in the USA it gives rise to a lower participation rate, and in the UK to higher rates of part-time working. However, there are racial/ethnic differences between women. In the USA, black/African American mothers have the highest employment participation rates (compared with white, Asian and Hispanic/Latino mothers) (Bureau of Labor Statistics 2007). In the UK, all BME women have lower participation rates than white women, but black Caribbean women have a stronger tendency to work full-time (Aston et al 2004). In terms of where we find women employed, it should be no surprise that gender segregation is deeply embedded in both the UK and USA—women are heavily concentrated in management, professional, sales and office occupations and under-represented in blue-collar, manual occupations (see below for more on this).

Without a doubt, one of the other most significant demographic issues facing the USA and UK concerns the increased racial/ethnic diversity of labour markets that indeed many other countries are also witnessing. However, the extent to which this is a new phenomenon varies from country to country, but certainly it is 'new' in the sense that it is now firmly on the policy agenda. In 2006 in the USA, 11 per cent of the workforce was black, 14 per cent Hispanic/Latino and 4 per cent Asian, meaning that combined minority ethnic groups comprise 29 per cent of the workforce. In comparison, the size of the UK BME workforce is small at approximately 8 per cent. Arguably these demographic profiles render the business case for equality and diversity (in relation to race/ethnicity) more compelling in the USA compared with the UK. For example, the larger BME population of the USA makes it a bigger consumer group with greater purchasing power.

In the UK and the USA, it is not only the *composition* of the workforce that is racially/ethnically diverse, but it is also the case that the labour market itself is *segmented* by race/ethnicity. For example, in the USA, black/ African American and Hispanic people are less likely than are white and Asian people to be employed in management and professional occupations (Bureau for Labor Statistics 2007). In the UK, whilst over the last decade or so there has been some improvement in the representation of minority ethnic people in the more highly prized professional and managerial jobs, some groups are faring better than others. So, for example, men of Indian background are more likely than white men to be in this type of work, but black Caribbean men are far less likely to be so (Heath et. al. 2001). Even at the margins of the labour market—the unemployed—the picture is racialized in both countries. In the USA, black and Hispanic/Latino people have disproportionately high rates of employment, as do black and Asian people in the UK.

The other main demographic issue is the ageing nature of populations in industrialized countries. In 2001, there were more people aged over 60 than below 16 in the UK. By 2051, it is estimated that one in four people will be over age 65. The main reasons are a fall in average family size and increased life expectancy. The ageing population has enormous social and economic implications, but the impact is expected to be less pronounced in the UK than in most other developed economies, but likely to be greater than in the USA where the age structure is younger (Select Committee on Economic Affairs 2003). A report by the Government's Select Committee on Economic Affairs emphasizes the economic importance of increasing the labour market participation of older workers (defined as over 50). It states that employment participation declines sharply after 55, and the majority of men have left the labour market before the state pension age of 65. Some of this early withdrawal is thought to be voluntary insofar as people with good personal or occupational pensions, those who dislike their jobs or are in poor health, may choose to retire early. Also, some employers use early retirement incentives to shed workers—so-called 'natural wastage'. The report claims that there is no separate labour market for the over 50s; in other words, the labour market is not segmented by age. For example, older men are most likely to be found as managers and senior officials and professionals, indicating that many have succeeded in climbing the career ladder. The proportion of men employed in skilled trades remains stable across age groups. Similarly, the proportion of women employed in the most highly feminized occupations remains stable across age groups, with the exception of sales and customer service, where older women are under-represented (Kirton and Greene 2005a). But, the Select Committee report does state that there are skills issues, in that some older workers who are made redundant from traditional industries (especially men) may see themselves as ill-equipped for the 'new' service sector jobs and may experience long-term unemployment. Among its recommendations, the report calls for the government and employers to encourage equal access to workplace training and lifelong learning. The report acknowledges that age discrimination exists, but states that the 'fact that persons of a particular age may be under-represented in a specific employment cannot, on its own, be taken as evidence of age discrimination' (Select Committee on Economic Affairs 2003: 29). However, it is felt that a move from age-based to competency-based criteria for recruitment and promotion will require a profound cultural shift. Indeed, research by the Chartered Institute for Personnel and Development found that 40 per cent of people believed they had been discriminated against on age grounds, compared with 14 per cent who cited gender (CIPD 2003).

CHANGING FAMILIES AND HOUSEHOLDS

One of the major social changes of the last couple of decades has been changing family and household types. Our interest is in the inter-relationship between this and employment participation. All the evidence reveals that women's employment is affected by age, life stage and family formation to a much greater extent than men's. The Organization for Economic Co-operation and Development (OECD 2001) identifies four types of families with two parents living in the same household. In both the UK and USA, there has been a marked decline in the post-war ideal-type 'male breadwinner model' and a similarly marked increase in the 'dual full-time earners model'. However, in the UK, the most common family/household type has a male breadwinner working full-time and a woman working part-time. The other main family/household type identified by the OECD as significant is one-parent households, of which the most common sub-type in the UK has a woman who is not in the workforce. Women in this family/household type are also less likely to work full-time than women living with a male partner and are more likely to depend on state benefits at least to supplement wages.

Against the existence of different family/household types, another significant change within the family is the smaller number of children per family that most industrialized countries are witnessing. The average number of children per woman in the UK stands at about 1.74, although certain BME groups (Pakistani and Bangladeshi) have a greater tendency to have more than the average number of children. Smaller family size is without a doubt related to women's increasing employment participation as stated above (although whether increased female employment participation is a cause or effect of a lower birth rate or vice versa is unclear). There is also a growing tendency among British women, especially the highly qualified, to delay having children. Despite an increase in teenage pregnancies, the average age of the mother on the birth of her first child is 27, increasing to 30 for married women (ONS 2007). Mothers' employment participation rates are lower in all OECD countries except Iceland and Sweden, where arguably there is a more supportive legal and social policy regime (see Kirton and Greene 2005a: Chapter 10). The younger the child, the less likely the mother is to be in paid work, and in most countries mothers are more likely to be in work once their child reaches the age of compulsory schooling. Women in the UK with children under age 6 have a slightly lower than average rate of employment among the OECD countries, and, as stated, mothers of dependent children, especially the less highly qualified, have a strong tendency to work part-time. Even in the absence of a family-friendly public policy and employment regime, in the USA, women with dependent children, even single parents, are far more likely to be working full-time than their British counterparts. Thus, family takes different shapes and has different effects on female employment patterns in different countries.

In the UK, the aggregate statistics on family formation and employment participation conceal ethnic differences. For white women, the presence of children and/or a partner has a far greater impact on employment participation than for other ethnic groups. For example, black women (of Caribbean, African and 'other' origin) are more likely to be single (meaning not married or cohabiting) and to be raising a child without a partner. Nevertheless, as stated above, this group of women also displays high levels of full-time working even when children are young and even when a partner is present. Conversely, Pakistani and Bangladeshi women are more likely to be partnered, but have very low levels of economic activity regardless of life stage, but particularly once mothers (Lindley et al 2004).

CHANGING LEGAL AND POLICY CONTEXT

The USA has a highly deregulated labour market, and as discussed in Chapter 2 there has been a pulling away by the polity from the moral arguments for equality reflected in the Civil Rights Act (Kelly and Dobbin 1998). This has resulted in a weakened legislative climate for equality issues, and the emphasis is now more firmly on employers' voluntary efforts, grounded in the business case. In the UK, the legal and policy contexts are rather different and reflect the influence of multiple actors, including the European Union (EU), but also the business lobby. A complex body of equality law has accumulated in the UK over a long period of time (more than 30 years), and so this section can merely summarize the main issues. It is important to state at the outset that the legal and macro-level policy contexts are necessarily influenced by the political orientation of the government of the day. The fact that the Conservative Government (1979–1997) did not sign the Social Charter agreement of the EU (which provides the basis for a range of social and employment provisions and regulations) symbolizes that particular government's hands-off approach to employment and equality regulation. In contrast, the Labour Government signed the Charter in 1997, and without it the UK would not have seen many of the later legal regulations and provisions (some of which are described below) that enhanced legal protection for certain groups, advanced equality generally and improved employment protection for many.

UK Legal Context

The principal pieces of British anti-discrimination legislation are set out in Table 3.1, but this must be supplemented by the Equal Pay Act (1970), designed to ensure equal pay between men and women and also by various pieces of legislation such as the Employment Act 2002. The latter introduced measures, such as paternity leave, adoption leave and the right to request flexible work, aimed at helping parents maintain access to employment during the early childrearing years (when women are mostly likely to drop out of the labour market). As stated, equality legislation has emerged over an extended period of time (see Table 3.1) and has been derived both legally and conceptually from a range of sources. For example, race discrimination law was influenced by USA civil rights law, although it did not go as far as allowing affirmative action (AA) (Keter 2005).

Table 3.1 Equality Strands Covered by British Legislation

Equality Strand	Act/Regulations	Year Enacted
Sex discrimination	Sex Discrimination Act	1975
Race discrimination	Race Relations Act	1976
Disability discrimination	Disability Discrimination Act	1995
Transsexual discrimination	Gender Reassignment Regulations	1999
Religion or belief discrimination	Religion or Belief Regulations	2003
Sexual orientation discrimination	Sexual Orientation Regulations	2003
Age discrimination	Age Regulations	2006

Despite evidence of a degree of shift towards market values and an obvious concern with economic performance, the EU has a stated commitment to the moral arguments of equal opportunities. Indeed more recent pieces of British legislation have emanated from European directives. In terms of stakeholder involvement, the EU also has a strong tradition of encouraging member states to involve the social partners (government, employer organizations and trade unions) in policy-making (European Commission 2005). In the UK, the government uses a variety of mechanisms for consulting interested parties on proposed regulatory change, for example, 'White Papers'. In 2002, the government consultation document, *Equality and Diversity: The way ahead*, sought stakeholder opinion of the proposal to disband the three equality commissions on gender, race and disability and to create a single body responsible for all equality strands. Responses were received from organizations as diverse as the Confederation for British Industry, the Local Government Association, the Trades Union Congress, Age Concern and the Evangelical Alliance.

As can be seen from Table 3.1, the scope of equality legislation has been widened enormously since the introduction of the anti-sex and anti-race discrimination acts in the mid-1970s. However, although much of the legislation has been driven by an underlying need for social change, the legislation generally creates rights for individuals (although importantly on the basis of social group) in the form of legal protection against discrimination and the right to sue should it occur. Thus, British equality law considers discrimination to consist of individual acts perpetrated against individual victims who should have some means of seeking compensation. Individuals who believe they have experienced discrimination may take their complaint to the Employment Tribunal (ET); however, class actions (as in the USA) are not permitted. The number of cases accepted by the ET within the various equality strands is shown in Table 3.2.

The individual complaints-based nature of the system is the source of one of the main criticisms of British equality law (see Dickens 2000). As important as it is for individuals to have a channel for redress and compensation, this

Table 3.2   Employment Tribunal Statistics

Claims Accepted	04/05	05/06	06/07
Sex discrimination	11,726	14,250	28,153
Disability discrimination	4,942	4,585	5,533
Race discrimination	3,317	4,103	3,780
Religion/belief discrimination	307	486	648
Sexual orientation discrimination	349	395	470
Age discrimination	N/A	N/A	972

Source: Employment Tribunal Annual Statistics 2006–2007.
www.employmenttribunals.gov.uk/publications

Table 3.3 Employment Tribunal Success/Compensation 2006–2007

Basis of Claim	Successful at Employment Tribunal	Average Compensation Award
Sex discrimination	2%	£10,052
Disability discrimination	3%	£15,059
Race discrimination	3%	£14,049
Religion/belief discrimination	2%	N/A
Sexual orientation discrimination	5%	N/A
Age discrimination	0%	-

Source: Employment Tribunal Annual Statistics 2006–2007
www.employmenttribunals.gov.uk/publications

approach does very little to *promote* equality. Instead, employers are required to avoid discriminating, but beyond that, private sector employers do not have to do very much in order to comply with the law. Indeed, employers are not *allowed* to exercise AA, and the weaker tool, positive action, is only possible in limited circumstances. Most employers have interpreted the law as requiring them to take a more formalized, procedural approach to recruitment and selection in order to avoid prejudice and bias from influencing decisions—an important, but not highly proactive, policy position. Add to this the fact that, as can be seen from Table 3.3, even if employers are found guilty of discrimination, the average compensation awards are very small and what we are left with is a minimalist legal context.

That said, this has changed recently for most public sector organizations where so-called equality duties on race (RED—2002), disability (DED—2006) and gender (GED—2007) have been introduced within the relevant acts. These duties require most public bodies to *promote* equality. It is important to note that private sector employers are not covered by these duties. The introduction of positive duties represents the most fundamental change in British equality law since the 1970s. Instead of identifying a perpetrator and compensating a victim, the duties require the restructuring and transformation of institutions without any attribution of blame (Fredman 2002). The equality duties stipulate a 'general duty' to eliminate discrimination and to promote equality in relation to the particular strand and also set out 'specific duties' within each strand to help public bodies meet the general duty. For example, the RED requires 'race equality schemes' and the DED 'disability equality schemes'. Public sector employers are also required to assess and consult on the likely impact of their proposed policies on the promotion of equality and to monitor for any adverse impact. The results of the assessments and consultations must be published (see http://www.equalityhumanrights.com/ for more information). Most commentators and stakeholders have welcomed the equality duties as a step forward for British equality law (see further discussion in Chapter 4) even if the fact that private sector employers are not included is lamented by some.

Another fundamental criticism of British equality law that conceptually chimes with DM and its claim to broaden the agenda is that the plethora of single strand pieces of legislation does not grapple easily with the now widely recognized multiple and intersecting nature of inequalities. As a simple example, if a black woman experiences discrimination, which piece of legislation should she use in order to make her complaint? Is it really so simple a task to disentangle race from sex discrimination, and why is it necessary to do so? The dissolution in October 2007 of the individual equality bodies (publicly funded, but independent of government)—the Equal Opportunities Commission (EOC), the Commission for Racial Equality (CRE) and the Disability Rights Commission (DRC)—and their replacement with a single equality body—the Equality and Human Rights Commission (EHRC)—goes some way to addressing the concern with intersectionality. As well as taking on the work of the previous three commissions, the new EHRC is responsible for other equality strands covered by law—religion and belief, sexual orientation, age—and human rights, meaning that an intersectional perspective can be taken. The single equality body approach mirrors that of a number of other countries, including New Zealand, Australia, Canada and the USA. A proposal for a Single Equality Act which would harmonize the law across the different equality strands is also now on the political table for discussion. It has been argued that the EHRC will not work without a Single Equality Act. In practical terms, the way that legislation has developed over a 30-year period or so has resulted in a large and complex body of law that arguably requires considerable expertise to operationalize and to interpret (Keter 2005). At the time of writing, the government's consultation on the Single Equality Act has closed, but the timetable for putting the bill through parliament has stalled, and it is unclear what this will now be. The fact that a general election is not far off reminds us of the political nature of equality and diversity as the Conservative opposition has yet to make its intentions in regard to the Act known. Thus, the legal context of equality and diversity continues to evolve in the UK.

Similarly, the broader government-led policy context continues to evolve. There is evidence that the government has embraced the diversity paradigm. For example, the various consultation documents issued by the Department for Business, Enterprise and Regulatory Reform (BERR, formerly the Department for Trade and Industry) now typically contain reference to workforce diversity and to the importance of the business case. The report of the major government-commissioned 'Equalities Review', published in February 2007 and intended to inform the modernization of the British equality machinery, also talks about the importance of the economic arguments for equality and diversity (Equalities Review Panel 2007). The Equalities Review also proposes a new framework for equality that is resonant with many aspects of DM, particularly an emphasis on individual differences. This framework has prompted mixed reactions from the social partners. For example, the CBI approved of the weight given to individual choice in determining life chances. In contrast, the major trade union Amicus (now part of Unite, the UK's largest trade union) was more critical. It felt that the proposed new framework was too individualistic and ignored the impact of class, poverty, discrimination, occupational segregation and family responsibilities on the choices available to people. The union believes that the policy focus needs to be firmly on traditional concepts of equality of access and outcome (Kirton 2007). These criticisms echo those lodged against DM by many critical academic voices (see Chapter 2).

CHANGING INDUSTRIAL RELATIONS

As discussed in Chapter 1, industrial relations is a field of study and an area of policy and practice that is generally associated with male-dominated heavy industry, trade unions and strikes (Kirton and Greene 2005a). Historically, because women have been under-represented in all three areas, this has meant a neglect of gender, women's and equality issues in industrial relations research, policy and practice (Wacjman 2000; Greene 2002). Because many of the organizations that participated in our research were unionized, we have a particular interest in the role that unions play in workplace equality. Historically, the unions' record is not wholly positive. For example, the bargaining priorities of UK and USA unions during the 1980s and early 1990s were widely criticized for being white-male biased (Ellis 1988; Cockburn 1991; Rees 1992; Briskin 2002; Cobble and Bielski Michal 2002), and therefore unions were held to have a 'mixed record' on challenging discrimination and inequalities (Dickens et al 1988). As suggested above, the social and economic contexts of industrial relations have changed enormously, and the unions have by and large responded to the feminized, more diverse workforce with proactive strategies to address the concerns of different groups. For example, most UK unions now have a range of equality campaigns, and they have also actively lobbied government for enhanced legal provision on equality issues (Greene and Kirton 2006).

However, the climate facing unions over the last 25 years or so has been fairly hostile, on a variety of fronts, weakening their ability to exert influence on working life generally and on employees' terms and conditions specifically. One of the major features of the contemporary industrial relations landscape is the steep decline in trade union membership that most industrialized countries have seen over the last 25 years or so. Trade union membership declined in both the UK and USA in the 1980s and 1990s, along with the manufacturing industry, but government economic, labour market and industrial relations policy and employer-led initiatives played a large role in the decline of trade unionism in both countries. This is a problem for trade unions as the framework for industrial relations in the UK and USA can be characterized as voluntaristic, meaning that there is only a weak legal framework for trade union recognition and collective bargaining. This means that in both countries unions are dependent for their strength and power on high workplace membership levels.

In the USA, overall union membership now stands at about 12 per cent, down from about 20 per cent in 1983 when statistics were first systematically collected (Bureau of Labor Statistics 2007). Thus, union density in the USA has historically been at a relatively low level, whereas in the UK it was once over 50 per cent (it peaked in the late 1970s at about 55 per cent), but is now 29 per cent (Grainger 2005). Membership losses have left the union movements in both countries severely weakened. The face of union membership has also fundamentally altered and is now heavily concentrated in the public sector in both the USA and the UK. In the USA, 40 per cent of public sector employees are union members, compared with only 10 per cent of private sector. In the UK, the figures are 59 per cent and19 per cent, respectively. Thus, the overall relatively low density level conceals the sectoral disparities that mean that unions have greater influence in the public than private sector. As we might expect from the patchy membership rates and no national legal framework for collective bargaining, the proportion of UK employees whose terms and conditions are influenced by collective agreements is about 35 per cent overall, but a very high 71 per cent in the public sector, compared with 21 per cent in the private sector (Grainger 2005).

In terms of the demographics of membership composition, in the USA, men are still more likely to be union members than women, but the gender disparity has narrowed over time. However, in an historical turnaround, in the UK, trade union membership has become increasingly feminized with membership among women now standing at about 30 per cent while for men the figure is about 28 per cent. In fact in the UK, the slight increases that we have seen in the last few years in overall union membership are because women's membership is increasing (Grainger 2005). BME people are also an increasingly significant membership group for trade unions. In the UK, black employees are slightly more likely to be union members than white, but black women have the highest union density overall when compared with women and men in other ethnic groups.

Despite the current low membership levels in the UK and the consequent constraints on unions to have an influence at workplace level, unionized workforces are still generally characterized by less pronounced inequalities than non-union ones (Colling and Dickens 2001). Further, Colling and Dickens (ibid) argue that the political and policy contexts post-1997 under a Labour Government has held out opportunities for joint engagement on equality issues. They link this not only to the current government's somewhat more favourable orientation to unions, but also to the promotion of joint engagement that is part of the European agenda that they argue has resulted in a renewed legitimacy granted to unions by current public policy (ibid: 150). Combine this with the increasingly diverse workforce and it is clear that unions can no longer ignore equality and diversity issues and indeed that they are (at national level at least) using whatever power they have left to advance an equality agenda.

CHANGING PERCEPTIONS AND DISCOURSES OF EQUALITY AND DIVERSITY

Changing perceptions of equality and diversity on the part of the general public and the polity represents an important aspect of the political and social context in which DM is developed and implemented. The kinds of policies that will be acceptable to or resisted by employees will inevitably reflect attitudes towards the issues. One report, produced in 2003 at the time when the government launched its review of Britain's equality law framework, gathered the general public's understandings and perceptions about equality issues (Howard and Tibballs 2003). The research found that people are comfortable with the idea of equal *opportunities* or protection from discrimination, but that they are less comfortable about the idea of using policy measures to attempt to achieve equal *outcomes*. This general attitude fits well with DM and its retreat from a focus on group-patterned disadvantage and group-targeted policy initiatives. The study also found that people are aware of which groups are considered as disadvantaged—for example, women, black and ethnic minority people, gay men and lesbian women and so on—but that they did not necessarily agree that this was the case. In particular, the study found little support for the idea that women as a group are unequal in society today. Most people believed that the fact that women might have less well-paid jobs or do more work in the home was a function of individual choices or natural gender differences, rather than any bias in society as a whole. Howard and Tibballs (ibid) conclude that professional equality policy-makers are in danger of losing touch with the 'audiences' they aim to reach and serve. They caution that the fact that the general public is not on board with current equality approaches suggests that there is little will from the general public to change. For example, the findings suggest that there would be little support for measures such as positive action. The authors suggest that equality policies need to be developed in consultation with ordinary people, rather than purely by professional policy-makers, in order to achieve a greater consensus of what needs to be done. It is clear that the general public's views on what, if anything, should be done to tackle different inequalities have changed over time and that these changing public discourses of equality influence policy-making, but it is also possible for policy-making and policy-makers to influence attitudes and perceptions.

The government commissioned Equalities Review (see above) identified the lack of consensus on equality as one of the major reasons why inequalities still exist. The report stated that, despite the fact that there is broad political consensus that greater equality should be an essential element of Britain's future, there is a lack of awareness and understanding about what equality means, how it relates to what organizations do, what is required or permitted under the law and who is responsible for delivering on this. It also stated that anxiety exists in UK society about whether greater fairness for some might mean reduced freedoms for others and that this inhibits unequivocal support for measures to promote equality. Therefore, the Equalities Review concludes that one of the ten steps to greater equality is building consensus.

Where does the discourse of diversity fit in with these debates? In Chapter 2, there was a detailed discussion about what DM is that will not be rehearsed here, but it is relevant to say that the promulgation of the new discourse of diversity might represent an attempt at consensus-building on equality on the part of various policy-makers and stakeholders. Thus, it might either reflect changing perceptions of equality or it might be implicated in causing such changes. We have argued elsewhere that language frames employment relations issues and problems insofar as talk usually precedes action, and therefore the talk of the actors defines the policy agenda and shapes actual policy initiatives. Discourses are also powerful resources with which different actors construct different realities, and consequently different policies emerge as seemingly rational and justified and therefore less likely to meet resistance (Kirton and Greene 2006). It is also clear that in describing and labeling things the way they do, organizational stakeholders seek to persuade others to accept or challenge policy and its measures or to change or reinforce certain attitudes or values (Hamilton 2001). On this point, it is important to note that the business case is at the core of DM and that organizations can use various resources to seek to persuade stakeholders that the business case is sacrosanct and should drive equality and diversity policy-making. However, as we have discussed in Chapter 2, the business case has inherent major weaknesses that mean that its prospects for advancing the equality project are limited. Thus, we argue that building a consensus around the business case is problematic, if not damaging, for the equality project.

KEY EQUALITY AND DIVERSITY
ISSUES AND CHALLENGES

Our research is located at the organizational level, but its industrial relations perspective means that our primary interest is in the impact that labour market contexts and equality and diversity policies have on employees. In this section, we turn our attention to the implications of the external contexts described above for organizational-level policy and practice in the equality and diversity area. We do this by outlining what we consider are the key equality and diversity issues and challenges as they impact on employees in the organizational context.

Discrimination

Although the key issues and challenges we briefly consider in this section are not presented in any hierarchy of importance, we address discrimination first because in the era of the diversity discourse, when all the political rhetoric presents differences as positive and valued, we feel it is vitally important to state very clearly that discrimination remains widespread in the UK labour market. As the Equalities Review made clear, all the available evidence confirms that discrimination on the range of grounds now covered by British equality law remains prevalent—gender, race/ethnicity, disability, religion, sexual orientation and age. Discrimination can take different forms. It can, for example, manifest as a job or promotion refusal or it can involve harassment, meaning that discrimination can have economic effects, as well as impacting on psychological well-being and generally having a negative effect on working lives. Thus, it is not sufficient simply to look for economic indicators or measures of discrimination; the impact that it has on people's subjective experiences of employment is just as important from a policy perspective.

A recent UK study found that significant proportions of BME people report that they have been refused a job on racial grounds. In addition, there was a significant level of self-reporting of unequal treatment at work, particularly by black African women. The same study also found high levels of self-reported racial prejudice among white employers and managers; differences between sectors were generally not great (meaning that even where there was a significant BME workforce it was still high), but the level was lower in public administration, education and health (Heath and Cheung 2006). The annual statistics produced by the Employment Tribunal system give some indication as to the level of discrimination claims being brought against UK employers (see Table 3.2). Many commentators would rightly argue that this doubtlessly represents only a small proportion of actual experiences of discrimination. The difficulties involved in bringing a legal case are immense and success rates extremely low (although cases are often settled in favour of the claimant out of court). Further, recent research on race discrimination claimants indicates that many have negative experiences of the process itself, adding further to an already stressful situation (Aston et al 2006). Even for those who are successful, as can be seen from Table 3.3, compensation awards are relatively low, and therefore the prospect of compensation is unlikely in itself to act as an incentive for legal action, but neither is legal action an effective remedy. Therefore, discrimination remains a key challenge for organizational policy-makers and stakeholder groups such as trade unions. It continues to be necessary for organizations to monitor for patterns and instances of discrimination and to develop policies and procedures designed to minimize the scope for discriminatory behaviours. The continued need to consider group-patterned disadvantage is thus highlighted.

Discrimination is of course morally wrong and, as stated, can be extremely harmful for individuals, but it also has a structural effect in that it is part of the explanation for labour market segregation.

Labour Market Segregation

The labour markets of all industrialized countries are highly segregated by gender and to some extent at least by race/ethnicity, meaning that women and men and different ethnic groups tend to be concentrated in different employment sectors and occupations and at different levels of organizational and occupational hierarchies. For example, across Europe, women are concentrated in a limited range of occupations and industries, in the public sector, in small private sector firms and in particular modes of employment such as part-time work (Fagan and Burchell 2002). In the UK, women are especially concentrated in the public administration, education and health sector; for black Caribbean and black African women, this sector is by far the most common. BME people are overall more likely to be found in the distribution, hotel and restaurant sectors than white people, and for people of Bangladeshi background, there is a very heavy concentration in that sector (Heath and Cheung 2006). In terms of occupations, in the USA, almost three-quarters of women are employed in management, professional, sales and office occupations, compared with about half of men. However, black and Hispanic people are far less likely to be employed in management and professional occupations and more likely than white people to work in service occupations (Bureau of Labor Statistics 2007). In the UK, the most common occupational group for women is administrative and secretarial work. But UK women's representation among managers and senior officers and professional and technical employees has grown so that nearly one-fifth of women are in these two types of job (Aston et al 2004). Within the private sector, there is a clear pattern for BME people overall to be under-represented in professional and managerial occupations and over-represented in semi-routine and routine occupations. These patterns are not so marked for BME women and are not found in the public sector. But, there are ethnic variations; for example, Indian men outperform white men in terms of their representation in high and low professional and managerial jobs as compared with semi-routine and routine. Similarly, black Caribbean women slightly outperform white women in terms of their representation in high and low professional and managerial jobs. Part of the explanation for the latter lies in the fact that black Caribbean women are far more likely to work full-time than are white women (and most professional and managerial jobs are organized on a full-time basis). Further, a high proportion of black Caribbean women in this broad category are actually located in lower level professional and managerial occupations such as nursing. In contrast, Bangladeshi women are far more likely to be in semi-routine or routine jobs than any other ethnic group (Heath and Cheung 2006).

As stated above, although in the UK women's labour market participation has grown enormously, full-time, continuous employment remains relatively uncommon for women with pre-school children, and many women continue to work part-time well beyond the early childrearing years. Part-time work is highly sex segregated, and women who work part-time often end up stuck in low-level, low-paid work and suffer a lifetime earnings disadvantage (Glover and Kirton 2006). There is an ongoing debate about whether women *choose* part-time work because they prefer to prioritize family and home-making over paid work careers (Hakim 2000) or whether this 'choice' is made in the context of lack of real alternatives, that is, it is a constrained choice. Because of the high cost of childcare in the UK, many families depend on informal childcare arrangements involving partners and grandparents that facilitate part-time work, but make it difficult for lower skill women to work full-time.

The question for us to consider is the extent to which labour market segregation is an issue that organizations could or should be tackling. Clearly some of the reasons for segregation are beyond the scope of employers and need to be tackled with pre-labour market policies, such as education and training, and careers services. However, employers do play a role in reproducing job segregation as Collinson et al (1990) showed in their seminal study of sex segregation in the late 1980s. This occurs through what the authors termed the '3 Rs'—the vicious circles of job segregation. The first 'R' is reproduction—for example, informal recruitment practices, managerial control strategies and ideologies, patriarchal control strategies and ideologies and managerial divisions. Much of the informality in recruitment and selection that was prevalent at the time of the Collinson et al's study has now been replaced by more formal recruitment procedures, but the recruitment process remains vulnerable to subjectivity and bias. The second 'R' is rationalization—blaming the victim, blaming society/history, benefiting the victim and controlling production. This is where managers making decisions deny and deflect responsibility for job segregation by invoking factors beyond their control. The third 'R' is resistance—involving personnel managers, external candidates, internal candidates and trade unions. Here, the possibility for breaking the vicious circle is highlighted. The idea is that various actors in the process can act in ways that disrupt traditional, historical norms and patterns. We argue that organizations need to be alert to the '3 Rs' before they can begin to develop initiatives to break down segregation. So, why does labour market segregation matter from an equality perspective? Labour market segregation by gender and race/ethnicity is not simply a neutral fact of life. Not only does it restrict individual choices and freedom, but one of the major issues is that the sectors and occupations where women and BME groups tend to be concentrated are generally lower paying ones.

Pay Gaps and Undervaluation

The lesser access to higher paying jobs experienced by women and BME people in both the USA and UK is a major policy issue. However, we argue that policy should not simply be concerned with pushing or coaxing women and BME people into higher paying areas, but that there also needs to be consideration of the (lack of) value attached to certain types of jobs, especially those done by women (Grimshaw and Rubery 2007).

But let us look at the facts on pay. The USA shows some of the highest rates of low-paid full-time working women, especially in the wholesale and retail trade, restaurants and hotels and community services (Robson et al 1999). In the UK, it is part-time women workers who experience the highest rate of low hourly pay. Arguably the service sector in both the UK and USA has expanded by creating low-paid jobs (often part-time in the UK) for women (Robson et al 1999). Comparing the pay of full-time workers, women in the USA earn about 79 per cent of average male earnings, while black workers earn about 80 per cent of white average earnings and Hispanic workers about 70 per cent (Bureau of Labor Statistics 2007). Occupational segregation is estimated to account for about two-thirds of the racial gap among women in earnings in the USA (Kim 2002). In the UK, full-time working women earn on average 82 per cent of the average male salary, but there is variation between sectors, between occupations, between women with and without children and between women of different ages (Glover and Kirton 2006). Even higher education qualifications do not protect women from the gender pay gap. Purcell (2002) analyzed the occupational outcomes of UK graduates 3 1/2 years after graduation and showed that women graduates can expect to earn 15 per cent less than their male counterparts by the time they reach the age of 24. Closing the gender pay gap is a major gender equality policy issue within the EU, and the European Employment Strategy now includes a requirement that member states take policy action to achieve a substantial reduction by 2010 (Rubery et al 2005).

When it comes to race/ethnicity in the UK, it is not a simple case of all white people earning more than all BME people. For example, Chinese and Indian people have the highest hourly earnings of all ethnic groups, while Bangladeshi men have the lowest. black African and black Caribbean men have shortfalls of around 10 per cent when compared with white men. Interestingly, most BME women (with the exception of Pakistani and Bangladeshi women) earn more than the average hourly rate of white women. This is because white women in the UK have such a strong tendency to work part-time, and, as stated, part-time work is so poorly paid (Heath and Cheung 2006).

This complex picture of gendered and ethnicized pay gaps points to the ongoing need for policy initiatives that are sensitive to the disparities and the needs of specific groups.

Flexible Working Patterns and Work-Life-Balance

Flexible working and work–life balance policies are firmly on the equality and diversity agenda and are now commonplace in UK organizations (Walsh 2007). They have the active support of the trade unions (see http://www.tuc.org.uk/work_life/), many employers (see http://www.employers-forwork-lifebalance.org.uk) and government, but whether and how these policies contribute to the equality and diversity project is keenly debated. Flexible working has proved a double-edged sword for women. On the one hand, it has enabled more women to enter the labour market, but, on the other hand, it reinforces the role of women as carers and 'slow track' employees (Purcell 2000). In order to avoid these kinds of negative associations that position women as less committed workers, the contemporary fashion is to frame work–life balance policies in gender neutral terms, even though it is women who are most likely to take advantage of them. In a recent report, the EOC (now encompassed within the EHRC), stated:

> The flexibility agenda is unfinished business for 21st Century Britain. While flexibility is on the increase, it's not happening fast enough or in the right ways to deliver what people, businesses or the economy really want and need for work and life now and in the future. So far the increase has largely been a flexing of the traditional model of working and this is not enough—more radical transformation is required. (EOC 2007)

The EOC report reasons that Britain has already witnessed two 'generations' of flexible working, the first of which was about time flexibility and based mainly on part-time working. Evolving from this, the second generation, according to the EOC, was also focused on time, for example, relaxing the nine to five boundaries, but with some consideration of space and technology usage, such as home-working. It is argued that both of these generations of flexible working were inextricably linked to caring and therefore to women (the so-called 'mummy track' was one employer response the EOC mentions here), but that this resulted in the stigmatization of employees (usually women) taking advantage of flexibility as less career-minded. The EOC claims to have come up with a multi-dimensional model for a third generation of flexible working that it says can benefit individuals and business. The model consists of four categories of flexible worker and four dimensions of time, space, lifetime and lifestyle. The model emphasizes different types of flexible worker with different needs (for example, young people, parents, older people and mid-career workers) and also the multiple ways in which employers can benefit (such as through reduced overheads, employee retention and reduced absenteeism). A number of 'good practice' case study organizations are presented in the report, but it remains to be seen whether the EOC's optimistic vision of work transformation via a third generation of flexible working will be realized for the benefit of everyone. As discussed in Chapter 2, when policies are premised on the business case, it is always questionable as to what will happen if the economy or the business takes a downturn. Will flexible working *for* employees still be a priority or will the belt be tightened so that it is flexibility *of* employees that becomes the prevailing model? Whilst we are not making an argument against flexible working and work–life balance policies, we do believe it is necessary for research and policy to engage critically with the realities of the flexible workforce, rather than simply base policy recommendations on an idealistic, upbeat vision of what could be.

CONCLUSION

What do we take forward from this chapter into the reading of the empirical research presented in this book? First, it is clear that organizations and their stakeholders do not and cannot operate in a vacuum. The external political, economic, social and legal contexts shape the contours of inequality and diversity and influence the policies and actions of the key actors—government, employers and trade unions. Second, the labour market is not a level playing field. Deeply embedded inequalities are ever present, and to a large extent an individual's employment chances and experiences are influenced, if not determined, by primary characteristics especially gender and race/ethnicity, but also by other factors as reflected in the main equality strands. In the light of the political, economic, social and legal contexts briefly described in this chapter, our research is interested in whether, as the new paradigm for equality and diversity policy-making, DM can make progress on equality and diversity, in particular the key issues and challenges outlined.

4 Diversity Management in the Public Sector

This chapter considers diversity management (DM) within the context of the public sector in the UK. Developments and trends in public sector management and industrial relations over the last 20 years or so are outlined. The effects of these developments on approaches to equality and diversity policy-making within public sector organizations are considered. The chapter then presents findings from a case study of the UK Civil Service.

THE CONTEXT AND INDUSTRIAL RELATIONS OF THE PUBLIC SECTOR

In order to understand developments in equality and diversity policy-making in the public sector, it is necessary to consider the distinctive features of public sector industrial relations as shaped by the particular political and economic conditions within the UK (Bach and Winchester 2003: 286). First, it should be stated that despite substantial job losses since the 1970s, the public sector is still a considerable force within the UK labour market, accounting for 5.7 million or one in five (20.4 per cent) of all workers in the UK in 2008 (ONS 2008).

While change predated the Conservative Government of 1979 (Wilson and Iles 1999), there is no doubt that major changes were made to the structure, culture and management of public services during their administration (1979–1997). Bach and Winchester (2003) provide a useful review, outlining the key features of the public sector during the 1960s and 1970s and the reforms of subsequent decades. In summary, looking at the pre-1979 period, the traditional characteristics of the public sector involved: (i) a commitment to the welfare state and its provision of services; (ii) the development of an ethos, whereby the public sector took on the mantle of 'model' employer (Pendleton and Winterton 1993); (iii) high levels of trade union membership; and (iv) hierarchical and bureaucratic management structures, where work was organized by reference to rules and regulations within routinized regimes (Cunningham 2000: 701). Public sector industrial relations in the post-war period rested on the relative absence of market pressures, whereas post-1979, the influence of the market appears paramount.

From 1979, an accelerated programme of public sector reform was initiated which included rationalization, commercialization, de-regulation, decentralization and privatization (Blyton and Turnbull 2004: 203). A major part of this involved substantial job losses (while 30 per cent of the working population of the UK was employed in the public sector in 1979, this had declined to only one-fifth by the mid-1990s (ibid). This programme of reform also included a critique of public sector management values and policies and a government attempt to set a different kind of example as the 'model' employer (ibid: 205). In particular, the emergence of what has been termed 'new public management' (NPM)—'the importation of private sector concepts and techniques into the public sector' (Wilson and Iles 1999: 27)—is a major characteristic of the period (see also Branine 2004). Various features are seen to characterize NPM. First, the the role of management was elevated, with the associated increase in the authority, status and pay of senior managers (Bach and Winchester 2003). Second, the public sector should take on more characteristics of private sector management. Wilson and Iles provide a useful summary of these characteristics involving 'a central core of resource accountability, monitoring and measuring . . . mission statements, customer care, decentralization, quality, innovation, entrepreneurialism and a perceived link between culture and performance' (1999: 28). In practice, departments and functions were decentralized, budgets delegated and authority devolved (particularly for HR issues) to local/line-managers. Third, the new public sector should have a competitive market-driven approach to management, with a diffusion of market-type mechanisms across public services. This involved departments competing with each other for resources and contracts in the National Health Service (NHS) and Civil Service, processes of compulsory competitive tendering (CCT) in local authorities and outsourcing of certain public services to the private sector. Finally, although trade unions have fared much better in the public sector than they have in the private, in the wake of public sector industrial unrest in the late 1970s, the wider Conservative programme of reform also included an explicit attack on trade union power, through legislation that directly limited the ability of trade unions to organize and mobilize members and a gradual exclusion of trade unions from national policy-making (Bach and Winchester 2003).

To the disappointment of public sector trade unions, the *Modernising Government* agenda of New Labour (published in March 1999) accepted much of the Conservative reform programme (see http://archive.cabinet-office.gov.uk/moderngov/). This agenda set out key policies and principles underpinning the Labour Government's (elected 1997) long-term programme of reform to modernize public services. A major feature was action to improve service quality, thus moving away from the Conservative Government's narrow focus on cost minimization (Bach and Winchester

2003). In addition, Bach and Winchester argue that some of the worst excesses of the market-driven approach were abolished, such as CCT in the NHS. However, the monitoring and target-based focus of NPM has been maintained and even heightened with the tightening of service standards. This has seen more rigorous scrutiny of organizational performance, for example, the introduction of continuous performance reviews in local authorities within 'Best Value' regimes (ibid: 290). In addition, further involvement of the private sector in the delivery of public services has been encouraged, for example, through 'private-public partnerships' (Blyton and Turnbull 2004). Korczynski (2002) also highlights another consequence, namely the redefinition of public service users as 'customers', and their role as a key assessor of the performance of service providers. Indeed, the *Modernising Government* agenda specifically enhanced the role of customers in this regard, aiming to 'deliver public services to meet the needs of citizens, not the convenience of service providers' including their direct participation through the 'routine monitoring of customers' views on public services' (http://archive.cabinetoffice.gov.uk/moderngov/whatismg.htm).

Overall, the changes have arguably 'made the public sector less dissimilar from the private sector in terms of human resource management' (Branine 2004: 137). As a consequence of the reform programme, the public sector has become a much more complex context in which to manage work and be an employee, largely because the public sector was not transformed, but became a hybrid of old and new models. Indeed, Bach and Winchester (2003: 310) point out that only partial convergence has occurred as there is still significant variety in the institutional arrangements and employment practices and outcomes. Moreover, the level of public scrutiny and political intervention in public services continues to make the public sector distinct. Part of this relates to the often contradictory nature of the reforms. Cunningham (2000) indicates the difficulties of the existence within NPM of two sets of inherently contradictory values—one that calls for improved performance and efficiency savings, and the other that calls simultaneously for people-centred and empowered managers. Thus, at the same time as the need for competitiveness in public services saw both decentralization and devolution, the Treasury also demanded an unprecedented level of centralized control over funding and the management of service providers through strictly enforced cash limits and demands for annual efficiency gains (Bach and Winchester 2003).

In addition, despite the attack on trade union power, one area of continuity is that the public sector remains heavily unionized. Even with the overall decline of union membership in the UK, 59 per cent of or three in five public sector employees belong to a union (ONS 2008), and approximately 71 per cent of employees are covered by a collective agreement (Kersley et al 2006). This means that the public sector still provides a context in which the joint regulation of industrial relations is particularly salient, and therefore where we might anticipate greater involvement of trade unions in equality and diversity policy-making.

Part of being a 'model' employer also included action on equality, and the public sector is generally considered as having led the way in the development of equality policy (Dickens 1999; Bach and Winchester 2003; Kirton and Greene 2005; Maxwell et al 2001; McDougall 1996, 1998; Cunningham 2000; Creegan et al 2003). Policy commitment to equal opportunities (EO) in the public sector is longstanding, pre-dating key legislation of the 1970s (Equal Pay Act, Sex and Race Discrimination Acts). Furthermore, the development of NPM in the 1990s occurred in parallel with increasing interest in EO within central and local governments (ibid). WERS data indicates that the industrial sector characterized as 'public administration' is the one which is now most likely to have a formal equal opportunities policy in place (Kersley et al 2006). Indeed, WERS 2004 data indicates the near universal existence of formal policies in the public sector (at 98 per cent of public sector workplaces). Furthermore, with reference to the mismatch between formal policy and equality outcomes, there is clear evidence that EO policies are less likely to constitute an 'empty shell' (where formal paper commitment is not supported by practical policies, frameworks and structures) in the public sector as compared to the private (Hoque and Noon 2004).

Some reforms associated with NPM can be seen to have had specific equality dimensions. For example, the development of new and simplified national pay structures based on systems of job evaluation were designed to try and redress unfair discrimination embedded within the old structures (Bach and Winchester 2003). Similarly, attempts to address recruitment and retention problems in key professions such as nursing, teaching and the police service saw attention paid to family-friendly policies and non-pay awards (ibid). Certain areas of the public sector, particularly central and local governments, enthusiastically supported national campaigns such as Opportunity 2000 (now Opportunity Now) and Race for Opportunity (Wilson and Iles 1999: 29), and public sector organizations still stand at the vanguard of support for these initiatives and their successors. Take a cursory look at organizations that win awards for their diversity initiatives or who sign up for campaigns (for example, www.bitc.org.uk) and a large proportion come from the public sector.

In addition, diversity was clearly an integral part of the reform agenda outlined in the *Modernising Government* White Paper of 1999:

A truly effective diverse organization is one in which the differences individuals bring are valued and used. Currently we tend to minimize differences and to expect everyone to fit into the established ways of working. We should not expect them to. We should be flexible to allow everyone to make the best contribution they can. This has to be reflected in our ways of working, our personnel practices, the way managers manage. (http://www.archive.official-documents.co.uk/document/cm43/4310/4310–06.htm)

The focus within this agenda on a longer term perspective and on quality of service rather than short-term cost maximization potentially has some diversity benefits. In addition, while on the one hand attention to targets and increased accountability within NPM have been subjects of criticism, on the other hand monitoring (of demographic trends within organizations and the impact of policies) is seen as being key to successful equality and diversity action. Therefore, attention to accountability and monitoring under NPM may have positive effects. Indeed using WERS data, Adams and Carter (2007) have found that public sector organizations are twice as likely to undertake workforce monitoring as private sector organizations.

Yet, Cunningham calls NPM a 'two-edged sword' (2000: 710). While it could potentially offer scope to managers to find new and innovative ways to drive equality forward, it could just as easily mean pressure to cut back the scope of initiatives due to resource constraints and performance requirements. For Cunningham, the context in which equality management is now carried out has been made much more contradictory and difficult by NPM. Pressures on organizational performance under NPM mean that the business case for equality becomes ever more contingent and unlikely to be compelling (Creegan et al 2003). Creegan et al (2003) highlight the ways in which power and resources to deliver EO within local authorities were progressively undermined by the Conservative Government's reforms. Devolving responsibility and accountability to line managers (see discussion in Chapter 7) has meant that equality and diversity have to compete directly with other managerial demands on time and resources, such that the 'freedom to manage' can easily be 'freedom to ignore' (Cunningham 2000: 708). Creegan et al (2003), in their case study of race equality in one local authority, found that devolution of equality issues to line-managers was seen to have a significantly deleterious effect on the effectiveness of the race equality plan, in that it weakened and compromised the centralized monitoring role of the HR function. A contentious issue was the level of management discretion, leading to practice varying highly across the organization.

However, the public sector arguably has had a better record on equality and diversity issues because of its close proximity to equality legislation and given the dual role of the state as employer and legislator. This relates to the level of political intervention that Bach and Winchester referred to as an enduring distinguishing feature of the public sector (2003: 310). It is often the case that legislation applies first, or that requirements are applied with greater severity to the public sector. For example, recent amendments to discrimination legislation (see discussion in Chapter 3) have seen additional statutory duties to promote race, gender and disability equality applied to public sector organizations.[1] Under previous laws, action could only be taken against public bodies after they had been found to have discriminated. The new duties mean that they must take steps to actually *promote* equality.

EQUALITY AND DIVERSITY IN THE PUBLIC SECTOR

Looking at demographic patterns, the public sector is heavily feminized, with 66 per cent of workers being women (compared to only 47 per cent in the private sector) (Kersley et al 2006). A greater proportion of public sector workers also work part-time (30 per cent compared to 24 per cent in the private sector). In most parts of the public sector, inequalities such as the gender pay gap have declined over the last 20 years more quickly than in the private sector (Wilson and Iles 1999: 29). However, the public sector remains interesting as a research context because there is still much work to be done on equality and diversity. This sector might be progressive compared with much of the private sector, but it is still marked by inequalities, such as horizontal and vertical sex and race segregation (Wilson and Iles 1999: 30; McDougall 1996, 1998; Creegan et al 2003). Taking the Civil Service as an example, while policy initiatives have had some success in increasing the gender and ethnic diversity of employment, a lot of activity has been concentrated at basic entry grade-level posts, such that lower grades are significantly feminized and racialized (Wilson and Iles 1999: 34). Bach and Winchester (2003: 294) indicate that, despite the extra attention given to EO, 'employment in the public services expresses a complex pattern of gender segregation rooted in traditional—if changing—assumptions about appropriate employment for men and women'. The public sector has also been at the centre of campaigns that have highlighted the embedded nature of discrimination and inequalities within its organizations. A case in point is the concept of 'institutional racism' that emerged out of the MacPherson Inquiry into the police handling in 1993 of the murder investigation of black teenager Stephen Lawrence. While the concept and the policy initiatives flowing from it were situated originally within the police service, they have been adopted by a variety of public service organizations and by some in the private sector.

THE EMERGENCE OF DIVERSITY
MANAGEMENT IN THE PUBLIC SECTOR

The emergence of a diversity discourse (see Chapter 2) within the public sector has links to the public sector reform programme discussed above. If there is increasing convergence between public and private sector management practice and industrial relations, then there is likely to be increasing convergence between equality policy approaches. In a similar way as changes can be identified from old style public management to NPM, some changes within the approaches to equality are found. Dickens (1999) provides a useful summary of these tracing the way in which a bureaucratic and rules and procedures approach to EO gave way to one grounded in cost-based rationales and market imperatives. Creegan et al (2003) point to the way that the Conservative Government from 1979 explicitly promoted a business case approach to EO for both the public and private sectors. Chapter 6 outlines the traditional EO approach adopted by many public sector organizations, with specialist equality officers typically located in personnel departments or sometimes in equality units, with their work involving the monitoring of policies and practices, recommending policy changes and new policy initiatives and providing training on equality issues (see Cockburn 1991). The issue is the extent to which movement away from this traditional approach has occurred in the public sector. It is interesting to consider whether the distinctive features of the public sector imply that DM will have somewhat different implications in comparison to the private sector. To frame this discussion, we use the four key features of DM set out in Table 2.2 and discussed in Chapter 2, namely (i) business case rationale, (ii) systemic transformation of the organization, (iii) a broader range of individual and social group based differences, and (iv) positive imagery and celebratory rhetoric.

What is the Business Case for Diversity in the Public Sector?

At a purely theoretical level, we might question whether the business case emphasis of DM is appropriate and applicable to the not-for-profit public sector. However, there are obviously areas where a business case could be made in a public sector context. For instance, looking back to Chapter 2, attending to diversity issues could bring gains in terms of maximizing employee potential, in aiming to help recruitment, retention and promotion (Wilson and Iles 1999: 32), all areas needing to be addressed, especially in key public services such as nursing, teaching and policing, where there were significant recruitment and retention problems. Furthermore, given the emphasis of NPM on service delivery and quality, there could also be significant business benefits to recruiting front line staff with whom 'customers' can identify (ibid.)

However, there are various ways in which it is also difficult to make a business case in the public sector. On the basis of improved service delivery achieved through a more diverse workforce, Wilson and Iles (1999: 32) indicate the complexity of the 'customer' in a public sector context, which may make the business case less easy to make. For instance, unlike in the private sector, there are many more occasions when the 'customer' may be unwilling or have no choice of provider, or where there are multiple individuals concerned in any one service interaction or transaction, often with widely differing perspectives (for instance, a service employee, a carer, a family member or other professionals) (see also Korczynski 2002). Reforms introducing internal competition within public service departments only increase this complexity.

The need to make a business case for diversity also needs to be weighed up against the parallel demand for resource constraint and budget rationalization that were a key part of the public sector reforms under both Conservative and Labour Governments. Questions certainly arise as to what happens in times of economic hardship, both regarding the status and practice of diversity policies and also their impact (or lack of) on those facing inequality and disadvantage. It could be argued that a context of economic hardship could enhance a business case for maximizing the potential of existing employees or enhancing the performance (service delivery) of the organization by utilizing the talents of a more diverse workforce. However, the opposite could also be argued. Business case arguments are inevitably 'contingent, variable, selective and partial' (Dickens 1999: 10), and there is always the danger that a business case can be articulated against equality and diversity action. It is often the case that in times of economic hardship, equality and diversity policies become easy targets to lose funding, and that cutbacks and rationalization also disproportionately affect those at lower levels, and therefore those already facing disadvantage in the labour market (Creegan et al 2003; Wilson 1997; Woodall et al 1997). Indeed, while their research was based in a private sector airline, Bajawa and Woodall's (2006) central question of how resilient the business case for DM can be, when organizations are undergoing cutbacks and downsizing, is clearly also relevant to the public sector.

Systemic Transformation of the Public Sector

Moving to the second feature, DM calls for a systemic transformation of the organization, rather than just reliance on legal regulation and bureaucratic procedures. On the one hand, Wilson and Iles (1999: 36) indicate that the emphasis within NPM on measuring effectiveness and delivering outcomes fits more easily with a DM rather than an EO approach. However, have public sector organizations changed enough? Has such systemic transformation occurred within the continued bureaucratic structure of many public sector organizations? Can DM co-exist with the realities of an employer (the government) demanding resource constraint and downsizing? Furthermore, systemic transformation requires that DM becomes a key part of business strategy; however, Wilson and Iles (1999: 35) are pessimistic that this is possible in the very traditional organizations of the public sector, despite attempts at market-led reform. They argue that diversity issues remain an add-on to both the human resources or personnel function and the value system and culture of an organization.

Policy-Making Within a 'Difference' Paradigm

The third and fourth features involve thinking positively about difference and expanding views about what differences should be considered beyond the traditional social groups to encompass more elements of individual diversity. All of the reasons discussed in Chapter 2 as to why it would be positive to think more broadly about difference, as well as the dangers it poses, would clearly apply equally to the private as well as to the public sector context. However, more specifically to the public sector, we have already argued that this sector is more closely linked to legislation and is often more closely scrutinized for compliance. Therefore, as the legislation is largely concerned with group-based discrimination, it is worthwhile considering whether there is a better policy fit with more traditional EO notions of social group-based disadvantage in the public sector context.

A CASE STUDY OF EQUALITY AND DIVERSITY IN THE UK CIVIL SERVICE

This section explores equality and diversity in the UK Civil Service, drawing on findings from our case study of one government department that we call PSO. As there are later chapters dealing specifically with line-management, employee and trade union perspectives, this section will primarily present a critical review of equality and diversity strategy and policy at PSO. The questions we address include: do understandings of, rationale for and policy approaches to DM reflect any of the distinctive features of the context outlined above? Is there any evidence that there have been changes as a consequence of the public sector reform programme or any impact of the context of resource constraint? What role do different stakeholders play in DM development and implementation? Finally, given the higher levels of unionization, do we see significant trade union and employee involvement in the public sector?

The Equality and Diversity Context in PSO

PSO monitors its workforce by gender, ethnicity, disability, age and part-time status. The latest available workforce monitoring data at the time of the research was for the year up to 2001, and, where possible, we have managed to update some of this with publicly available data sources. At the time of research, the composition of the PSO workforce was 43 per cent female, meaning that women were just slightly under-represented relative to their share of the national workforce. Black and minority ethnic (BME) workers were over-represented (relative to the national workforce) at just under 15 per cent (but not relative to the BME population in London which is at least 29 per cent, where the majority of employees at PSO were based), while disabled people were about 5 per cent of the total PSO workforce (in keeping with the national average). However, when the workforce is broken down into the various Civil Service grades, there are a number of observations to make.

First, Tables 4.1–4.4. show the latest available statistics on the demographic composition of PSO headquarters staff by grade (Band A being the

Table 4.1   Staff Breakdown by Gender November 2007

Level	Female	Male
Band A	63%	37%
Band B	45%	55%
Band C	38%	62%
SCS	33%	67%
Fast Stream	53%	47%
Overall Workforce	45%	55%

Table 4.2   Staff Breakdown by Ethnic Origin April 2001

Level	White	BME	Unknown
Band A	55.4%	30.7%	13.9%
Band B	72.7%	13.6%	13.7%
Band C	84.5%	4.5%	11.1%
SCS	91.7%	1.3%	7.1%
Fast Stream	74.2%	7.2%	18.7%
Overall Workforce	72.4%	14.8%	12.8%

Table 4.3   Staff Breakdown by Ethnic Origin November 2007

Level	White	BME	Unknown
Fast Stream	27%	7%	66%
Overall Workforce	56%	13%	31%

Table 4.4   Staff with Disabilities November 2007

Level	Percentage of Total Staff at This Level
Band A	12%
Band B	9%
Band C	6%
SCS	4%
Fast Stream	7%
Overall Workforce	8%

lowest and Senior Civil Service (SCS) the highest). As can be seen, women, BME and disabled people were over-represented (relative to their total share of PSO workforce) in the lowest grade and under-represented in the two highest grades. In addition, BME and disabled people were particularly under-represented in the 'fast stream', graduate-level entry category (note that there has been a significant improvement for women in the fast stream from 43 per cent in 2001 to being in the majority in 2007).

Second, PSO had an overwhelmingly full-time workforce, but part-time employees were fairly evenly distributed across the grades. There was a small over-representation of part-timers in the lowest grade (relative to their total share of the workforce) and in the SCS, suggesting a concentration of part-time work at the lower skill levels, but possibly that there were also opportunities to work part-time once seniority had been achieved.

Third, as would be expected, younger employees were concentrated in the two lower grades, but also comprised the overwhelming majority of 'fast stream' employees. Older workers (55 plus) were over-represented in the lowest and highest grades, suggesting a polarization between lower skilled, lower paid older workers (who possibly need to continue working until at least statutory retirement age) and higher status older workers.

PSO also monitors the outcomes of the bonus schemes, promotions and progressions, including an initiative to encourage individuals to train and apply for promotion called the 'Accelerated Development Plan'. This data reveals that female promotions were more numerous than male, indicating the success of the various initiatives discussed below, to improve the position of women in PSO (the increase in the number of women in the fast-stream grade from 2001–2007 has already been noted). However, the data reveals that white workers were more likely to be promoted than BME from which it is clear that the organization has some way to go before race equality of outcome is achieved. In addition, the overwhelming majority of promotions were among full-time workers and among the 25–44 age group, with older workers under-represented, the latter suggesting that PSO careers have a tendency to plateau after age 44. This also suggests that people opting to work part-time could end up in a career cul-de-sac.

Looking at bonus distribution, it is skewed towards white, non-disabled, full-time, male workers. In 2001 (the latest data we have access to), only 7 per cent of employees who received £500 or more were known to be BME, only 31 per cent were female, only 5 per cent worked part-time and 6 per cent were disabled. Finally, the monitoring data for the 'Accelerated Development Plan' show that 62 per cent of those selected were women, 8 per cent were BME and 8 per cent were disabled. It seems that women and disabled employees were benefiting disproportionately (relative to their share of the PSO workforce) from this particular initiative.

It should be noted that there were some significant gaps in the availability of monitoring data. Indeed, PSO trade union representatives we spoke to complained about the incomplete nature of monitoring data on ethnicity. We had difficulty ourselves getting hold of recent data on the ethnic composition of the workforce by grade (whereas this was readily available for other diversity strands), and indeed PSO recognized it had a problem with regard to the availability of ethnicity data, stating in a Diversity Impact Assessment document of 2007 that they did not have ethnicity data on some 37 per cent of staff and were having to take specific action to try and address this. This explains the large percentage labelled as 'unknown ethnicity' in Table 4.4. Clearly we can only speculate on the reasons why it has been difficult to gather this data, but perhaps this relates to the level of suspicion and fear that we sensed employees felt around ethnicity issues, perhaps making them less willing to be open about their ethnicity, and which is discussed in detail in Chapter 8.

Overall, therefore, PSO replicated the demographic patterns that exist within the wider public sector. In particular, there was significant vertical sex and race segregation with a concentration of women and BME employees in the lower grades. In the revised PSO Equality Scheme of 2007, the continued problem of the over-population of women in lower grades is acknowledged, while the last Equal Pay Review in 2003 revealed a narrower pay distribution among female staff and that women were less likely to be found at or near the pay maxima for their grades. There has, however, been some notable progression of women with regard to some promotion programmes and entry at the graduate level.

The Civil Service and the PSO Policy Context

Given the discussion of the economic and industrial relations context above, it is worthwhile noting that the Civil Service (and PSO more specifically) faced a context of particular hardship at the time we conducted fieldwork. Bach and Winchester (2003) note that, as part of the wider public service reforms over the 1990s and into the 2000s, the Civil Service in general faced particularly harsh demands requiring budget cuts and rationalization. Reform of pay, for example, was more comprehensive in the Civil Service than other parts of the public sector. In 2003, driven by an 'efficiency agenda', the government launched major reviews into the operation of the Civil Service. The Lyons Review[2] (2004) into the location of civil servants recommended significant dispersal from London and the South East to other regions of the UK where salaries and other costs were lower. Plans were also announced for significant cuts in the Civil Service workforce, and the Gershon Review[3] examined a series of 'efficiency measures' designed to reduce Civil Servant numbers. Therefore, just 3 months before we began the case study research at PSO, the government announced, as part of its Comprehensive Spending Review, that there would be gross cuts of 84,150 Civil Service posts by 2008 and relocation of 20,000 civil servants (BBC 2004). The Spending Review also announced that PSO would specifically face a 15 per cent cut in its running costs and redundancies of approximately 16 per cent of the total workforce. The downsizing programme would culminate in a restructuring into a new streamlined department. This whole process was finally completed in mid-2007.

The context of PSO was therefore one of economic hardship and increased central scrutiny for the short to medium term. It therefore provided an interesting context in which to explore the fate of DM (its profile, development, effects and practice) when the organizational imperative had turned towards significantly reducing workforce numbers.

PSO Strategy and Policy

In terms of exploring the impact of the public sector reform programme, we have already stated that diversity issues were central to the reforms required under the 1999 *Modernising Government* agenda, and following this, each Civil Service department had to draw up action plans that established how they would deliver on this agenda. The Civil Service Management Board committed departments to action on the basis of six key themes (http://archive.cabinetoffice.gov.uk/roleofcentre/modagenda.htm), two of which clearly had diversity issues at their core, namely: theme (iv), a dramatic improvement in diversity; and theme (v), a Service more open to people and ideas. In particular, there was a specific commitment to a dramatic improvement in the Civil Service record on diversity, and to raising diversity awareness, whilst also developing policies to enable staff to achieve a better balance between their work and private lives. Moreover, there were clear echoes of a difference approach in the following extract from the *Modernising Government* agenda document:

> Civil Servants need exposure to wider thinking and new ideas. The Reform programme aims to target the areas with the greatest need for innovative thinking, broader horizons and different skills. The Programme is also about creating a Service which values people and develops them to their full potential, at all levels, gives them more challenging opportunities at all stages, and helps outstanding performers to progress rapidly. (http://archive.cabinetoffice.gov.uk/roleofcentre/ modagenda.htm)

In looking at how this broader framework was translated into policy at departmental level, the formal Equality and Diversity policy document of PSO defined diversity as:

- About individuals and including everyone.
- Not treating people less favourably because of obvious differences, e.g. age, race, gender, disability, accent, religion, belief or non-visible differences such as responsibilities and/or skills.
- Valuing differences. It aims to harness those differences to the benefit of both the organization and the individual.
- About *all* differences; not just those based on gender, race, disability or sexual orientation.
- Aiming to create equality of opportunity for *everyone* whilst recognising that some people face barriers that others do not.
- Better understanding of the diverse needs of the customer.

We can see from this that PSO included in its conception of diversity the social group-based issues traditionally associated with EO (for example, gender, race, disability and so on). Indeed, one aim of the policy was to tackle the concentration of women and BME employees in lower grades and to improve their progression rates. The mention of 'barriers' indicates recognition of discrimination and disadvantage. However, there were also elements drawn from the diversity concept, such as broadened categories and individual differences, specific mention of valuing and utilizing difference and the business case, fitting in with the aims of the broader *Modernising Government* agenda.

PSO's policy also expanded the agenda to look outside of the organization, namely to the customer, a development in tune with the shift towards a diversity paradigm (see earlier discussion and Chapter 2). The PSO approach was also reflected in the interviews with diversity practitioners from other public sector organizations who typically stated that the business case for diversity was to gain a workforce that was more reflective and/ or representative of the customer/service base, and thus improve customer service. They stressed that the focus on the customer and service delivery was a significant difference from traditional EO's internal focus on staff.

PSO equality and diversity policy can thus be characterized as multidimensional and hybrid, involving a mix of EO and DM approaches. It is interesting to note the extent to which a traditional compliance-based approach was dominant, however. Overall, many of our public sector research participants, including the majority of PSO line managers (as will be discussed further in Chapter 7) had a fairly limited understanding of the business case, associating it largely with the need to comply with legislation and avoid litigation. For some, this was *the* crucial rationale for the policy, whereas others felt it was important to move beyond legal compliance towards a business case.

Key PSO Policy Initiatives

Overall, the PSO Equality and Diversity Policy contained most of the elements that would be expected of a 'good employer' in the 2000s. However, despite its definition of diversity as involving broader categories and individual differences, central to the PSO policy were three programmes of action on traditional social group-based issues: (i) disability, (ii) race, and (iii) women's equality. Race/ethnicity and gender seemed to be given highest priority. There was, however, some broadening of the agenda, such as the positioning of work–life balance and flexible working (for all) as diversity issues. In addition, elements of the programmes of action extended beyond the workplace; for example, in the disability programme, a specific reference to customers was made. However, overall there was little evidence of a transformation to take on more radical broadening of the agenda around individual differences. Key elements of all three programmes of action included raising awareness, training, career development, promotion and progression and internal and external recruitment. PSO had identified

Table 4.5   Benchmarks for Women by Band within PSO

Year	1999	2002	2004	2005
Band B	40%	43%	47%	50%
Band C	26%	32%	38%	40%
SCS	21%	28%	33%	35%

Table 4.6   Benchmarks for BME staff by Band within PSO

Year	1998	2001	2003	2005
Band B	11%	14%	16%	18%
Band C	3.6%	5.5%	6.3%	8.5%
SCS	0.5%	2%	3.5%	4%

benchmarks for measuring progress on women's and race equality (see Tables 4.5 and 4.6). In addition, the disability programme included the working environment, information technology and people with disabilities in the wider community. The women's programme included cultural barriers, alternative working patterns, caring responsibilities and double disadvantage (on the basis of gender and ethnicity).

Monitoring data indicated that, despite the overall context of constrained resources, the 2005 benchmarks for women (Table 4.5) were close to being met, and the benchmarks for BME staff were almost reached for Band B and Band C (Table 4.6). It is significant that the benchmark for the SCS level was not met, however, as it lends support to Wilson and Iles' (1999) assertion that much equality and diversity policy action in the public sector has been targeted at lower organizational levels (i.e. getting people into the organization) to the neglect of more senior levels, leaving these lower levels heavily feminized and racialized. Reflecting this, trade union respondents commented on the extremely low numbers of BME employees in senior positions and their concentration in the lowest grades in the organization.

Some of the policy initiatives are worthy of more detailed attention, namely: the 'Diversity Season', diversity objectives in performance reviews and work–life balance initiatives.

i)   Diversity Season: this was an annual 2-week period of equality and diversity events that all members of staff were invited to attend, and specialist employee groups related to the diversity strands were invited to host events to promote and publicize their role.

ii)   Diversity Performance Objective: PSO also operated a performance management scheme which specifically included a diversity objective. This is particularly noteworthy because the lack of accountability of managers and other employees for DM is a common criticism within practitioner and academic literature (see, for example, Kandola and

Fullerton 1998: 83). The aim of this initiative was to embed diversity into all employees' roles to signal that diversity was everyone's responsibility. Accordingly, all individuals completed an annual performance review that had to contain a diversity objective to be agreed with the individual's line-manager. Examples of possible diversity objectives were provided by HR on the intranet, but people were encouraged to develop their own. Examples given to us by respondents included concrete activities such as attending a diversity training course or participating in an employee network; other examples were more aspirational, such as 'improve sensitivity to diversity'. All respondents were aware of the diversity objective, however, while it is held up by the organization as a particularly progressive initiative, nearly all the stakeholders indicated some level of difficulty with it. For some, it was simply a 'tick box' exercise that led to little understanding of what diversity meant for their job:

> I'll just put something very general, like 'keep up-to-date with diversity'. I think it's meaningless and pointless, but you have to put something and I can't think of what else to put. (Line-manager, white woman)

A couple of managers reported that groups of people put down the same diversity objective, undermining the intention for it to reflect an individual's work. Many were concerned about problems of measurement and evidence, claiming that it was impossible for someone not to achieve their diversity objective and that it was usually glossed over in the performance appraisal interview anyway. For managers, this meant that there was considerable variability in the way that they understood what was required of them and therefore how they incorporated DM into their own everyday work.

The ways in which involvement in DM could be demonstrated by workers in the lower grades was clearly a problematic issue. Many non-management employees had little sense of what they could claim as a diversity objective. Indeed, some indicated that participation in our focus group interviews would be something they would include, which in our view would not necessarily indicate anything about their role in implementing DM. One white, male non-management employee reported that he found it very difficult to meet the diversity objective because of the nature of his work: 'As someone at the very bottom of the ladder, I don't see where there is any application of diversity'.

Overall, the employees we spoke to felt that they did not get enough help in understanding how they might meet the diversity objective. This issue was also discussed at a 'Valuing Diversity' training course, where participants were asked to think about what they might include as their diversity objective, and we observed that most found this very difficult. When participants asked if more detailed examples of objectives could be posted on the intranet to provide further guidance, the course trainer was opposed to the idea because it would mean that people would cut and paste, rather than develop their own. However, clearly people found developing their own objectives difficult and seemed very concerned about the possible negative consequences of not meeting this objective.

iii) Work–Life Balance Initiatives: Under the remit of work–life balance, PSO offered a range of policies and flexible working arrangements, including (i) special leave for time off for dependants or domestic problems; (ii) a career break scheme; (iii) part-time working (with all advertised posts available for part-time or job share and the possibility of temporary part-time working during a difficult period); and (iv) flexi-time, home working and term time working. It was emphasized that all flexible working patterns were available to those with or without family or caring responsibilities, thus explicitly moving beyond the traditional EO focus on working parents towards individual difference. In practice, however, it was clear that the policy did not always live up to its aims. A significant problem raised by trade union representatives and non-management employees was that line-managers must agree on any individual arrangements. While most interviewees felt that there were now more opportunities for flexible working at PSO than there had been in the past, it was perceived that it was more difficult for lower grades to get their line-managers' agreement. For managers, too, there were difficulties with the whole issue of work–life balance. There was a sense of frustration that the culture of the organization had not kept pace with the policy. One issue for managers was the widely held perception that to progress in PSO involved working long hours and showing commitment and dedication to the work. This 'long hours culture' often meant that line-managers felt under pressure and disinclined to take on anything that they saw as extra work, such as the diversity agenda, particularly against a background of staff cuts. As is discussed in more detail in Chapter 7, the difficulty of needing to work long hours was exacerbated for women line-managers.

Stakeholder Participation and Involvement

It was noteworthy that the action programmes related to the Equality and Diversity Policy at PSO identified specific roles for Groups/Head of Management Units, Staff Directorates, Line-Managers, Employee Groups and Individuals (Employees). Thus, emphasis was placed on the need for everyone within the organization to be involved in DM implementation. With regard to trade union involvement, our overall conclusion was that PSO had fairly progressive relations with its trade unions compared to many unionized organizations. For example, trade union representatives and non-management employees were invited to comment on initial drafts of the policy. An example of the difference that trade union involvement can make was that PSO trade union representatives had argued for a continued focus on discrimination and disadvantage and for this to be reflected in the title of the DM policy. Following consultation, a title of 'Equality and Diversity Policy' (rather than just 'Diversity') was agreed on. Further, monitoring data was made available to the recognized trade unions, and much of this was also publicly available on the PSO web site, indicating some considerable level of commitment to transparency, although as indicated above there were acknowledged difficulties with the availability of ethnicity data.

Another significant mechanism for involving employees in DM was via employee groups. PSO had established four groups on women, race equality, disability and lesbian, gay, bi-sexual and transsexual (LGBT) issues. The employee groups were formalized structures with reporting channels to, and representatives on, the central bodies responsible for decision making in the diversity arena. Management and non-management employees were able to participate on equal terms, and the groups were resourced by the organization both in terms of a budget and time off from normal work duties for participants. Furthermore, efforts were made to communicate with employees more generally so that they understood the impact that such consultative groups had. Most importantly, it also appeared that these groups were seen as having some effect on policies, with group participants reporting changes made to policy documents or initiatives put in place in response to feedback.

The disability group was the largest with approximately 90 members, the LGBT group had about 35 members and the women's and race equality groups each had about 25 members. This particular employee involvement structure was therefore based around social groups rather than the individual. These groups were designed to be and had developed to be more than support mechanisms, for example, they were specifically invited to make recommendations on the equality and diversity policy and give advice on the content of relevant training. Additionally, during the 'Diversity Season', there was a particular role for the employee groups in hosting events in order to promote and publicize their role. It was also intended that the groups would facilitate self-development and networking among members, and groups were encouraged to liaise with each other. This aim for networking arguably indicates a desire to move beyond merely legal compliance towards a deeper 'transformation' of the organization. However, it should be noted that while the employee groups were formally well established and resourced, only a small minority of the non-management employees we interviewed seemed to know about them, and even fewer were actively involved themselves. Nevertheless, the establishment of employee groups is important and is indicative of a commitment to multi-channel forms of communication and consultation that genuinely seemed to be trying to engage employees proactively.

Policy Reviews

PSO had conducted two major reviews in the period immediately preceding our fieldwork—a general Diversity and Equality Review in 2002 and a race equality report in 2003. In addition, at the time of research, PSO's Race Equality Scheme was under review. It should be noted that all of these reviews were conducted before the announcement of the Comprehensive Spending Review of 2004 and its associated resource cuts. Looking at the documents, our general view was that the PSO reviews seemed to be reflexive and critical in nature, rather than simply self-congratulatory. The reviews identified areas where PSO had made equality and diversity advances, but also areas where more work needed to be done. So, for example, the Diversity and Equality Review identified strengths and areas for improvement. Many of these identified areas of weakness included issues that were raised by stakeholders in our interviews. For example, the importance of consulting employee groups on policy initiatives was emphasized. The inclusion in the performance review of a diversity objective was also seen as an important initiative, but it was believed that good practice in this area needed to be better communicated across PSO, a recommendation that tallied with some of the comments of stakeholders we spoke to. It was also acknowledged that employees in lower grades were not taking up flexible working, possibly because some managers were not prepared to enter into negotiations with them about flexible work arrangements. There was therefore formal recognition of the difficulties that trade union representatives and non-management employees had indicated to us (see Chapters 8 and 9 for more detailed discussion of trade union and non-management employee perspectives).

The 2003 Race Equality Report outlined PSO's work on internal and external race equality. Of particular note, it was stated that the race equality employee group was consulted on a number of new policy initiatives, including bullying and harassment guidance and the development of a new PSO Race Equality web site. In addition, a conference on minority ethnic issues—'Lifting the Barriers'—was held, from which some recommendations were taken forward, including a commitment (i) to design and pilot training and development for the lower grades, (ii) to develop additional management courses in harassment and bullying, and (iii) to introduce pre-coaching for BME staff for the fast stream promotion track.

FUTURE DIRECTIONS

Clearly, the DM context at PSO was heavily influenced by the wider context of restructuring and threats to jobs. There is detailed discussion of the perspectives of line managers, non-management employees and trade union representatives at PSO in Chapters 7, 8 and 9, respectively. In summary here, the context of restructuring was clearly at the forefront of the minds of those we spoke to. Trade union representatives and non-management employees were specifically concerned that measures to cut staff numbers would impact disproportionately on BME employees. It was interesting to note that line-managers were more concerned about the impact the restructuring would have on their workloads, and not one specifically mentioned the potential effect of the restructuring on BME staff or any other group.

In looking at the potential impact of the restructuring on the DM agenda within PSO, it should be noted that there are some limitations in terms of the time frame of our research fieldwork. We conducted the case study fieldwork late in 2004 just 3 months after the plans for proposed restructuring were announced. However, we did subsequently have access to a wide variety of publicly available documentary data relating to the periods when we were not present at the organization. Two main questions are relevant to our analysis of this documentation. First, could we gain any sense of the status of diversity issues, looking in particular if there was any indication that resources had been significantly decreased or increased for example? Second, did there appear to have been any direct impact on staff from particular diversity strands (especially given the clear concern of trade union representatives and non-management employees about the potentially detrimental effects on BME staff)?

It was clear that the central Civil Service Diversity Agenda continued to make demands on individual departments to improve their diversity record. A key initiative was the 'Delivering a Diverse Civil Service: A 10-Point Plan' (Crown Copyright 2005) which was introduced in 2005, committing individual departments to ten key areas for action on diversity and targets for progress to making the Civil Service more diverse. So, for example, PSO was required to work towards a target of improving the diversity of the Senior Civil Service to 37 per cent women, 4 per cent BME and 3.2 per cent disabled people (Crown Copyright 2005: 2). Individual departments were expected to indicate how they were going to meet these targets and areas for action, and they were required to report back to them through a variety of forums including the Annual Report and Equality Schemes (relating to the positive duties legislation). Within this, there was a continued focus on the need to 'mainstream' diversity issues as a key business issue, for example, in getting diversity to form part of departmental business plans together with an emphasis on departments having 'meaningful and measurable diversity objectives linked to reward systems' (Crown Copyright 2005: 8). As a consequence of the 10-Point Plan, the PSO Annual Report of 2006 notes that the diversity strategy of the department was refreshed. Looking at the Race, Disability and Gender Equality Schemes produced by PSO in 2006–7, the continued level of resourcing for the diversity strategy even during the period of cutbacks is evident. For example, all the schemes mention the delivery of a new programme of mandatory diversity training for all staff across PSO to be rolled out in 2007–8. The PSO Annual Report details the appointment of a designated diversity training provider and the requirement for it to monitor and report on take-up, attendance and participant feedback every quarter. In addition, there are examples of investment in additional training, for instance, after reporting in the Disability Equality Scheme on feedback from disabled staff that line-managers lacked understanding of access requirements, training was planned for line-managers of disabled staff. The Annual Report also details the funding of a new leadership development programme designed to encourage staff from underrepresented groups to progress to the Senior Civil Service. In all of the documents, consultation exercises with the employee groups and trade unions are also evident. Since our fieldwork ended, the women's group has been disbanded, but the race, disability and LGBT groups are reported as strong, and an additional group on multi-faith issues has been set up. The Race Equality Scheme is explicit about the continued difficulties found with gathering data on ethnicity: 'we recognize the need to improve the percentage of staff that declares ethnic origin to the Department' (ibid:16). There had been a consultation exercise with other organizations to share knowledge about how to improve declaration rates and a planned exercise to improve this data across the department to be rolled out in 2008. We also note that there has since been a follow-up strategy to the 10-Point Plan, namely, *Promoting Equality, Valuing Diversity: A Strategy for the Civil Service* which was launched in July 2008, just as the manuscript for this book was being produced (http://www.civilservice.gov.uk/about/diversity/index.asp). Given the recent publication of this document, we will not engage with much discussion about it; however, at the very least, it indicates continued commitment to the DM agenda in setting out what the Civil Service wants to achieve in equality and diversity in employment over the next 3 to 5 years. It is also notable that there is further supporting evidence of commitment to a DM policy agenda based around social groups, with the document stating specifically that 'By diversity we mean people who are in one or more of seven diversity groups' (http://www.civilservice.gov.uk/documents/pdf/diversity/diversity_strategy.pdf: 5).

Moving back to the specific context of PSO, the 10-Point Plan also specifically had a requirement for departments to assess the impact of the restructuring process 'to ensure that no particular group of staff is unfairly discriminated against' (Crown Copyright 2005: 9). One way in which this requirement was attended to in PSO was through a Diversity Impact Assessment on the Restructuring Process conducted in 2007, produced in order to comply with the department's duty as a public sector body to assess and consult on the likely impact of proposed policies on the promotion of equality. This document details the way in which during the development of the restructuring proposals through 2006, trade unions and diversity employee groups were consulted before the trade unions were formally involved in the statutory consultation process from September 2006. While this did not appear to have been recognized by the line-managers we spoke to, the

Diversity Impact Assessment document acknowledged that as proportionately more posts were being cut at the lower grades, the groups responsible for looking at selection of posts in each Business had analyzed that there could be a potential negative impact on the diversity of the department. In particular, women, people with disabilities and people from BME backgrounds might be disproportionately adversely affected (ibid:12). In addition, it was concluded that an adverse reduction of disabled, women and BME staff could result in the department failing to meet its commitments under the various Equality Duties and the targets of the 10-Point Plan. This led to more detailed impact analysis, consideration of policy changes and mitigating factors being undertaken. This had practical outcomes in that, for example, sickness absence records were to be disregarded for staff with long-term health conditions or a disability. Also, an assessment that performance appraisal markings tended to be lower in the lower grades led to a disregarding of these markings so as not to unfairly discriminate against disabled and BME staff. The document presents in detail the comprehensive measures taken to mitigate compulsory redundancy and facilitate redeployment with the effect that, in the end, only around 2 per cent of cuts had to be achieved through compulsory redundancy. Overall, the before and after comparison of statistical data, along with the broader assessment, allowed a conclusion that the process did not have an adverse or disproportionate impact on grounds of gender, disability or ethnicity.

CONCLUSION

Our first question involved the nature of DM at PSO and whether it reflected any of the distinctive features of the public sector discussed earlier. In many ways, DM strategy and policy at PSO was what would be expected from a government department given the public sector's long-standing focus on equality action and its role as a model employer. PSO had an impressive range of initiatives included within its equality and diversity strategy. However, although the portfolio of initiatives was comprehensive at PSO, the policy approach remained fairly traditional, perhaps because of the close proximity of legislation to the public sector. In parallel with the NPM reform programme, there was some inclusion of 'diversity' elements at the margins (for example, an emphasis on issues such as flexibility and work–life balance for all, and the role of the customer). However, largely the policy resembled traditional EO. There was limited evidence of concrete efforts to engender culture change and limited attention to individual differences or intersecting inequalities, in the way that might be expected within a DM paradigm. Nor was it a policy that had much in the way of 'radical' EO; indeed, the relative absence of initiatives based on strong positive action was noteworthy. Despite significant improvements for women within the organization, as is discussed in detail in Chapter 8, there were obviously still problems concerning BME staff and significant perceptions of gradism amongst lower grade employees. We would argue that for substantive change in the fortunes of under-represented, undervalued groups to occur, there needs to be stronger accountability and stronger initiatives to push structural change forward. Attempts to achieve greater accountability such as the diversity objective in the performance review had significant weaknesses in practice, which militated against the initiative acting as a way to change mindsets and embed diversity into the everyday practice of employees. Nevertheless, these are important initiatives, and only trial and error can improve their application.

In terms of our second question regarding the impact of the downsizing exercise, when we conducted fieldwork at the organization, it did not appear that the restructuring associated with the Spending Review had led to any immediate changes to the policy environment or reduction in the importance of DM initiatives (except the obvious additional pressures felt by line-managers; see Chapter 7). In addition, our analysis of the documents during and after the restructuring exercise seemed to indicate continued emphasis on and resourcing for DM initiatives. In their case study of a private sector firm, GlobalAir, Bajawa and Woodall (2006) found that the downsizing exercise was handled in a way that was proactive and sensitive to the issues of EO and DM, endeavouring to implement the process in a way that sustained the diversity of the organization. In many respects, there are signs that PSO handled their exercise in a similarly sensitive way, at least formally. However, clearly our later assessment of PSO is being made purely on the basis of formal, publicly available documents, and if we had been able to talk to the participants at this stage, a very different story may very well have emerged. As was the case with GlobalAir, it is problematic to compare the before and after organizations because they have changed considerably in terms of shape and structure. While the demographic data indicates that there had been no adverse changes in overall representation of BME, women or disabled staff (in fact ratios had increased from 2006 at PSO), the reliability and scope of this monitoring data was acknowledged as weak in some areas to begin with. Moreover, Bajawa and Woodall (2006: 58) point out that while overall proportions of workforce diversity may have been maintained, the cuts in absolute numbers of staff may take years to redress, may have diversity implications, and will require commitment and resourcing to ensure that progression and promotion will continue in the future.

Our interviews with line-managers (see detailed discussion in Chapter 7) indicated that, bearing in mind their uneven levels of understanding and buy-in and ever increasing pressure on them in terms of time and operational targets, the restructuring exercise could potentially have meant that diversity issues were pushed even further down their list of priorities. Certainly, this was the fear of the trade union representatives and the majority of the non-management employees, who clearly saw line-managers as the main conduit for implementation of diversity policies. However, there is evidence that overall resourcing for diversity issues did not appear to have been affected by the restructuring exercise at PSO, indeed, the opposite seems to be the case, with renewed emphasis on these within the business plans of PSO and plans to roll out new training programmes and other initiatives. As Cunningham (2000: 705) points out, 'success in maintaining and developing equal opportunities policy and practice in an environment of changing and contested values is contingent to a large extent on how well it was developed and legitimized prior to organizational reform'. Therefore, the longstanding and embedded nature of equality and diversity policy-making at PSO may very well have meant that it would be very difficult for this to be abandoned at this stage in the organization's development.

Part of the resilience of DM at PSO during the downsizing exercise, can also be attributed to our third question, namely the role of wider stakeholder involvement in DM policy. The open approach of the various diversity events and groups was a significant feature of the PSO policy. Management and non-management employees were given diversity awareness training alongside one another; they could attend various diversity events together and could participate in the employee groups on equal terms. These are in theory important opportunities for the different grades to share and hear each other's experiences. PSO was also an organization where stakeholder involvement was taken seriously and where proactive attempts were made to involve trade unions and employee groups. In this regard, PSO stands apart from the 72 per cent of workplaces in the UK where no negotiation, consultation or dissemination of information on equality occurs, but in line with the 78 per cent of workplaces with recognized trade unions, where employee representatives are negotiated with, consulted or informed about EO issues (Kersley et al 2006).

However, as discussed in subsequent chapters, this is not to say that the picture on stakeholder involvement was all rosy. It is clear from the research (as is discussed in later chapters) that trade union representatives and non-management employees in particular felt that their participation, opinions and voices were often less valued by the organization than those of more senior grades. There seemed to be a widespread perception that the equality and diversity policy did not serve the needs of non-management, lower grade employees. In particular, while significant progress appears to have been made on gender equality, one of the most pressing equality and diversity issues for trade union representatives and employees was that of the situation of BME employees within the organization. Therefore, it is important not to downplay the obvious representation gap that was alluded to by non-management employees and which clearly needs to be addressed in the longer term. However, trade union representatives we spoke to were themselves positive about the level of involvement they had in the diversity policy arena, and the post-restructuring documents also demonstrate the continued involvement of trade unions and the employee groups and some evidence of the impact they had in terms of contributing to fairer sets of criteria in the downsizing exercise.

In addition, it is important to see the way that an emphasis on legislative compliance also offered a stronger support for continued DM action. While it is important not to overestimate the importance of legislation (Dickens 1999: 12), the requirement for PSO to comply with legislation, particularly the statutory duties to promote equality, seemed to have meant that it would be difficult for PSO not to keep diversity issues at the centre of the restructuring process. Our documentary analysis indicated that the need to comply with this legislation affected the process right from the beginning and led to changes being made to the way the restructuring was conducted. This legislation only applies to the public sector, and it is interesting to reflect on its potential importance in keeping diversity at the top of agendas, and therefore how useful it would be to have in the private sector. In this regard, PSO provides a good example of the way that Dickens' three strategies for addressing equality action (business case, legislative and social or joint regulation) worked together in the case of PSO to provide a more secure foundation for DM than might otherwise be seen.

5 Diversity Management in the Private Sector

By Deborah Dean

INTRODUCTION

We know that over the last 15 to 20 years increasing numbers of both private and public sector organizations across Europe and the USA have introduced equality policies that shift emphasis away from non-discrimination towards valuing diversity (European Commission 2005; Konrad 2003; Kelly and Dobbin 1998). As discussed in detail in Chapter 2, this shift has largely been based on 'business case' arguments, but in the European context has also been influenced by increased legal regulation in the equality and diversity area. However, the central points of the business case have become pervasive as rhetoric and in many cases as (attempted, sporadic) practice, particularly in larger organizations (Maxwell et al 2000; Subeliani and Tsogas 2005; Hoque and Noon 2004). The business case has been explicitly labelled a 'privatised approach' to equality (Dickens 1999: 9), and private sector pressures to generate profit put the business case under its most revealing spotlight. In specifically UK terms, these pressures are shaped by an institutional investment and governance context that prioritizes short-term financial returns, often referred to as 'shareholder' capitalism (Jacoby 2005).

In this chapter, we look in detail at the development and introduction of DM in one organization. In the first two sections of the chapter, we consider the specificities of the UK private sector in relation to diversity issues. We then look more closely at our case study organization—ServiceCo—its culture, policy, initiatives and perceptions of the people who work there. The findings support and extend existing literature on the principal obstacles to DM within organizations and the persistent gaps between policy aims and workplace realities.

THE UK PRIVATE SECTOR CONTEXT

At the end of 2007, just over 80 per cent of the UK workforce, some 23 million people, were employed in the private sector (ONS 2008). The majority of private sector workers, 59 per cent, are men (compared with

65 per cent women workers in the public sector), and the age profile is younger than that of public sector workers (62 per cent 35 or over as compared with 72 per cent). The proportions of both black and minority ethnic (BME) and disabled workers are approximately the same in both sectors, at 7 per cent and 13 per cent, respectively (ONS 2008). The private sector is characterized by significant and persistent inequalities. The data indicates continuing advantage in being a so-called 'standard' worker (i.e. full-time, white, male, non-disabled) in relation to employment progression and pay (TUC 2007a; TUC 2007b; Berthoud 2008). For example, despite narrowing of the overall gender pay gap—currently standing at 23.4 per cent—the disparity in weekly earnings between full-time men and women remains widest in the private sector. The full-time gap in the public sector is 13.3 per cent, but 22.5 per cent in the private sector, and in banking, insurance and pension provision it is as high as 41 per cent (Hurrell 2006: 22). Further, 42 per cent of working women are in part-time employment (as compared to 9 per cent of working men), and the pay gap between women working part-time and men working full-time is 38.4 per cent (Hurrell 2006: 19).

Ethnicity, disability and age also all significantly affect contractual status, occupational location and rates of pay (Platt 2006; DRC 2006). For example, only half of disabled people overall are employed, compared with four-fifths of non-disabled people (DRC 2006: 4). However, BME disabled people are on average 15 percentage points less likely to be in paid employment than white disabled people (Sefton et al 2005: 66).

Occupational segregation has been identified as one of the principal explanations for inequality (see Women and Work Commission 2006), and in European Union (EU) countries horizontal segregation by gender is particularly apparent. In 2005, six (service) sectors employed over 60 per cent of all women in work, with men's employment spread more evenly across a much larger and more diversified range of sectors (Franco 2007; for a similar picture of the USA labour market, see Chao and Rones 2007: 26–27). The long-term systemic nature of these divisions is illustrated by a clear example of vertical sex segregation in the UK, where women comprise only 3.8 per cent of executive directors of FTSE 100 companies. All of those women are white, and of the 102 women non-executive directors (13.7 per cent), only four were from BME groups (Singh and Vinnicombe 2006).

The situation of persistent inequality exists despite the UK's framework of anti-discrimination legislation, which is regarded as comparing favourably with many other EU member states (European Commission 2007) and, in line with wider EU discourses on 'flexicurity' (European Commission 2006), encouragement of working practices that recognize the diverse positions of workers (*inter alia*, relating to work–life balance issues as in the Work and Families Act 2006). Nevertheless, this legal regulation is viewed as weak in effecting comprehensive change for a variety of reasons (Dickens 2006), and there is less compulsion to comply with legislation in the private than the public sector. This is in keeping with law as part of a national institutional framework characterized as a liberal market economy, privileging short-term returns on investment and unilateral managerial governance (Soskice 2005).

However, if the wide variation in private sector managerial practice in the UK (see, for example, Boxall and Purcell 2000), is recognized it is evident that broad categorization of economies can result in too static an analysis: 'For example, liberal market economies may tolerate more local experimentation, such as the coexistence of 'high road' labour practices alongside 'low road' adversarial relations, whereas choices may be more constrained in coordinated market economies' (Deeg and Jackson 2007: 156). There are obviously clear differences between countries in terms of the culture and structure of organizational equality and diversity practices and their relationship with broader legislative regimes and industrial relations climates (Konrad et al 2008). For example, where employer practices are firmly constrained by strong legal regulations or national collective regulations (as typically in coordinated market economies such as Denmark Campbell and Pedersen 2007), changes in regulations will have a direct effect on organizational policies. Where the regulatory framework is looser, the pace of change depends much more on the individual initiatives of the organization (Rubery et al 1999: 62; see also Marginson et al 2007 on host/home country and sectoral influences on employee voice in multinational companies).

Formal attention to equality and diversity issues is widespread in large private sector organizations in the UK. The most recent Workplace Employment Relations Survey (WERS) 2004 indicates that over two-thirds of UK private sector workplaces have equal opportunities (EO) policies, with large workplaces (1,000 employees or more) being significantly more likely to have a policy than small workplaces (100 employees or fewer) (94 per cent as against 46 per cent; Kersley et al 2005: 238). However, review of both the current and previous (1998) WERS data indicates that there remains a substantial mismatch between an organization's possession of an EO policy and organizational action in translating the policy into practice (Dickens 2006: 446; Hoque and Noon 2004). For example monitoring, both of the workforce and of policy initiatives, is widely regarded as essential (if insufficient) in transferring measures from page to practice (European Commission 2005). Yet, the overwhelming majority of UK workplaces with a policy do not monitor its implementation—only 14 per cent of UK private sector workplaces in the WERS survey did so (Kersley et al 2005: 247), a pattern repeated in private sector organizations across the EU25 (European Commission 2005: 6). There is more variation in that, for example, it has been found that organizations are significantly less likely to monitor disability than gender and ethnicity (Roulstone and Warren 2006: 121). Further, the number of private sector workplaces that undertake more detailed demographic monitoring, such as by gender within ethnicity, is less than half the number in the public sector (Adams and Carter 2007).

Finally, a significant structural difference between the private and public sectors is in relation to trade union presence. Trade union density in the UK private sector as a whole is 19 per cent, and terms and conditions of work negotiated through a collective agreement cover only approximately 26 per cent of private sector workers (Kersley et al 2005: 180). The relevance of these statistics for discussion of DM is that recent data suggest that recognized unions are positively associated with adaptation of equalities legislation into workplace practices (Dickens 2006), as well as earlier research indicating some positive associations between union recognition and equality outcomes (for a discussion, see Kirton and Greene 2005). Yet the low levels of union density in the UK private sector militate against this positive influence. These issues are considered in some depth in Chapter 9; here, they inform consideration of the realities of organizational policy development and stakeholder involvement.

DIVERSITY MANAGEMENT IN THE PRIVATE SECTOR

Chapter 2 delivered a detailed discussion of the concepts of EO and DM and the possible implications of these approaches. With regard to the identified shift from EO to DM, the latter is clearly becoming a policy concept of choice for organizations across the private sector in both the UK and the EU more generally (European Commission 2005: 12; Cornelius et al 2001; CBI 2008; Wrench 2007) as any survey of corporate web sites indicates (Singh and Point 2006; Bellard and Rüling 2001). The way the concept is presented, however, differs. Singh and Point (2006) found national variation in presentation of DM on the web sites of top corporations from eight European countries. For example, they found UK companies giving more emphasis to the 'competitive advantage' aspect of the DM discourse, as well as greater prominence to explicit categories of gender and ethnicity. French and German companies were more likely to refer to 'culture', which Singh and Point speculate may have been intended to allude to race/ethnicity (2006: 368). This is echoed in Bellard and Rüling's (2001) exploration of the transplanting of the USA-derived DM discourse into French and German corporate environments. Different aspects of this discourse were stressed by the 38 largest corporations in both countries, and, finding no systematic difference by industry, the authors argue for the importance of socio-cultural traditions and the national context. Stressing the business case dimension of DM draws on an implicitly unitarist argument that there is 'an identity of interest between employer and employee' (Edwards 2003: 10). Therefore, it might be expected that this element is not highlighted in the same way in European contexts where pluralism is the dominant industrial relations paradigm

A useful example of the spread and orientation of DM in the UK private sector context is the organization Business in the Community (BITC), which describes itself as 'a unique movement of over 800 of the UK's top companies committed to improving their positive impact on society'. BITC's member companies employ over 12 million people across 200 countries and in the UK, over one in five of the private sector workforce (BITC web site). It hosts a 'portal' web site to a wide range of employer web sites, most of which specify equality and diversity issues as important to their business. It is notable that 'diversity' in these web sites is commonly used to express the conventional business case drivers discussed in Chapter 2, in line with Singh and Point's (2006) assessment of UK corporate diversity emphases.

An enthusiasm for 'diversity' is in line with policy developments in companies based elsewhere in the EU and in the USA (see Grayson 2007). At the most proactive end of the spectrum of approaches, in 2007, the France-based food and drinks multinational Danone signed a worldwide 'convention on diversity' with the international union IUF, covering (unusually) specifics of HR practice. In contrast to dominant French corporate approaches as previously discussed, Danone's stated reasons for promoting diversity related directly to the business case, including opening up new markets and countries, encouraging innovation, responding to society's expectations and recruiting and retaining talented staff (Carley 2008). While it is too early to comment on the effectiveness or longevity of such 'international framework agreements' (Fairbrother and Hammer 2005; Riisgaard 2005), variants of which have been agreed by other multinational corporations (see European Industrial Relations Review 2006), they have been entered into voluntarily by the organizations involved, and their unlegislated-for existence is of interest in considering trends in private sector engagement with diversity issues.

The relatively long-standing existence of an organization such as BITC (celebrating its 25th year in 2008, with growing membership) is arguably testament to ongoing private sector engagement with issues around disadvantage and discrimination. However, one of the key problems is the enduring gap between the rhetoric of policy and the reality of practice. For example, consideration of workplace practice in US multinational corporations (MNCs) reveals the ongoing tensions. These include the sometimes contradictory relevance of size and resources in developing and implementing DM and the obstacle of competing agendas in translation of policy aims into outcomes (Wentling 2004; see also den Dulk and de Ruijter 2008 on managerial attitudes towards work–life balance policies in practice). Hoque and Noon's (2004) exploration of UK national survey data found that, although public and private sector organizations were as likely to have EO policies, private sector organizations were significantly less likely to have instituted practices supportive of policy, with national ownership relevant as to where practice is least likely; for example, 'the probability of having an 'empty shell' gender policy increases more than three-fold where

North American workplaces are concerned. . . . European Union-owned workplaces are more likely to have 'empty shell' ethnicity policies' (2004: 495).

Liff and Cameron's (1997) discussion of the influence of organizational culture on equality initiatives has been brought to life in the largest civil rights class action lawsuit in USA legal history. Despite proactive DM policies in several areas (see, for example, Peters 2006) and notably in light of Hoque and Noon's findings above, Wal-Mart, the largest private sector employer in the USA, was recently the subject of allegations of sex discrimination against its women employees (Greenhouse and Hays 2004). In line with findings on the ubiquity of DM rhetoric amongst large organizations, Wal-Mart's web site lists a range of diversity achievements, initiatives and goals. Yet the class action suit alleges systematic direct sex discrimination in levels of pay and promotions. Further, Wal-Mart has also been accused of employing illegal immigrants on unlawfully poor terms and conditions and having a secret plan to discriminate in recruitment against older, overweight people in order to contain health care costs (see discussion in Kirton 2008). The sex discrimination allegations have been explored as outcomes of an entrenched, traditionally masculine corporate culture (Schein 2007; Besen and Kimmel 2006). The other situations can be seen as privileging cost minimization strategies over either a business or social justice case for equality and diversity. This is a possibly unsurprising clash of corporate goals in a context of 'shareholder capitalism' (as outlined above) and also confirm that line-managers' well-established struggles with competing operational and policy objectives (Foster and Harris 2005; den Dulk and de Ruijter 2008; McBride 2003) are often in parallel with tensions at senior management level. The accusations levelled at Wal-Mart exemplify Dickens's argument that 'Unfair discrimination can be rational and efficient for an individual and the organization either because of perceived cost advantages or in terms of control of the labour force' (2000: 159).

The extant research literature indicates three main areas offering explanations for this rhetoric/reality gap, which are also supported by our case study findings: First, the difficulties of DM policy focused predominantly on the business case in a sector where generation of profit is the principal goal, thus making equality action (even) more contingent (Dickens 1999); second, the variable and often confused understandings of DM among organizational stakeholders responsible for implementing policy; and third, the top-down nature of DM and uneven wider stakeholder involvement. Aspects of these explanations are considered below.

Looking first at the business case more closely, the UK Chartered Institute for Personnel and Development (CIPD) found that, measured against 146 variables indicating level of 'sophistication' in DM, only 7 per cent of private sector organizations were in the top 20 percentile, compared to 34 per cent of public sector organizations and 18 per cent of voluntary sector organizations (CIPD 2007: 5). Whether this finding is related to causes or outcomes, the tensions between profit and equality action are apparent in the empirical research on DM in both the UK and USA private sectors. For example, Bajawa and Woodall (2006) address the difficulties faced by an international airline in maintaining DM objectives in the face of 'downsizing' strategies, highlighting the inbuilt inconsistencies of the business case for DM in a liberal market economy (albeit in a less extreme way than the Wal-Mart example above). Bassett-Jones et al (2007) found that effective DM in a telecommunications multinational was dependent on the existence of appropriate training, feedback, mentoring and decision-making mechanisms at and between all levels of the organization. This is a requirement that most organizations would find challenging to develop and maintain, particularly in a context of highly variable employee voice arrangements (see, for example, Marchington and Wilkinson 2005). Kalev et al (2006), analyzing longitudinal data from private sector organizations in the US, found that despite the lack of evidence that equality and diversity measures 'work' (in terms of increased managerial-level presence of minorities), 76 per cent of employers made some effort to promote diversity. However, they also found that the effectiveness of diversity programs was highly variable, with some common practices such as training having either small or negative effects (Kalev et al 2006: 602). Further research in USA-based MNCs points to the countervailing pressures of organizational size and competing organizational agendas as barriers to implementation of DM (Wentling 2004).

The two other areas of explanation, the level of understanding of DM by organizational stakeholders and the extent to which different stakeholders are involved in development and implementation of DM, are clearly closely connected. The key role of line-managers in DM is discussed in Chapter 7; however, Larsen and Brewster note that, in terms of devolution of HR responsibilities to line-management, the UK consistently comes near the 'least devolved' end of the European spectrum (2003: 240; Brewster 2007). This calls into doubt the translation of the DM paradigm's emphasis on engagement of line-management. On a different aspect of the same point, Foster and Harris (2005) found that line-management in a major retailing organization frequently did not understand what they were being asked to do and also found DM in conflict with their operational performance objectives. This finding can also be considered in relation to Rasmussen et al's (2004) contrast of responses to part-time work issues in Denmark, the Netherlands and New Zealand. The more positive outcomes for women in Denmark and the Netherlands were associated with established tripartite social regulation, involving government, trade unions and employers. As discussed in more detail in Chapter 1, Dickens argued that a tripartite approach was necessary to promote equality action in the first place and must involve 'complementary and mutually reinforcing' business case rationales, legal regulation and social regulation strategies (1999: 16). The limitations of each route would be mitigated by the different strengths of the others. This argument is revisited in the concluding discussion and in Chapter 10.

Given this brief indication of complex difficulties, why have private sector organizations responded to the DM discourse? The spread of this discourse from North America has been discussed as encouraged by 'common external factors' of increasingly internationalized competition, ongoing migration, demographic shifts and growth of the service sector (Wrench 2005: 74; European Commission 2006: 1). However, the 'social partnership' model of consultation between government, employer and union representatives at the EU level arguably facilitates more emphasis on social justice in the European context. As discussed in Chapter 2, in the USA, DM has been argued to be a creative response by EO specialists and advocates to the backlash against EO and affirmative action policies intended to redress embedded disadvantage of minority groups. 'Diversity' is rhetorically inclusive, extending to the white males who have been the dominant employee group in the private sectors of Europe, Australasia and North America. In the USA, Kalev et al argue that employers often use equality and diversity practices as evidence of 'good faith' to improve morale or to defend against litigation (2006: 610). Anti-discrimination legislation in both liberal market and co-ordinated market economies arguably necessitates ongoing engagement with realities of 'difference'. As DM can be presented and delivered in a variety of ways (as noted above; Singh and Point 2006; Bellard and Rüling 2001), employers can engage with this necessity in context-sensitive ways. For some, it could also be seen as substituting an individualist focus for the collectivist focus associated with trade unionism (Kirton and Greene 2006), glossing the variations in power possessed by individuals as members of different social groups (see Liff 1997). Fleetwood, in a related discussion of the contemporary prominence of the 'work–life balance' discourse, argues that 'flexibility' has been 'discursively rehabilitated' (without its former negative connotations) as representing individual freedom, thus legitimizing a range of employer-friendly working practices (2007: 388). However, in the way that strategic, policy and operational objectives can collide unpredictably in specific organizations, and given that DM may also involve employer costs (e.g. disruption to internal labour market expectations), it is important to be wary of blanket ascription of interests. Empirical investigation remains central to building understanding (Edwards et al 2006).

THE CASE STUDY: SERVICECO

This section explores equality and diversity in one large private sector organization, drawing on findings from our case study of a UK multi-sector MNC we term 'ServiceCo'. The case study involved fieldwork focused on the company's headquarters and three regional sites (HealthSite, RailSite and RoadSite) involving two business groups—Transport and Health. We will primarily present a narrative account of the development and implementation of the DM policy at ServiceCo, and while there are later chapters dealing in more detail with line-management, employee and trade union perspectives, which also draw on the empirical material from ServiceCo, a brief consideration of stakeholder views is central to this chapter, in contextualizing the company's policy framework.

The Equality and Diversity Context Of ServiceCo

ServiceCo had only been systematically monitoring the composition of its workforce since 2003, and improving monitoring data was stated by the senior manager responsible for the development of the organization-wide DM policy to be key to targeting appropriate initiatives. In 2004–5, there was monitoring by gender, ethnicity, age and length of service, but surprisingly, despite the existence of anti-discrimination regulations on this dimension of diversity, disability was not included (see discussion below).

The available data (Tables 5.1 and 5.2) showed that ServiceCo had a predominantly white and male workforce: in 2005, the composition of the ServiceCo workforce was only 24 per cent female, meaning that women were under-represented relative to their share of the national workforce (approximately 46 per cent; BERR 2006). The percentage of BME workers had increased from 4.2 per cent in 2003 to 7 per cent, in line with the national workforce figure. However, monitoring statistics were not broken down by region, despite the fact that regional variations are likely. Official UK statistics on geographic distribution of BME groups indicate that, for instance, the West Midlands region (where much of the fieldwork for this study was undertaken) has the largest BME population outside London, at 13 per cent (ONS 2003).

Table 5.1   Staff Breakdown by Gender

Year	Female	Male
2003	19.3%	80.7%
2004	23.1%	76.9%
2005	24.5%	75.5%

Table 5.2   Staff Breakdown by Ethnicity

Year	White	BME
2003	81.5%	4.2%
2004	78.9%	4.7%
2005	78.7%	7.0%

Looking at Table 5.3, ServiceCo also had an unusually young workforce, with 43 per cent under 30 years of age and 66 per cent under 40, with the largest proportion of the workforce being under 20 years at 24 per cent. It is also clear from the monitoring data in Table 5.4 that the workforce was very transient (34 per cent of employees were employed for less than 1 year) with relatively high turnover rates, particularly for BME, female and young employees. However, the monitoring data were not detailed enough to cross reference between turnover rates and demographics. So, for example, it was not possible to determine whether the 34 per cent of employees who have been employed for less than 1 year were also disproportionately female or BME.

Further, there was no monitoring across occupations, levels or grade boundaries, or by business sector. Thus, the organization had no concrete information on patterns of occupational segregation (for example, whether women were concentrated in the lowest pay bands) or whether ServiceCo Health is more feminized or has a larger proportion of BME employees than other business sectors. Thus, the available monitoring data provided only a very partial picture of workforce composition. This reflects the broader situation captured by WERS 2004 (noted above), which found that within the small proportion of private sector workplaces that did monitor, there was significant variation according to activity (for example, monitoring promotions) and which characteristics were monitored (such as ethnicity or age) (Kersley et al 2005: 248). ServiceCo certainly used these monitoring statistics to inform policy, but the very limited range of data and lack of a basis for making relevant comparisons could not give a full enough picture to produce the desired 'focused' initiatives. For example, while ServiceCo appears to have been successful in recruiting staff under the age of 20 years (18 per cent), it was losing them at a much faster rate, with this

Table 5.3   Staff Breakdown by Age

Year	<19 years	20–29 years	30–39 years	40–49 years	50–59 years	60+ years
2003	14.2%	14.6%	23.1%	24.7%	18%	5.3%
2004	21%	14.9%	18.3%	20.5%	16.9%	5.6%
	16–25 years	25–35 years	35–45 years	45–55 years	55–65 years	65+ years
2005	24.2%	18.8%	22.8%	19.9%	16%	1.3%

Table 5.4   Staff Breakdown by Length of Service

Year	< 1	2–3	3–5	5–11	11–15	15–19	19–25	25+
2003	37.4%	17.4%	7.3%	11.0%	8.4%	4.5%	5.6%	8.3%
2004	45.5%	17.2%	7.4%	10.8%	5.7%	3.8%	3.2%	6.4%
2005	34.0%	24.2%	10.6%	11.9%	4.7%	4.7%	3.0%	6.8%

group forming 40 per cent of leavers in 2005. Importantly, this flags up the fact that recruitment alone is not an indicator of equality: increasing workforce diversity does not mean that the firm is an EO employer when wider indicators are considered such as retention of staff or the changing of workplace cultures.

Despite the gaps in monitoring data, it was clear that managers were aware of distinct patterns of gendered and racialized occupational segregation across the organization. This included statements that women were over-represented in human resources (HR), largely absent in Transport, disproportionately concentrated in the lowest-earning jobs in Health and under-represented in company-wide management, with no women at the most senior level. BME workers were similarly concentrated in the lowest-earning jobs in Health and Transport and were also more or less absent from management. The senior manager responsible for the DM policy (a white woman) acknowledged that ServiceCo was overwhelmingly white and male and described the gender split as the biggest single issue facing the organization: 'We shouldn't joke about it but we do—we go to [ServiceCo] conferences and if it wasn't for HR people and lawyers there'd be no women there'.

The Impetus for and Development of DM at ServiceCo

When our research started in 2004, diversity issues had only recently become a part of ServiceCo's formal policy agenda. A launch campaign for the policy took place mid-2004 with the intention of rolling it out to all areas of the business through 2005 into 2006. Hoque and Noon note that the likelihood of a policy having substance rather than simply existing as a paper policy 'depends largely on the reasons for its introduction' (2004: 483; see also Subeliani and Tsogas 2005 and exploration of what drove policy introduction is developed below). However, a closely related, if indirect, consideration is how policy is developed and by whom.

In 2003, the white, female Head of Employee Relations (ER) who had a long and varied employment history in the company took over responsibility for equality and diversity from a senior management colleague:

> I volunteered to pick up the equality banner from one of my colleagues who was dropping it because he'd got some other pressing issues to deal with from a work perspective. So I stuck my hand in there and that's how I got equality.

From this quote, it appears that the DM policy did not have a particularly strategic or co-ordinated start. Further, it should be noted that diversity responsibilities were taken on in addition to her other ER and HR duties. This is not an unusual practice: recent research by the (CIPD 2006: 8) found that 53 per cent of those with responsibility for diversity in their organization reported that they were not contracted to work exclusively on diversity.

From this point, reporting to the Group HR Director, the Head of ER, together with two assistants in the HR office, developed the company's equality and diversity policy. The Head of ER—who had had no background or training in these issues—said that she and her assistants focused on what they could learn from 'best practice' advice from ACAS, from ServiceCo employment lawyers, from a fellow organizational member of BITC and from relevant web sites:

> We got examples from past lives and all sorts of stuff. So anywhere we could grab bits of information from, obviously the Internet is abound with this stuff. So primarily that's where we were coming from, in terms of putting a policy together. . . And we just swamped ourselves with information and then went into a darkened room and wrote a policy.

The policy thus developed in a fairly ad hoc fashion and notably with little stakeholder involvement. Indeed, as is discussed further later, there was no formal input requested from the recognized trade unions, from line-management or non-management staff, despite the existence of employee involvement mechanisms such as consultative Staff Forums.

It is possible that this was a function of the central impetus for the policy. According to the Head of ER, there were a number of 'drivers' for the development of this policy, but a recurring theme from her and from most interviewees was consciousness of the costs of falling foul of anti-discrimination law (there had been some high-profile and costly cases taken against the organization in the recent past) and a perception that employees were both more aware of their rights and more ready to take action through Employment Tribunals. Some drivers mentioned also had echoes of a conventional business case, including the desire to be an 'employer of choice' in a tight labour market for skilled workers, extensive work with the public sector and that sector's expectation of equality and diversity policies, and the increasing importance to city investors of equality and diversity measures as indicating a 'sustainable organization'. These tally with the DM drivers discussed by Bellard and Rüling (2001) in drawing on DiMaggio and Powell's (1983) findings on organizational isomorphism in response to changing investment pressures (2001: 18). Certainly other organizations' practice around both diversity and 'employee voice' issues were frequently cited. The Head of ER also, however, expressed opinions that this was 'the right thing to do' (the social justice case). This belief in social justice coexisted with organizational pragmatism.

After drafting the policy on the basis of a self-taught, essentially crisis-management approach, it was sent to other senior HR directors within the company for feedback. This was a process that, according to the ER manager, was carried out 'quite quickly, because everyone was particularly mindful that what we'd got at that time was not particularly robust'. Again, despite the citing of business case drivers, there was no evidence of the sort of strategic planning that Wentling (2004) found was regarded by diversity managers in US MNCs as crucial in preventing the failure of diversity initiatives.

The DM Policy

The final version of the document was termed the Equal Opportunities and Diversity Policy—the significance of the title is discussed later. Its main aims were stated as:

- At ServiceCo we operate and make every effort to ensure that a working environment exists where all employees are treated with courtesy, dignity and respect irrespective of gender, race, colour or sexual orientation.
- All efforts are geared to eliminating all bias and unlawful discrimination in relation to job applicants, employees, our business partners and members of the public.
- To complement ServiceCo's 'core values' of 'openness, collaboration and mutual dependency'.

The objectives were to:

1. Match the diversity of our society.
2. Create a working environment free from discrimination, harassment, victimisation and bullying.
3. Ensure that all employees are aware of the Group Equal Opportunities and Diversity Policy and provide any necessary ongoing training to enable them to meet their responsibilities.
4. Strive to become an organization that will recognise, value and understand diversity and provide its employees with genuine opportunities to improve and reach their full potential.

The aims of the policy are broad and 'diversity' is defined as what Bellard and Rüling call, in relation to the public discourse of large French and German companies, 'a general and diffuse value-related category' (2001: 11). Some analyses see this lack of precise definition as part of the reason for the appeal and spread of diversity discourses (see Noon 2007: 780). The predominantly vague understanding at ServiceCo of the concept (considered below) lends some support to this argument.

At the same time, with the exception of the final objective above that indicates a more recognizably 'diversity' approach, the main thrust of the ServiceCo policy reflected a conception of DM focused mainly on traditional EO issues. Such issues, as noted in Chapter 2, commonly include policies in line with anti-discrimination legislation in relation to, for example, recruitment and selection procedures. This is indicated by the objective of 'matching' the workforce to wider societal diversity (with its implied focus on certain groups). The wording of the second objective also implies that some groups need protection. However, of note is the fact that at the time of the research in 2004, disability, religion and age were missing. This was surprising, given that legal compliance was emphasized as a primary impetus for the policy and the fact that legislation already existed on disability (Disability Discrimination Act 1995) with more imminent (Disability Discrimination Act 2005) and regulations publicly in the pipeline on religion and age. The omissions are possibly less surprising given the non-strategic, time-pressured development of the policy by a non-specialist. The main aim was to defend the company against discrimination claims. The Head of ER explained:

> I guess the biggest strength of [the policy] is we know it's robust, because we've had it tested by all sorts of professionals that say, *as a policy this is a robust policy* . . . In terms of compliance, would it go through tribunal?

There was also acknowledgement by the Head of ER of the potential impact on ServiceCo of the existing and (at the time) forthcoming public sector duties to promote equality in respect of race, disability and gender (in force from 2001, 2006 and 2007, respectively). These public sector duties apply to the private sector in limited circumstances, such as where a private organization carries out functions contracted out to it by a public authority. ServiceCo is extensively involved in such activities, including various public-private finance building initiatives (PFIs) and in managing housekeeping and catering facilities in a number of National Health Service hospitals. However, there was no awareness apparent amongst ServiceCo's senior managers of the implications of these impending duties. Indeed, the challenge of taking a proactive approach to DM is suggested by the perspective of HealthSites's Chief Executive (a white man): 'I guess you could say if a lack of cases in a legal sense is a success, then we are very successful'.

At the same time as the Head of ER had been given responsibility for drafting the policy in 2003, ServiceCo was putting together a major PFI bid in the Health Group:

> And of course they [*public sector Primary Care Trusts*] automatically say to you . . . 'And what's your policy on equal opportunities?' And when [we] were first putting the bid together [the manager] who was running the bid couldn't find anything. And then all of a sudden we sort of pulled the rabbit out of the hat with our new equal opportunities

policy. And the Primary Care Trust was so impressed and we actually won that work and [the manager] was absolutely convinced that one of the reasons we won it was because of the content of the policy.

This was a clear example of an unvarnished business case. Rather than an aspiration that employing a diverse range of people would result in unspecified organizational improvement, it was recognized that the *declared intention* of doing so and of not discriminating would immediately result in an improved chance of securing a new contract. So the picture of legal compliance as separate to proactive pursuit of business outcomes is not necessarily consistent: the public sector duties to promote equality enable ongoing focus on equality and diversity in some private sector companies, potentially stimulating the isomorphic tendencies noted above as contributing to the spread of the DM discourse.

However, despite the overriding impetus of legal compliance, the Head of ER acknowledged that ServiceCo needed to move away from a defensive and narrow legal impetus towards building a business case. Within the business case and her argument for becoming an 'employer of choice', she stressed that recruitment and retention were central concerns for ServiceCo:

> A lot of our bids are actually around our people. That's what we sell because we haven't got a tangible product . . . Gender is a big issue. Race is a big issue for us . . . we need to open up our talent pools to wider audiences. And there's a lot of Luddite sort of response that I get occasionally that says 'Ah yes but they don't do the sort of degrees that we want.' Which in part is true but I think for me it's an education process that says, unless it's something that's very very specific, why do they need to have that particular degree? Why can't we go for something that's a bit broader?

Her arguments had implicit echoes of the social justice case (recognition that organizational structures are not 'neutral' and effectively operate to advantage the dominant group); however, her articulated orientation was to make an appeal to the business case. As noted previously, the business case for both EO and DM has been criticized mainly for its contingent nature, reliant on short-term business conditions (Dickens 2000; Noon 2007). We therefore asked the Head of ER to explain why she thought senior management would be convinced:

> Because they see the business value of caring . . . And that's what they're responsible for let's face it. They're responsible to our shareholders . . .

Responsibility for DM policy implementation was not placed directly with HR in ServiceCo, but was supposed to be given to Heads of the different business groups and then 'cascaded' down through the organizational hierarchy. This suggests that, in line with DM discourse, policy was intended to relate to core business strategy. However, senior management support of DM is widely regarded in mainstream diversity discourse as necessary for effective implementation (for example, Gilbert et al 1999; CBI 2008). It was significant therefore that nobody on the ServiceCo executive board had any formal association with the development of the DM policy. In line with common Anglo-Saxon organizational practice, the person designated responsible for employee-focused issues was not a member of the executive board (see Sisson and Marginson 2003).

The Head of ER made it clear she had to 'sell' the policy company-wide, particularly to senior managers. However, despite her sincere enthusiasm for equality and diversity, her position can be conceptualized as 'liberal reformer' in that she did not seek to use her resources to push through any radical organizational change, but regarded modification to existing structures as sufficient (Kirton et al 2007). An indication of her lack of transformative intentions was the decision, about a year after the company's DM project started, to change the policy title from solely 'diversity' to include 'equality'. She said that this was because people in the company understood the idea of equality but had no understanding of 'diversity'. This amendment was therefore based on helping understanding and so presumably acceptance within the organization—it did not reflect a paradigm change. In this regard, it contrasts with the situation at our public sector case study, PSO (see Chapter 4), where the term 'equality' was apparently specifically retained due to the influence of the trade unions, which were critical of the language of diversity.

Key Policy Initiatives

One of the most striking features of the launch of the DM policy was the relative absence of concrete initiatives to support its aims and objectives. An equality and diversity training session had been developed and was delivered by (non-expert) ServiceCo staff. Bassett-Jones et al's study suggests that 'peer trainers' can be more effective than specialist trainers, as they can be better at contextualizing issues 'thereby, concretising them and rendering the issues more transparent' (2007: 64; see also Roberson et al 2003 for a discussion of trainer credibility). However, they recognized that this initiative was one of a range of supportive and explicit DM measures within an organization that had already done a great deal of work in addressing workplace inequalities. The Head of ER at ServiceCo, in contrast, acknowledged that 'a lot of the programme stuff has still got to be formulated and put together' and that the main thrust would be dissemination of information through training days. 'We took the approach that each business will build their own action plan for implementation, because they know what's best for their business'. There was no strategic or longer-term consideration of how the policy might be put into practice in any integrated or consistent ways across the company. For example, at the time of fieldwork, there were also no mechanisms being considered to monitor the businesses' separate action plans. While it is possible that this might have developed subsequently, the lack of explicit consideration beforehand suggests a lack of appreciation of the potential complexities involved.

The main ServiceCo initiatives were to raise awareness of the policy (publicizing its launch through leaflets, cards and in the company newsletter) and to roll out training, first for senior and line-managers and subsequently to employees. In enforcement rather than dissemination terms, it was also intended (according to the Head of ER) to 'challenge' the Heads of the businesses at established twice-yearly Project Review Meetings by asking them how they have performed on equality and diversity issues. However, no specific goals or targets were mentioned as desirable, and performance management was specifically mentioned as an area that was not connected to any of the equality or diversity issues discussed in the company training programme. Therefore, the onus was apparently on individual senior managers to work out what was needed, with no structured monitoring of processes or outcomes. This has echoes of Foster and Harris's (2005) study in the retail industry where line-managers apparently did not know what they were meant to be doing within DM policy. As will be discussed below in consideration of policy implementation, expectations of ServiceCo managers were based on a misplaced assumption of understanding of both concepts and organizational objectives.

Other initiatives mentioned were an intention to improve monitoring data and the fact that sub-contractors were contractually required to abide by the policy. However, the policy did not require specific action, and sub-contractor compliance was unmonitored. While the use of contract compliance to further social policies has been discussed largely in relation to the public sector (see, for example, Orton and Ratcliffe 2005; Fee 2002), its use in the private sector in the UK has been relatively unexplored in recent years except in Northern Ireland, where USA pressure led to the requirement for USAMNCs to have regard in recruitment to underrepresented (religio-political) groups in their workforces (McCrudden 1986). In light of the other data from ServiceCo, it appears that the requirements they placed on contractors were largely driven by awareness of legal vulnerability and consciousness of the linkages between corporate social responsibility, reputation and investment.

While we found some limited instances of workplace-based initiatives (such as language courses for non-English speaking staff at HealthSite), at policy level, the focus was on awareness training and thus arguably an assumption that once people were made conscious of the issues, existing practice would improve. However, conflicting initiatives were also apparent. Participants in an employee consultation session we observed talked about career progression and the ServiceCo 'fast-track' leadership programme. To general agreement, one participant (a white woman) described it as ageist, as the maximum entry age was 35. This staff developmental tool had clearly not been 'equality-proofed', highlighting the way that a piecemeal approach to DM can lead to inconsistency and therefore a lack of legitimacy. It also emphasized the problems of not having a coherent strategy coordinated across management areas of responsibility within which to attempt to implement DM (see Wentling 2004: 176). The constant emphasis on legal compliance is also arguably revealed as simply that—as a short-term calculation of protection from *current* legislation rather than, for example, consideration of the implications of the then-imminent Age Regulations.

Stakeholder Involvement in the DM Policy

As noted earlier, unions at ServiceCo were not perceived as potential partners in developing and implementing DM or even useful communication conduits for management practices relating to equality and diversity issues. There was certainly no consideration of unions affecting ServiceCo's cost/benefit analysis of equality and diversity issues, as suggested by Dickens (1999: 14), in the sense of the cost of employer inaction increasing if unions are able to organize employees around the issues. On the contrary, the Head of ER made it clear both that the recognized unions were not involved in any policy development and that none of the unions had pressed for an equality and diversity policy before ServiceCo management developed one:

> On the basis that I work from—'here's something we prepared earlier' when we're talking to the trade unions, rather than getting them to help with the design. Yes they can contribute to it but this is the way that we will do things around ServiceCo. And frankly I don't think there's anything in our policy and what we're trying to achieve, that the trade unions will have nothing but support for.

Maxwell et al found in a public sector organization that both managerial and non-managerial employees were either unfamiliar with or did not understand the term 'managing diversity' (2001: 477). In our research in the public sector (see Chapter 4), we found variable understanding amongst managers, but limited understanding amongst non-managerial staff. In the private sector context of ServiceCo, we found a generally low level of understanding amongst *all* categories of staff, including those working in the organization's various HR departments. Line-managers, as with most other stakeholders at ServiceCo, equated equality with treating people the same, believing that this resulted in treating people fairly (the 'liberal' approach discussed by Jewson and Mason 1986). However, some managers seemed to lack even this very basic awareness: 'I've heard of equality but no, I don't understand' (Supervisor, Health, white man). There was almost no awareness of the concept of 'diversity', with, for instance, line-managers at RoadSite relating it to ServiceCo's work organization or job roles, and one manager (a white man) saying he 'didn't connect diversity and equality at all'.

We also found uncertainty of understanding of the term DM among workplace union representatives at ServiceCo. When questioned directly, they were confused by the term, so, for example, one comment from a representative in Health (a white man) was: 'Racial understanding. I don't really know; I presume it's something to do with how the managers and the workforce get on'. As we found with managerial staff, the equal opportunities label was more familiar to the representatives. The union representatives in the Health sector were not even aware of ServiceCo's DM policy when we spoke to them, surely indicating a failure of the dissemination and implementation strategy. In Transport, one union representative (a white male line-manager) had recently been to the equality and diversity training course associated with the roll-out of the policy. However, his recall of the content of the course was very vague; when pressed on what he had taken away from it, he commented:

> To think, stop and think . . . If I want someone to come and work for me, I want to give everybody an opportunity to apply, irrespective of race, colour, creed, religion or whatever. And by putting the wrong word in or the wrong description in you can, indirectly, discriminate against someone. That's the point.

The focus here is again implicitly negative: being wary of unintentionally breaching a legal regulation, rather than the conceptually positive DM approach of actively encouraging diversity in recruitment. Almost everyone interviewed saw this approach as both the core and the boundary of these issues; that is, few people thought that 'fairness' could be defined or achieved in any way other than as same treatment.

The uncertainty and legal compliance focus of the union representatives suggests that some unions still do not see equality and diversity issues as central to engagement with employers or with employees. Furthermore, the representatives had not received any equality and diversity training or information from their unions' regional or national offices, suggesting that they were ill-prepared to engage with ServiceCo's DM policy. This is interesting in light of research indicating that UK trade unions at the national level generally have a politicized awareness of DM and suggesting that activists are important for equality awareness and education within union structures (see Kirton et al 2005).

It appeared that non-managerial employees had been given absolutely no opportunity to be involved in the development of the DM policy.

Fairly limited employee involvement mechanisms existed throughout the organization (although this varied by Business Group and site). One organization-wide mechanism was an annual attitude survey called 'The Great Debate'. This was ServiceCo's name for the company-wide technologically interactive employee consultation exercise (according to the Head of ER, in line with practice in Cadbury, British Aerospace and Nokia). In addition, samples of employees from every Business Group were selected for participation in group sessions of approximately 20 at a time. Participants were given issues to discuss and asked questions by facilitators that they responded to via electronic keypads, the results appearing instantly on-screen as percentages. At the time of fieldwork, equality and diversity issues were not directly addressed, although the Head of ER indicated that the intention was to feed in equality questions into all company-wide employee consultation exercises. However, non-management participants in the 'Great Debate' expressed the feeling of not being listened to by management. During a discussion about the company's annual attitude survey, one participant (a white man) commented: 'The questions are a lot too open. For example, the question "am I listened to" should be "when I'm listened to is anything done about it?"' This perception resonates with research into the realities of employee involvement mechanisms (Butler 2005; Marchington and Wilkinson 2005).

Other employee involvement mechanisms included a variety of staff forums and briefing groups, but again nothing explicitly on diversity. We asked a meeting of the Health manager/employee consultative Staff Forum to indicate what 'diversity' meant to them. There was a complete lack of response from employees who had not been through the initial round of equality and diversity training. This suggested both individual and organizational lack of awareness of the ideas and issues. Generally, the short discussion in the Forum on these issues produced either (what seemed to be embarrassed) silence from the group or conventional sexuality/gender jokes from the senior manager chairing the meeting. These comments played on stereotypes and seemed unlikely to encourage the culture change that the HR manager and Chief Executive said they regarded as important. For example, asked about his meeting schedule later, the late middle-aged white male senior manager chairing the session (who had attended the equality and diversity training) leaned towards the young (early 20s) white female and apparently uncomfortable HR assistant and said, 'I've got a date today—my colleague is going to give me some HR advice'. Again, when asked later about a particular procedure, he responded, 'My colleague on my left [HR assistant] is going to speak for me, she's much prettier than I am'. The use of gendered humour in organizational meetings has been discussed as a strategy of repressive power (Mullany 2004), and its use here suggests two things. First, that the Head of ER accurately identified attitudes and behaviour as a central problem in implementing DM and second, simultaneously, that ServiceCo failed to recognize that 'awareness' training on its own is commonly insufficient (see discussion in Roberson et al 2003).

Policy Implementation at ServiceCo

As discussed in Chapter 7, within the DM paradigm, line-managers are central to successful implementation, but at the same time the literature suggests that engaging managers is the greatest challenge organizations face. In light of these debates, the extent to which line-managers took ownership of the DM policy at ServiceCo and subscribed to its declared objectives was a key focus of the research.

In principle, we found that most managers had positive perceptions of what they knew of the ServiceCo policy, and there were very few criticisms. However, awareness of policy objectives and initiatives became more limited further down the managerial hierarchy, to the point where supervisors and line-managers with direct responsibility for non-managerial employees were almost completely unaware of any specific initiatives. As noted above, this was probably because there were few if any 'headline' initiatives that engaged with change in existing structures, processes or behaviour, in combination with the variability and ineffectiveness of the 'cascading' dissemination method. Some managers saw the DM policy as simply *labelling* existing managerial practices that they had carried out for years and had thought of simply as managing people, trying to treat people fairly and as one white male line manager put it, 'staff welfare, HR-side issues'.

However, there was also a general perception amongst managers that ServiceCo was serious about ongoing equality and diversity training for staff and that therefore managers would comply by carrying this through. This perception of the company as genuinely committed to training staff suggested potential for change in internal culture, or possibly to the receptiveness of some individuals:

> I like to think that I am pretty tuned in to it anyway. It won't be anything that I am not really used to and understand. It's times when you have to be careful what you say and what you do. You have to meet different people's needs, personalities, religion, gender, sexuality and everything. But I could be wrong. I am sure I will find out on the course. (Manager, RailSite, white man)

Reflecting previous research (Foster and Harris 2005), managers also supported the predominant rationale of legal compliance for equality and diversity action:

I think ServiceCo will want us to realise at the back of our minds, we have got to be able to understand the warning signs if you think somebody is possibly storing up information to make a claim on yourselves. (Manager, RailSite, white man)

I think probably [the diversity training was] to make us aware how if we do things wrong, the company can be prosecuted. I think that was the general impression I got when I left . . . It's got to be done properly otherwise you can be taken to the cleaners, as they say. (Manager, RoadSite, white man)

This was borne out in observation of the equality training course for managers, where legislative pitfalls were stressed, illustrated by a recent case where ServiceCo was found guilty of racial discrimination, resulting in a large financial penalty. However, it did not seem that managers in general felt that they had to be any more proactive than this. It is possible that these perceptions were also shaped by the nature of the training, which, for instance, was delivered to the Health senior management team by an HR manager and an HR assistant. The HR assistant (a white woman) was asked who had trained her in the issues, and she laughed and said, 'No-one. I think [site HR manager] had some training'. Our observation notes of the training session at ServiceCo HQ highlighted trainer inexperience and parallel lack of facilitation, in that there was a long list of relevant issues but no explanation as to what was meant by or how to engage with each one. Surprisingly, given the emphasis of the training, we also noted inaccurate and incomplete information on equality and anti-discrimination legislation. Research by the CIPD indicates that lack of formal training for those with a 'responsibility for training' has been a common weakness of DM to date (CIPD 2007: 15).

With regard to implementation, managers at HealthSite perceived the greatest practical difficulties of DM as in relation to race/ethnicity: for example, some managers talked about difficulties managing cover for Goan staff (most of whom were related to each other) who requested an extended period of holiday at the same time each year in order to visit family in India. Not only did this create operational difficulties, but they felt that this also generated resentment from other staff at perceived special treatment, notwithstanding the Goan staff group's apparent willingness to work unpaid overtime throughout the rest of the year. The complexities of managing difference were also mentioned, a frequent example given being ServiceCo's translation of signs (into the specific staff group's first language) and subsequent discovery that the majority of this group were illiterate. It was noted repeatedly by many in HealthSite that the company had taken this situation seriously and arranged access to language training. Managers regarded this as an example of the company's positive approach towards equality, although a senior operational manager (a white man) at first did not perceive any specific DM issues in HealthSite, despite an acknowledgement (and acceptance, in line with other stakeholders) of the gender and race segregation. Indeed, he went on later to reveal direct discrimination in recruitment and selection:

> One of the problems with having a kind of a chauvinist Estates department is that any female electrician is going to be immediately disadvantaged. So I don't recruit female electricians, you know, which is sad because I am probably missing out on a real talent pool of really good people because they might feel a bit intimidated coming into an all-male environment.

The manager thus conflated his own discriminatory position with speculative assumptions about the attitudes of women engineers. While he did see this as problematic in terms of limiting the 'pool of talent' they had to recruit from, he looked to the equality and diversity training to resolve these sorts of issues by changing people's attitudes, without any apparent awareness of his own less than straightforward opinions.

CONCLUDING DISCUSSION

So was ServiceCo's policy simply an 'empty shell' in Hoque and Noon's (2004) terms? Certainly, there were few formal practices, either instituted or planned, to give effect to the policy. While reasons for introducing DM policy and organization-appropriate policy implementation have been identified as important in the literature and supported by this case study, ServiceCo's experience also emphasizes the relevance of who develops policy and (therefore) how. What seems to emerge from consideration of ServiceCo is that the absence of practices does not necessarily connote the absence of 'good' intent, but possibly unreflective acceptance of the status quo, limited awareness of the complexities of equality and diversity issues and rational responses to the variable strength of business case drivers.

As discussed in Chapter 2, the key dimensions of the dominant understanding of DM are the centrality of the business case, applicability to a wider range of categories than group-based identities and systemic organizational cultural change. We noted at the start of the chapter that the business case rationale is put under particular scrutiny in a private sector context. In ServiceCo, the business case was rhetorically central, but there were varying perceptions of the existence and strength of the business case, often because there can be both short- and long-term objectives (distantly echoing Jewson and Mason (1986) and Cockburn (1989) on EO approaches). Thus, the criticisms of this driver as variable and thus unstable were exemplified (Noon 2007; Dickens 1999). Kochan et al (2003: 17) found that there is almost no evidence to support a straightforward claim that diversity is good for business, and, given the national economic and institutional constraints discussed earlier in the chapter, it may be that potential rewards would need to be clearer before a company like ServiceCo sees DM as worth implementing in any comprehensive way.

In relation to the inclusion within DM of a broader range of differences, there were limited attempts at broadening awareness of multiple dimensions of 'difference' through company-wide training sessions. Raising awareness of diversity issues has been described as one of the more distinctive aspects of DM policy (Liff 1997: 22), but the argued parallel encouragement of seeing difference positively was not evident in ServiceCo, where there was a more traditional emphasis on complying with anti-discrimination regulations in order to avoid legal action. There were apparent attempts at DM approaches; for example, in the 'core values' section of the policy document, which referred to recognizing, valuing and understanding diversity of stakeholders. Also, aspects of the diversity training seemed to be intended to encourage a rethinking of the contribution of 'difference'. However, these were far from constituting a wholesale attempt at what a large modern corporation now knows to be mainstream DM. DM has been argued to be a way of 'selling' EO to managers in general and private sector managers in particular (see Kelly and Dobbin 1998; Liff 1997: 23), but it seems that in the absence of legal compulsion to promote equality as in the public sector, organizations pick and choose what they want to buy and when. This is facilitated by the DM discourse's neutral aspiration to recognize the diversity of individuals. DM re-conceived as recognition of the heterogeneity of disadvantage might be a more productive way of framing this aspiration and engaging with the realities of institutional and organizational contexts (for related developments in EU equality strategies, see European Commission 2007).

The third DM dimension of organizational change was, unsurprisingly given the above, absent. There was very little perception of any need for internal culture change, with inequalities often seen as natural or ascribed to external society and therefore as not 'manageable'. This highlights a factor that can be underestimated in focusing on the obstacles of organizational strategies, agendas and conditional motivation. We found limited (and sometimes no) comprehension of the concepts of equality and diversity and usually no awareness of this understanding as limited (similar to the experience of ACAS advisers: ACAS 2005: 1–2). Dickens (2007: 473) notes that a long-standing weakness of British legislation is its understanding of equality as same treatment, and this official formulation appears to have structured people's understanding and expectations. This has implications for how policy is developed, how it is implemented and how it is sustained over time. If 'equality' (seen in ServiceCo as the basis and context for 'diversity') is about treating people the same, then a top-down approach to policy formulation and implementation is unproblematic, and there is no need to involve trade unions or employees directly or explore the responsibilities of organizational structure in sustaining inequalities.

Developing Foster and Harris's (2005) identification of operational managers' confusion over the concept of DM, we have seen that this fragmented understanding extends through every level and within every occupational group in ServiceCo. This constrains ability and willingness to act and of course, identification of issues to act upon. For example, there is frequently emphasis in research literature on line-managers having conflicting objectives, such as immediate, 'hard' operational targets versus 'soft' developmental equality goals. However, this assumes that line-managers make informed choices in prioritizing one over the other. Our findings suggest that there may be no equivalence of understanding and therefore that conception of obstacles to line-managers' implementation of DM must be more nuanced and context-dependent.

We noted above Dickens's argument for a three-pronged (business case, legal and social regulation) approach to equality action to 'engender a preparedness to take EO action in the first place' (1999: 9). Consideration of ServiceCo—where the employers were prepared to and did take action—supports an extension of this reasoning. Given the restricted relevance of the more proactive elements of equality and diversity legislation to the private sector, compliance was largely understood as company self-protection (itself a business case of sorts of course). However, a direct merger of organizational benefit and (proxy) legislative drivers was seen in ServiceCo's response to the public sector tender, a combination that potentially offers a pragmatically enlightened route for some private sector organizations. The shortcomings of policy development and implementation highlighted the importance of the absent third prong of joint social regulation. A multilateral approach comprising internal organizational rationales framed and animated by more developed legal and social regulation that takes account of the realities of national institutional context would seem to be a minimum response to the diversity of organizational contexts, interests and objectives in the private sector.

6 Diversity Practitioner Perspectives

INTRODUCTION

There is little literature focusing on the people who do diversity work. This might be because within the diversity management (DM) paradigm, with the business case at the centre, the role of senior and middle managers is seen as more critical to policy implementation and effectiveness. Reflecting this philosophy, the growing body of UK-based research on DM tends to investigate organizational policy and practice, particularly in relation to the role of managers in implementation (Cornelius, Gooch et al 2000; Maxwell, Blair et al 2001; Maxwell 2004; Foster and Harris 2005). Nevertheless, it is clear that diversity practitioners play a central role in policy development and implementation (Lorbiecki 2001; Kirton, Greene et al 2007).

Before proceeding to consider what the literature has to say about diversity practitioners, it is worth stepping back to examine what the shift from equal opportunities (EO) to DM has meant for diversity work. Within the EO paradigm, many larger private and public sector organizations employed specialist equality officers typically located in personnel departments or sometimes in separate equality units. Equality work typically involved monitoring policies and practices, recommending policy changes and new policy initiatives and providing training on equality issues. Most equality officers came from leftist community/political activist backgrounds and were often feminist women and/or black and minority ethnic (BME) people, who brought with them personal experiences of discrimination and harassment. They were generally viewed as progressive, politicized people who identified with particular disadvantaged social groups and had a clear social justice agenda. It was their personal experiences (rather than professional training or qualifications) that gave them the credibility, the authority and, arguably, the expertise to lead EO policy (see Jewson and Mason 1986; Cockburn 1991). Cockburn (1991: 235) argued that equality officers were 'inserted to be an interface between a particular constituency of interests and the management system'. Thus, there was an opportunity for equality officers to translate personal commitment, beliefs and values into policy efforts geared towards making a difference to working lives. However, Cockburn (ibid) found that EO work in mainstream organizations proved to be an area of intense contestation, often arousing hostility, conflict and backlash. Therefore, to make equality initiatives more palatable, EO officers often articulated not only a social justice case for equality, but also a business case, and they also forged alliances with senior white men in order to increase the acceptability and credibility of policy initiatives. In this sense, equality work did not look so different from diversity work.

However, research indicates that in many countries, including the USA, Australia, New Zealand and the UK, diversity specialists have replaced the former equality officers (Sinclair 2000). Further, there is also evidence of the expansion of diversity work into the consultancy industry and of the creation of new categories of practitioners including diversity champions. In our research, we were interested in what the shift towards DM means for the people who do diversity work in the 2000s. Does the current generation of diversity specialists simply have a new label or have their characteristics, roles and perspectives altered? Who are diversity champions and consultants and what do they do? From previous research on people who do diversity work, it is not clear that the more overt business case within the DM paradigm necessarily implies that people who do diversity work have less commitment to social justice than held by the earlier generation of equality officers. For example, based on research in the USA, Litvin (2002) explores the compromises that diversity consultants have to make in order to supply the 'product' their corporate clients want. She found a dissonance between the diversity consultants' beliefs about what needed to be done and the more business-focused objectives of their clients. Similarly, Sinclair (2000: 239) finds Australian diversity specialists critical of the more 'palatable language' of diversity, which they accused of trivializing discrimination. In New Zealand, 'Equal Employment Opportunity' (EEO) practitioners contested the individualistic approach of diversity and fought against its substitution for EEO (Humphries and Grice 1995). Based on research in the UK, Lorbiecki (2001) positions what she calls 'diversity vanguards' (people doing diversity work in mainstream organizations) as 'outsiders-within', because she found them to be people who felt compelled to speak out against discrimination and yet who also had to uphold the organization's business objectives. Also, in the UK context, Lawrence (2000) finds that equality and diversity specialists use the business case to argue for equality initiatives within their organization, but their personal commitment to equality issues often also has a moral basis. Based on our research, we have argued elsewhere (Kirton et al 2007) that diversity practitioners sometimes need to temper any radical ideals and objectives they might have in order to be taken seriously by management within a context of a closer alignment between business and equality and diversity goals. Thus, we begin this chapter's exploration of diversity practitioners' perspectives from the position that the DM paradigm has altered the context in which people carry out diversity work, which in turn has impacted on the type of people doing the work and the actual work they (are able to) do.

This chapter explores the perspectives of diversity practitioners in a broad range of public and private sector organizations. The organizations that took part in this strand of the research and more details on the research methods can be found in Chapter 1. Given the stakeholder focus of the research, it is relevant to note that 27 of the 34 participant organizations had trade union presence/recognition. The chapter first considers who does diversity work and what it involves. It then investigates what qualifies people for diversity work. Next, the perspectives of different categories of diversity practitioners—specialists and champions from within mainstream organizations, consultants and campaigners on the outside of mainstream organizations—on various aspects of diversity work are examined.

WHO DOES DIVERSITY WORK AND WHAT DOES IT INVOLVE?

As can be seen from Table 6.1, we have developed a categorization of four types of diversity practitioners, which captures the people involved in our research: specialists, champions, consultants and campaigners. Diversity specialists are individuals whose job title contains 'diversity' or whose job is largely dedicated to equality and diversity work. They are responsible for DM policy development (generating new ideas and initiatives), overseeing policy implementation, monitoring impact and effectiveness of policy initiatives and advising other departments on equality and diversity matters (for example, discipline and grievance cases, compliance with the law). In our research, specialists' status in their organizations varied—a small number were at a relatively low level in the organizational hierarchy (sometimes called advisors), others were middle managers and some were very senior, earning high salaries. Some of the specialists were the only person working dedicatedly on diversity in their organization, whereas others worked with a small team and a small number with a larger team. For example, one senior level public sector specialist had a team of about 40 people working under him. Most of the specialists were located in human resources (HR) departments, but we found that some organizations have positioned DM away from HR either in Corporate Social Responsibility or in a stand-alone diversity unit. The latter were found in both the private and public sectors. The positioning of DM outside of HR symbolizes the idea within the DM paradigm that diversity is not simply concerned with the employment relationship or the sole responsibility of HR, but core to business strategy and the responsibility of all organizational stakeholders. In the latter model, diversity specialists took responsibility for both HR and business/service delivery equality and diversity issues. For example, some were involved in developing initiatives to broaden the customer base to 'minority' groups or to ensure that the needs of different local communities were being met.

Table 6.1   Characteristics of Diversity Practitioners

N = 48	Diversity Specialists	Diversity Champions	Diversity Consultants	Diversity Campaigners	Total
Female	20	7	2	4	33
White	16	7	2	2	27
BME	4	0	0	2	6
Male	3	12	0	0	15
White	1	10	0	0	11
BME	2	2	0	0	4
Total	23	19	2	4	48

Diversity champions are senior, middle or occasionally junior managers who have the role of 'championing' diversity in their departments. In our research, some champions had put themselves forward for their diversity role and others had been selected by senior management. Occasionally it had been necessary to persuade individuals to take on the role, but most took it willingly out of personal interest. They were found in both the private and public sector organizations and existed essentially to give credibility to the DM policy, but also to spread the message that diversity is good for business (Johnstone 2002). It was expected that, as experienced operational managers themselves, they could understand and be seen to understand the issues facing other managers. They were also expected to demonstrate that as managers they 'buy into' diversity and therefore they would lead by example ('modelling' appropriate behaviours) and take responsibility for promoting the benefits of diversity more widely in the organization. They were usually involved in some kind of equality and diversity forum where policy was discussed and formulated in conjunction with the diversity specialist(s). The creation of diversity champions fits well within the DM paradigm, where the pivotal role for senior management in lending top level commitment to diversity and for line-managers in implementing the policy on a day-to-day basis is emphasized (for example, Cornelius et al 2000).

External diversity consultants work with internal diversity specialists in aspects such as research and design of new initiatives. It is clear from the literature and from our knowledge of the diversity field that organizations are making increasing usage of external advice in the HRM area (Sisson 2001) including DM. In the USA, diversity consultancy is vast (Metzler 2003). A 'google' search in October 2007 for 'diversity consultants' produced over 1 million results when confined to the UK alone, indicating a mushrooming of diversity consultancy that is part of the broader trend towards outsourcing of HR activities. Being on the outside looking into organizations is obviously a very different role where potentially there is more freedom to be critical without falling foul of organizational politics. However, it must be remembered that consultants have to sell services and 'products' that organizations want to buy which undoubtedly influences and perhaps constrains them (Litvin 2002). Only two diversity consultants participated in our research; therefore, we are obviously not able to draw any conclusions about the work of consultants. However, we do argue that they are often important allies and support for specialists, particularly those who feel isolated or marginalized within their organizations (see Kirton and Greene 2009; Kirton et al 2007).

Finally, diversity campaigners are also outside looking in; they work for public and voluntary sector organizations that have some kind of campaigning or lobbying role in the equality and diversity area. Their aim is to influence businesses, organizations, government and sometimes trade unions to develop and implement effective DM policies.

The demographic characteristics of respondents are worthy of comment (see Table 6.1) as we believe this is something that is changing under the rubric of DM. The main point is that our data does not support the findings of one UK study (Lorbiecki 2001), where it seems that BME people were better represented among people doing diversity work. On the other hand, another UK study (Lawrence 2000) found, as we did, that the majority of practitioners in the area were white women. Our research also supports that of Lawrence (ibid), in that there were far more women than men involved professionally in DM and far more white than BME people. This pattern was particularly pronounced in the large private and public sector organizations. Although we do not claim that our sample is representative, it was large enough to be indicative. This finding also confirms our impressions gained from attending a number of diversity events over the past few years. This demographic profile is also quite different to the EO era (as stated above) and also to the USA, where diversity work is dominated by BME people, especially African-Americans. In the USA, the DM paradigm is rhetorically more inclusive yet is often used essentially as a kind of depoliticized code for race equality work (Kelly and Dobbin 1998). We can only speculate about the reasons for the apparent under-representation of BME people in diversity work in the UK. It might be partly at least to do with the general disappearance, or at least dilution of distinct strands of equality work that we saw within the EO paradigm, and with it the lesser likelihood of separate race equality officers existing, who were obviously BME people themselves. In general, we found that diversity work in the UK now involves working across the equality strands and therefore although being of a BME background would not disqualify someone from the role, neither would it necessarily be seen as a prerequisite. Thus, part of the reason for the relative absence of BME diversity practitioners is likely to lie within aspects of the diversity discourse itself. The mantra that diversity includes everyone implies that diversity work should not be the preserve of those who have personally experienced different types of discrimination and disadvantage. There are also likely to be a range of other reasons, like the greater vulnerability of BME workers making it more dangerous career-wise to take on a role that is potentially unpopular and that people in organizations are suspicious of (see Kirton and Greene 2009; Kirton et al 2007). However, as we can see, these issues do not seem to act as a deterrent to white women. Following this discussion, where quotes are used, the gender and 'race'/ethnicity of the respondent are shown in order to enable the reader to set the comments against the respondents' identity characteristics. This also has the effect of highlighting the fact that, regardless of their own identity characteristics, we did not find diversity practitioners to be a highly politicized group. However, as discussed later, this did not mean that social justice goals were entirely absent.

WHAT QUALIFIES PEOPLE FOR DIVERSITY WORK?

This brings us to a consideration of what qualifies people for diversity work. Given that there are currently no recognized formal qualifications for diversity practitioners, it is relevant to explore the kinds of work and personal experiences that people bring to the role that (they believe) qualify and equip them. Firstly, looking at actual profiles, respondents' work backgrounds were highly varied, indicating that a broad range of people are now involved in diversity work. Of particular note is that our data show that this area is no longer the preserve of activists; there are signs that it is becoming professionalized within the broader HRM field, but at the same time increasingly occupied by people with prior mainstream business and management experience. Prior to their current role, it was very common for respondents, regardless of their own identity characteristics, in both the private and public sectors to have held some kind of management position in a mainstream organization. Some of the specialists had previously been operational managers, some were previously HR practitioners (either generalists or with another specialism), but significantly only a minority of the white women had a longer history of equality and diversity work and for very few did this involve political, community or trade union activism. Many of the specialists had been recruited internally to their present role from other parts of the business/organization. The champions were all experienced operational line-managers, so although they did not have a professional background in equality and diversity work, some had worked as volunteers in various community organizations (particularly disability groups) or had undertaken a volunteer role, such as school governor. The two consultants, both white women, had very different backgrounds from one another. One was possibly atypical in that she was a former trade union official who had specialized in equal opportunities and was now working as a consultant with a range of public, private and voluntary sector organizations. The other was a management consultant, with a prior HR background, now specializing in diversity consultancy. As might be expected, three of the campaigners, two of them white women and the other a black woman, had a long history of community and political activism largely in women's, trade union and political groups. The other campaigner, a black woman, had a mixed work history of equality and diversity work, but also general management positions in the public sector.

With regard to what they *believed* qualified them to do diversity work, different personal qualities and types of work experience were most frequently mentioned. Only one respondent, a diversity specialist (a white woman), mentioned her academic qualifications as relevant; she was studying towards a Masters degree in Race and Ethnic Relations which she had found extremely useful for her work. On a more general level, many respondents talked about needing to have a lot of patience, personal commitment and passion for the work combined with a 'natural' interest. This was felt necessary because the role often started with a 'blank sheet' and so required creativity and tenacity often in the face of opposition (primarily from middle managers) to new initiatives. However, a prior business and management background was also regarded by most specialists and champions as essential in order to be able to persuade the organization, from the standpoint of actual 'hard' business knowledge and experience, of the business benefits of diversity. Some saw HR experience as useful, but the 'softer' image of HR work meant that those with this type of background felt that they were often seen as less qualified for the role within the DM paradigm. Very few respondents talked about political, community or trade union activism as relevant to their diversity role. The few who did were more likely to be consultants and campaigners and were therefore working on the outside of mainstream organizations, while a small number working in the public sector talked about prior involvement in community groups. As a case in point, one specialist in the public sector (a BME man) put his head in his hands and said 'awful, awful, awful' when in the course of the interview, the interviewer made a comment to the effect that in the 1980s equality officers were typically activists. He went on to say that he specifically did not want that 'type' working in his unit because he did not see the relevance of that kind of background. Further, we found it interesting that not a single respondent among the diversity specialists referred to their own identity characteristics (for example, being a woman or black) or personal experiences (such as of discrimination or harassment) as having a bearing on their 'qualification' for diversity work.

Often it was the champions who, ironically perhaps, stood out as exceptions here, and it was clear that many had a strong sense of citizenship and attached importance to making a contribution to public life. A couple of respondents had personal experiences of disability issues; a close relative or child with a disability, for example, meaning that disability rights were very significant personally for them. Other champions had previously volunteered for other 'extracurricular' duties in the workplace, such as health and safety officer. Some, however, had no such experience, but stated that they had become convinced of the business case for diversity and wanted to make their contribution to making DM work for the organization.

PRACTITIONER VIEWS FROM INSIDE ORGANIZATIONS

This section explores the perspectives of diversity specialists and champions on the discourse of diversity, on policy and practice within organizations and on stakeholder involvement. It is important to note that these practitioners' perspectives are highly relevant to the present state of DM policy-making because they are its architects and guardians. This is particularly true in the case of specialists. However, the caveat is that diversity specialists do not necessarily or indeed usually wield the kind of power and influence to single-handedly decide upon a policy course. They work within various structures of power and influence, and their work is vulnerable to political interference, especially in the public sector, but even in the private sector organizational politics come into play.

Perspectives on the Diversity Discourse

Reflecting the discussion of the paradigm shift from EO to DM discussed in Chapter 2, all the specialists and champions, irrespective of their own identity characteristics and of the sector they worked in, used the language of diversity in their work, but not necessarily to the exclusion of the traditional language of EO. Most respondents believed that DM and EO were interconnected, but saw DM as moving things on. They talked in terms, for example, of DM being 'a logical extension' of EO, a 'continuum from EO, through diversity to inclusion'. But, for most EO represented the 'building blocks' of DM, and mirroring arguments made in the academic literature (Liff 1999), some even felt there was a 'false dichotomy' between DM and EO. For example, two respondents commented:

> I see that there's almost like foundations to diversity, which are about removing discrimination, doing work around, say, harassment and bullying. I mean basic policies around equality and fairness. Then I think what you're building towards is much more an inclusive organization. (Diversity specialist, white woman, banking and finance)

> The first thing is to achieve equality, so that there are no barriers there. But when you've achieved that you should then be able to move on to diversity. So it's [diversity] actually genuinely seeking difference and harnessing that for business value. So, recognizing that you've got it and doing something with it and celebrating it. (Diversity specialist, white woman, banking and finance)

Thus, despite the existence of a large body of academic work that is fiercely critical of DM, diversity specialists and champions in our study were on the whole uncritical. This is in all likelihood related to the fact that most respondents were relatively new to the field and had brought with them fairly negative impressions of the EO paradigm, unlike, for example, the government-based EO practitioners in New Zealand who in the early 1990s apparently resisted DM (Jones et al 2000). In our study, only two (public sector) respondents, both white women, voiced clear and trenchant criticisms of the diversity discourse. Reflecting the academic critique (Prasad et al 1997; Kirton 2008), they were worried that DM was a façade for 'watering down' and de-politicizing EO in order to avoid dealing with some of the most challenging issues of discrimination and disadvantage.

Most respondents believed that the adoption of the diversity discourse signalled a policy shift, even though elements of EO were evident in their organizations' DM policies. For example, one of the key elements of DM-the expansion of the categories—included an increased focus on individual differences (visible and non-visible) and was reportedly centre-stage in most organizational policies. For example:

> We want to be looking much more at the individual and individual difference. Although we're doing some basic stuff that we need to do to make sure that we're coping with the broad requirements of certain groups, we are not trying to put people into boxes particularly. (Diversity specialist, white woman, general services)

> We don't specifically refer to different strands in our diversity statement because we want people to see that it's not necessarily just about four or five things, that it can be hundred things; it means different things to different people. (Diversity specialist, white man, banking and finance)

Generally, respondents perceived this individualization as a progressive aspect of DM as it a) avoided the backlash seen as connected to 'special treatment' for specific groups; b) did not 'pigeon hole' people, allowing instead recognition of multiple identities; and c) expanded the agenda to look at issues that they argued would not normally emerge within an EO paradigm, for example, work–life balance, flexible working, faith groups and broader identity issues:

> Well I think what we've got at the moment for equality and diversity work is the six strands that match the European Directives and the thinking on the Equality and Human Rights Commission and all that. But then running through the whole lot of it are things like diversity, things like class, things like identity, thinking around people's lives and what's going on in their lives. (Diversity specialist, white woman, local government)

Thus, most respondents saw DM as more proactive and inclusive than EO, as moving away from focusing simply on groups and legal compliance towards valuing individual differences. Respondents were also outwardly persuaded by the business case, but as in Lawrence's (2000) study, they did distinguish different types of business philosophies. For example, some respondents, particularly those in the private sector, argued that workforce diversity contributed to the 'bottom line', but when pressed to be more specific, most conceded that the benefits were largely qualitative, intangible and so had to be seen as long-term, rather than directly related to short-term profit. Again, these views speak to the importance of broadening and lengthening the business case, as discussed in Chapter 2. Most respondents articulated a business case for their own organizations, such as being an 'employer of choice', attracting an expanded pool of talent or, more typically, the benefits of having a workforce that reflected the 'customer' base. For example, for the police service, the business case was seen by specialists and champions as the need to improve engagement with different 'minority' communities; for one NGO, it was the perceived need to build a bigger and more diverse volunteer base; for the retail and banking companies, there was a perceived need to understand the needs of different groups of consumers in order to reach a bigger market. Some respondents articulated a broader business case that was part of an overall focus on business ethics or corporate social responsibility, suggesting that social justice and business cases can co-exist in practitioner thinking (Liff and Dickens 2000). These perspectives illustrated how diversity practitioners are attempting to build context-specific business cases which should, theoretically at least, go some way to ensuring that the rhetoric of the business case becomes a reality (see discussion in Chapter 2).

Perspectives on Policy and Practice

What kinds of policy initiatives did respondents believe should be prioritized? Interestingly, despite their generally enthusiastic engagement with the diversity discourse, especially its focus on a broad range of (individual) differences, the specialists and champions typically identified policy priorities as the six group-based issues of gender, race/ethnicity, religion, disability, sexual orientation and age clearly following the six strands of legislation. Within this, race/ethnicity and gender were generally given highest priority by specialists, but disability and age were also frequently mentioned by specialists and champions. Sexual orientation was rarely mentioned as a high priority issue. Most respondents specifically stated that gender imbalances and barriers to women's progression into senior levels were areas requiring policy initiatives. They also alluded to the expanded legislation and the need to keep up-to-date with requirements, demonstrating how the law continues to influence policy priorities. In the public sector, the need to respond to the relatively new race, disability and gender duties was a high priority.

Specialists and champions also believed that certain policy initiatives associated with EO also remained important, for example, dissemination of information on anti-harassment policies, equality awareness raising events, social group-based employee networks and positive action initiatives such as 'women into management' training programmes. These kinds of initiatives sit uneasily within a DM paradigm, but flexible working and work–life balance policies that included everyone were seen as a way of broadening the DM agenda beyond group-based issues. It was felt that a more inclusive approach would achieve the kind of culture change necessary to stop flexible working being stigmatized as only appropriate for less career-oriented women. For example, many respondents spoke of the need for the long hours' culture to be changed, and champions indicated that they were often asked to, or felt that they should, set a good example to other more junior managers by not working excessive hours themselves. This was something that male champions found easier to do.

In terms of policy implementation, a recurrent theme was the need for DM to be mainstreamed. One police service diversity champion (a white woman) used a compelling metaphor to explain this:

> It should be like an Intel chip. Until it's threaded through everything and becomes a natural part of every lesson that recruits have to go through, it's never going to be meaningful. Why do we have an EO/ diversity policy that's separate? It puts these things in a little block all on their own; whereas it should be part of the general way we work.

The appointment of champions was seen as part of the process of mainstreaming and spreading 'ownership' of DM. Respondents, particularly champions, felt it essential to avoid DM being seen as something 'done' to managers and staff by the HR department. Nevertheless, DM was based within HR in most organizations probably as a legacy of the EO paradigm. However, there were signs that this might be changing, with a minority of specialists situated within Corporate Social Responsibility or Corporate Ethics or a stand-alone unit; again this was usually seen as part of a mainstreaming strategy.

Another recurrent theme was the perception that DM needed to move beyond the reactive approach associated with EO (i.e. tackling discrimination) towards a more proactive strategy of culture change. Related to this, there was general disillusionment with traditional EO numerical targets and measures, captured by what one specialist referred to as the 'tyranny of measurement'. Some respondents, especially champions, felt that workforce audits were an example of the excessive 'red tape' associated with the EO paradigm, in itself a barrier to greater equality and diversity. On the other hand, data-gathering and impact assessments were seen by many specialists, especially those in the public sector, as the foundation stone of effective DM. Without the hard evidence, practitioners argued that appropriate policy initiatives could not be designed and that initiatives would have little credibility with other key stakeholders such as line-managers.

Perspectives on Stakeholder Involvement

A stakeholder approach provides a basis for seeing that organizations have a responsibility towards multiple groups, including employees (Liff and Dickens 2000). Encouraging broader ownership of DM via the involvement of internal stakeholder groups including senior management, line-management and non-management employees was a strong theme coming through the interviews. However, as is discussed later on in this section, it is significant that only a small number of respondents saw a role for the trade unions.

The sponsorship role of Chief Executive Officers (CEOs) is a particularly prominent theme in the USA literature (Gilbert et al 1999; Gilbert and Ivancevich 2000; Thomas 2004). The diversity specialists in our study were unanimous in believing that senior level commitment was essential, and most believed the support of their CEO had been critical in pushing forward the agenda. Echoing arguments in the literature, they believed senior level support gave DM initiatives legitimacy and credibility. However, getting line-managers on board was also extremely important, but again reflecting previous research (Dass and Parker 1999; Foster and Harris 2005), line-managers were often found to see pressures to increase workforce diversity as a threat. Although prejudice was seen to play a role in some line-managers' scepticism or outright hostility towards DM, most respondents indicated that, rather than vilifying line-managers as the problem, there had to be more understanding about *why* they were often so resistant to DM. Champions were seen to play a critical role in this regard by acting as role models and leading change. It was felt that fear of loss of power and autonomy, lack of training and awareness and, most importantly, heavy demands on time and resources were the main issues:

> I think sometimes you sort of need to be reminded of the fact that the priority for a manager won't always be diversity. (Diversity specialist, white woman, retail)

> They understand why they have to do it, but there's always something else fighting for time, space and resources, and budget. (Diversity specialist, white woman, airline)

Although the issues surrounding managing a diverse workforce do not seem to have attracted the same degree of negativity in the UK as in the USA (Pelled et al 1999; Bacharach et al 2005; Brief et al 2005), in terms of time pressures, many respondents felt that workforce diversity made day-to-day management more complex and therefore increased line-managers' workload:

> You're asking them, to manage in a more complex way. Asking them to start managing more flexible working arrangements or virtual teams or home working, so you are asking them to change habits of a lifetime in how they communicate, you know, how they performance manage. (Diversity specialist, white woman, banking and finance)

As previous research in the UK has argued (Foster and Harris 2005), one of the issues for line-managers is the lack of clarity within DM about what they should be doing, but yet it is widely believed that managers play a pivotal role in implementing DM (Maxwell et al 2001). Some diversity champions commented that there was fear among line-managers about being seen as prejudiced, and this sometimes meant that some everyday management issues were not dealt with appropriately. One example was BME staff allegedly not being given negative feedback at performance appraisals for fear of accusations of racism and the potential claims that might follow. In terms of how to tackle lack of line-management buy-in, most respondents put their faith in fairly conventional HRM tools, such as training and appraisal. Diversity training was recommended, but making courses compulsory was not generally favoured, as one respondent explained:

> I do not believe in the sheep-dipping of everybody, (a) because you can't do it, it's too expensive, (b) I think what we need to do is do a lot more integrated training; something that people feel relates to you know what they do on a day-to-day basis. (Diversity specialist, white woman, general services)

In terms of relating diversity to what managers do on a day-to-day basis, diversity targets sometimes linked to remuneration were a relatively new initiative that many respondents' organizations were experimenting with as a way of embedding diversity-friendly management practice.

With regard to involving non-management employees, all respondents commented on the importance of consultation so that DM does not simply become something that is 'done' by management to non-management employees. This is summed up by one quote:

> There is a tendency to do things from a central point of view or senior management point of view and the reality is something slightly different. I remember meeting somebody a little while ago and talking about what the issues for particular ethnic minority groups were. And this guy saying to me, 'I don't really care whether people know what I eat, or what I like to do in my spare time or about my religious observance particularly, unless it's necessary for my work'. And therefore, you know, that was an

interesting concept coz you thought, everybody produces these wonderful great cultural awareness guides with all the sort of minutiae about different cultures and different religions, but, this guy was saying that's not important. And I think in that way consultation helps you develop something that people actually feel that they can use and is meaningful. As opposed to doing a lot of work that people sometimes will feel is quite patronizing. (Diversity specialist, white woman, general services)

As stated above, the majority of organizations represented in the study recognized unions, but most respondents did not perceive any necessity or virtue in involving the unions in DM. At one extreme, there were a small number of specialists (mostly public sector) who stated that they were keen on union involvement because it provided additional resources and expertise. In some cases, specialists had formed a close working relationship with trade union officers and reported that the unions had played a significant and helpful role in the development of DM initiatives, for example, by advising on priorities and disseminating details of initiatives to employees. For example, one specialist from a major private sector company reported that she had signed a formal agreement to work with the union on a new anti-harassment policy. The union role was to gather membership views of the extent and nature of harassment in the company. It was felt that the consultation would be seen as more open if conducted via the union. At the other extreme were a small number of specialists who had not involved the unions at all and who stated that they would not consider doing so. The following specialist simply did not want union interference, even though she did not anticipate any union opposition to the organization's DM initiatives:

On the basis that I work from, 'here's something we prepared earlier', when we're talking to the trade unions, rather than getting them to help with the design. Yes they can contribute to it, but this is the way that we will do things around here. But, frankly I don't think there's anything in our policy and what we're trying to achieve, that the trade unions will have nothing but support for. (White woman, general services)

In the middle were most respondents whose organizations recognized trade unions, but who had mixed experiences of working with them. Some diversity champions expressed in principle support for union involvement, even though this had not actually occurred partly because no one (union officers, specialist and champions alike) had initiated it:

My view would be that it would probably be very useful because my experience from other places that I've worked is that the union can be incredibly helpful because most of the work that you do around diversity the union supports. (White woman, general services)

In contrast, some respondents perceived the unions as weak and uninterested in equality and diversity, or even disruptive:

> I think the unions seriously need to think about their contribution on this agenda. Coz the bit of them I've seen is almost always anti-cooperation. Whenever we're developing policies they will be part of the consultation process. But, if you do it as a really sound process you never hear anything from them. But then if you then go through a process of developing and think 'Oh must ask the unions what they think' and send it, you then get 'Oh you haven't asked us early enough we haven't been involved in this and you must stop this', is where they then come from. (Diversity specialist, white woman, local government)

Respondents also reported a range of other indirect staff involvement mechanisms that they had been involved in establishing or maintaining, for example, employee network groups organized according to equality strands. The specialists found these groups useful because if their support for initiatives could be obtained, there was less likely to be articulated employee resistance. Many respondents, particularly in the private sector, saw employee involvement as mainly concerned with gathering staff views; therefore, they favoured direct employee involvement mechanisms including staff attitude surveys. But, some respondents were sceptical about the real value of staff surveys, for example:

> We've had the vexed and thorny issue of staff surveys to get feedback which in an organization of 44,000 people is not the most efficient and effective way of trying to understand what's going on across the organization. The last time we had a corporate survey, by the time we got the results together and thought what we could do, the organization had moved on a pace. (Diversity specialist, BME woman, police service)

> The race perception survey was particularly important, but I don't think the response has been as it should have been. I feel, and I am sure a lot of black and visible minority ethnic staff certainly do, that it was just done because it had to be done. One of the comments made that really struck home was that the focus groups and the presentation of results were done in a dusty backroom and it wasn't very high profile. (Diversity specialist, white woman, local government)

Respondents also proudly reported a wide range of other direct involvement mechanisms including company newsletters and magazines, publicity campaigns, intranet and web sites (all regularly covering diversity issues) as well as specific issue-based diversity events and conferences. Whilst on the one hand any attempts to involve employees might be applauded, many direct involvement mechanisms that we observed as part of our research really seemed to be more about information dissemination—a traditional 'tell and sell' approach—than consultation. However, specialists and champions were noticeably uncritical of their organizations in this regard and were for the most part either leading, or happy to go along with, this approach to employee involvement.

PRACTITIONER VIEWS FROM OUTSIDE THE ORGANIZATION

This section explores the perspectives of diversity consultants and campaigners on the discourse of diversity, on policy and practice within organizations and on stakeholder involvement. The important point to note about consultants and campaigners is that, although they work with mainstream organizations, they stand outside them. Their careers are not directly dependent on any of the individual organizations they work with. In our research, it should not escape notice that all of the consultants and campaigners we interviewed were women, although it is clear that men have also entered diversity consultancy work.

It is obvious that consultants and campaigners have a vested interest in developing positive working relationships with mainstream organizations, in order to maximize their influence (particularly in the case of the campaigners) and their reputations, not least in order to secure future contracts for consultancy work (in the case of the consultants).

Perspectives on the Diversity Discourse

Consultants and campaigners expressed somewhat contradictory views on the diversity discourse even though they all used it in their work. On the one hand, to a large extent, they felt that the 'newness' and uniqueness of DM was exaggerated. They saw it as an example of the kind of linguistic change that can happen with management concepts, rather than as something fundamentally different from EO, for example:

> I've always thought that diversity is just an extension of what we've been calling equality of opportunity and that all the good practice that came about in terms of gender should actually be the model for a much more diverse workplace and society. (Diversity consultant, white woman)

From this perspective, respondents saw policy-makers continuing to develop new initiatives and consolidate older ones, much as ever, despite the new discourse. On the other hand, they also indicated that they saw DM as a distinct approach. For example, one respondent expressed this as EO being about rights and legislation and DM about the individual and the multi-faceted nature of identity. Moreover, similar to respondents in other research (Lawrence 2000), there was also a strong view that DM, firmly underpinned by the business case, signalled a departure from some of the traditional principles of EO:

It definitely makes it more commercially acceptable to talk about. And I hear people talk about it that wouldn't talk about what they would see as old-style equal opportunity. But I think the downside is that I think it definitely has watered it down a lot; you know everything's somehow all different; we're all completely different therefore we've got diversity. (Diversity consultant, white woman)

In terms of whether this turn in policy-making was a good or a bad thing, if DM opened up possibilities for talking about and acting on equality issues, respondents deemed it a progressive turn. Like trade unionists, they were prepared to be pragmatic and work with the diversity discourse even if they were critical of it (Kirton and Greene 2006; see also discussion in Chapter 9). On a more substantive note, most respondents felt that the strength of the diversity concept lay in its more inclusive nature. However, it was also felt that this greater inclusiveness could also be a weakness, possibly causing a dilution of the equality agenda or a lack of focus on the most critical issues:

It [diversity] is more complex [than EO] and that makes it difficult to sell. But there's all this about multiple identities which New Labour keeps telling us about—we have all got multiple identities which is true. But some of those identities have actually, I think, more relevance to us than others. (Diversity campaigner, BME woman)

Respondents felt that the business case was encouraging many organizations to develop DM initiatives. It was argued, for example, that a business-led approach (but coupled with the 'stick' of legislation) encourages organizations to compare their policies and practices with those of their competitors and that this in turns promotes the spread of 'good practice' as more organizations come to believe that good equality and diversity practice is essential for competitive edge. Writing in the USA context, Litvin (2002) has argued that consultants 'retell' the business case in order to motivate organizational members to adopt the changes and behaviours deemed necessary for a 'diversity-friendly' organization. However, Litvin (ibid) sees this approach as misguided because, she argues, the business case does not give rise to deep organizational change. Our respondents were not uncritical of the centrality of the business case within DM, but they were promoting a more multi-faceted business case that was not simply about the 'bottom line'. The essential message that consultants and campaigners in our study were 'selling' to employers was that diversity makes business sense, but that it is also 'the right thing to do'. Nevertheless, not all respondents were optimistic that this message was being absorbed, and there was some questioning of employer motives behind DM initiatives. Further, most respondents talked explicitly or implicitly about the dilemmas and tensions within DM (outlined in Chapter 2), and much of their effort seemed to be geared towards encouraging, supporting and helping organizations to reconcile these, particularly with regard to the involvement of line-managers (discussed later).

Perspectives on Policy and Practice

One of the critical issues for some of the respondents in this group was who they got to talk to in their dealings with organizations; generally it was the diversity specialist(s), but this attracted some criticism:

> I'm asked to go into an organization very often because they want the business case to be explored and developed. So the first person I meet is the equality specialist. Now, you tell me, if they believe it makes business and organization sense to develop that talent, who should I be meeting? Who should be driving this? The chief executive, the managing director, the finance director and so on. (Diversity consultant, white woman)

The above respondent was not arguing against having dedicated diversity specialists, but simply pointing out the irony inherent in the fact that a separate diversity post immediately establishes at least an implied distance between the core of the business and equality and diversity issues. Some respondents thought that disconnecting DM from HR would help to embed it in the business goals of the organization. In line with this perspective, there was some favouring of the positioning of DM within the broader business policy area of Corporate Social Responsibility, rather than within HR. Some felt that the time was now right to do this because they detected a greater interest from organizations in the relationship between equality and diversity, service delivery and ethical business practice as suggested by Liff and Dickens (2000).

When asked to talk about the type of policy initiatives they recommended, one campaigner, a black woman, repeatedly used the expression 'one size doesn't fit all'. Within the business case of DM, it was considered important to encourage organizations to take ownership of policy initiatives, and therefore in their roles some respondents were keen not to be seen to be imposing generic solutions on organizations, but to be more geared towards helping organizations find their own solutions. This perspective represents a departure from the traditional, bureaucratic approach to EO which urged all organizations to adopt more or less the same rules and procedures as a blue print for greater equality. The consultants and campaigners typically expressed a preference for a more nuanced, contextualized and flexible approach to policy-making. Some were only too aware from previous experiences of the shortcomings of an overly bureaucratic approach (as also discussed by Glover and Kirton 2006). The possibility for a more flexible approach to conflict with conceptions of 'best practice' that the respondents also talked about is evident and was noted by some respondents.

Most respondents continued to promote the benefits of certain traditional EO practices, but usually under the rubric of DM and the business case. For example, rigorous monitoring of workforce diversity was recommended as essential, ostensibly in order to ensure that everyone's talent and skills were being fully utilized by organizations. However, the respondents often had a hidden agenda to promote equality, rather than simply to help the organization harness the business benefits of diversity. One respondent explained how monitoring could identify patterns of indirect discrimination (as well as under-utilization of skills and training):

> One big organization I was working with—roughly equal numbers of men and women coming in at a certain level and then at a higher level it's just virtually no women. The assumption was well they're leaving and having children. Actually when we looked at the data that wasn't what was happening at all. They were entering in equal numbers, but very quickly the men were being promoted faster. So actually by the time the women had been in the organization a while, before they were even thinking about whether they wanted to have a family, they were already completely cynical. (Diversity consultant, white woman)

Respondents also recommended a policy of mainstreaming (a familiar concept within the EO paradigm). For example, organizations they worked with were encouraged to equality-proof and conduct impact assessments of all organizational policies. Another traditional EO initiative that respondents encouraged was awareness raising training courses. It was acknowledged that training can be very costly, but most consultants and campaigners saw it as the key to embedding equality and diversity within organizations. A couple were more circumspect about the capacity for training to bring about change, for example:

> The problem is not raising more awareness. The issue is about delivering equality and diversity in terms of mechanisms of change. It's not rocket science, but it sums up a very fundamental contradiction between the policy and public statements and what's delivered and therefore the credibility of the whole issue of equality and diversity in an organization. (Diversity consultant, white woman)

The above respondent was not arguing against equality and diversity training *per se*, but believed that the time, money and effort should be spent instead on more concrete mechanisms of change, which needed to be identified in the context of each individual organization. Reflecting the controversy reported in the literature (Cockburn 1991; Lawrence 2000), when it came to the more radical positive action initiatives, there was less consensus. On the one hand, there was a belief that positive action could help to address embedded disadvantage, as two respondents explained:

> One thing I'm worried is going to fall off the agenda of diversity and equal opportunities is positive action. I always worry about this word mainstreaming which is again part of the whole diversity thing. And you know, to me mainstreaming is putting equality at the hub of your policy and practice, that's it. Which isn't to say treating everybody the same; it isn't one size fits all. Positive action has to be there in terms of training programmes for people who are under-represented, for encouraging more people into the workplace. (Diversity campaigner, BME woman)

> I guess some people would still argue that you can't have a diverse workforce and treat everybody equally if you haven't got a diverse workforce in the first place. So it may be that you have to have some sort of positive action policies if you are not an organization that has a reasonable representation of women or minority ethnic groups or whatever. There may be recruitment policies like outreach or whatever. You might have to have policies targeting particular groups to make your organization more representative. But then when people are in the organization you don't then single them out for any different treatment because they come from different groups. HR policies should be equal. (Diversity campaigner, BME woman)

On the other hand, the second quote also reflects the more widely held ambivalent attitude towards positive action and differential treatment. Newer management techniques now being incorporated into DM also created some unease. Individual performance appraisal containing diversity objectives was seen as a potential instrument of change, but one on which respondents felt 'the jury is still out' in terms of whether it would prove an effective way of embedding equality and diversity in everyday organizational practices.

Perspectives on Stakeholder Involvement

The respondents agreed that there was a need to move away from the idea that diversity specialists 'own' DM. There was a perceived need to build relationships and alliances with and between different internal stakeholder groups including specialists, HR practitioners, senior and line-managers and non-management staff. Most consultants and campaigners saw top level (CEO) commitment and leadership as essential. From their experience, they typically believed that there is now genuine commitment to diversity at the most senior levels of public and (large) private sector organizations. They perceived gaining line-management 'buy-in' as the greatest challenge facing organizations. But, like the specialists and champions, their reflections and experiences caution against simply blaming line-managers for the failure of DM initiatives, as the quote below shows when the respondent alludes to the many pressures facing line-managers:

> The big challenge, I would say for virtually every organization is engaging the managers in the middle. That is very consistent within the private and public sector, central government; it's the same thing. The leadership at the top—absolutely committed, want to do it. People at the bottom—'please, do something'. And then you get the managers in the middle who are busy. The challenge is how do we develop support for them and get it as part of how we do business around here. (Diversity campaigner, BME woman)

An apparent line-management reluctance to engage with DM was also thought to stem from a lack of understanding about the issues, implying the need for more training:

> I think in some places what's happened is that management at the top, the chief executive, has said 'Oh God we have to have a diverse workplace, so get on with it.' So middle management has to put something in place and they really aren't sure what it is at all and it's difficult then to communicate that policy. (Diversity campaigner, BME woman)

The everyday tensions and conflicts facing line-managers were mentioned and therefore, the importance of establishing a dialogue on equality and diversity:

> But if you are valuing diversity and valuing the individual, sometimes you do have a conflict permanently or temporarily or whatever between people's performance, between the needs of the organization, between the rest of their lives. Being able to talk to people, generate options, maybe occasionally involve a staff counsellor or mediator without feeling that as a line manager you are giving away your power or something—that is a set of interpersonal skills that line managers ought to have, but increasingly it is clear that a lot of them don't have. (Diversity campaigner, white woman)

As stated earlier, respondents stressed the importance of monitoring, including monitoring the outcomes of processes that line-managers often take charge of, such as performance appraisal and recruitment and selection. However, it was also felt that monitoring can feel like surveillance to many line-managers, and therefore it was important to get them on board so that they would not interpret monitoring as 'Big Brother' watching them.

There was also general agreement about the necessity to involve non-management employees, and a variety of mechanisms were suggested depending on the circumstances of the organization. Respondents felt that trade unions should be consulted and involved where present. One consultant, formerly a trade union official, stated that while she felt that trade unions could make a positive difference in some organizations, this would only happen in practice where the union thinks beyond simply wage issues. She continued that in her experience it was not always the case that unionized organizations are better at 'doing equality and diversity' than non-union ones. Generally, respondents felt that involving non-management employees was positive as part of a 'grassroots' approach to DM. Many respondents argued that from their experience non-management employees often have little confidence in the DM policy to effect meaningful change. To increase non-management employee involvement, a number of fairly conventional HR-type policy tools were suggested including employee perception surveys, focus groups of employees and employee networks.

CONCLUSION

From our research, it seems clear that the DM paradigm has impacted on diversity work and the people who do it. One significant point is that diversity work is no longer the preserve of activists, although activists are still found, particularly working on the outside of mainstream organizations. A broader range of different 'types' of people now have significant roles in DM development and implementation. Perhaps this inevitably means that the characteristics and perspectives of people doing diversity work have altered. Of particular note is the fact that BME people were relatively absent in our range of organizations and that white men are entering an area that was previously seen as suited to 'minorities'. Added to this, there is now less of a sense that diversity practitioners are *activists* when compared with those doing equality work at the height of EO activity in the mid to late 1980s before the disillusionment with the EO paradigm (Cockburn 1991) really set in and before the diversity discourse took hold. There was from our research little sense that *personal experiences* of discrimination had politicized and spurred the practitioners into working in the field of DM. That said, what we detected was a *shift*, rather than a seismic movement, away from traditional equality goals and values. For example, most of the specialists and champions espoused the business case as the main driving force behind their own diversity work and what they thought should be organizational priorities. But many also had social justice goals, but they saw the business case as the vehicle or at least the discursive device for achieving these. Therefore, there was some suggestion that social justice and business cases could co-exist (as suggested by Liff and Dickens 2000). Certainly, the all-female consultants and campaigners were promoting a multi-faceted and complex business case that moved beyond thinking solely in terms of the bottom line to include ethical business practice. However, one problem with this was that the general failure of respondents, particularly those on the inside of mainstream organizations, to engage critically with the diversity discourse meant that there was very little confronting of the fact that DM makes management, not disadvantaged social groups, the primary constituency, such that diversity specialists probably do not act as an interface between management and employees in the way that equality officers did (Cockburn 1991). Yet, nearly all the respondents in all groups of practitioners were aware of the potential and capacity for line-managers—the primary constituency of DM—to disrupt or subvert policy initiatives. Therefore, it was clear that for most specialists, consultants and campaigners, allies were rarely found among line-management, with the exception of those who had stepped forward to take a visible leadership role—the diversity champions who were disproportionately male.

On the whole, practitioners saw the business case of DM as a progressive development, one that would win over senior and middle managers, where the social justice case of EO had failed to do so, especially in the case of middle managers. On the other hand, it is important not to exaggerate the impact of DM on equality and diversity work. Even though very few respondents were prepared to speak up for EO either theoretically or in practice, it was clear that what we might classify as EO initiatives lived on, even if they did have another name—for example, equality awareness training morphing into diversity awareness. Further, (EO) initiatives aimed at achieving procedural and legal compliance or positive action initiatives targeted at certain social groups—particularly women and BME workers—continued to feature on the list of priorities for most respondents, not least because of the changing and complex legal context that the UK has witnessed (see Chapter 3). Thus, what we are left with from our investigation of diversity practitioner perspectives is a complex, multi-faceted picture of diversity work, but one where the business case seems to have, for now at least, a firm grip.

7 Line-Management Involvement in Diversity Management

INTRODUCTION

This chapter explores the involvement of line-managers in diversity management (DM). A specific focus on line-management in particular, and as distinct from senior management, is justified because of the key role that line-managers play within the discourse of Human Resource Management (HRM) more broadly and consequently within the discourse of DM.

It is worthwhile beginning with a definition of line-managers as there is some lack of clarity in the literature, with a range of titles being used often for the same, or a very similar, role, for example, 'line-manager', 'first-line-manager', 'front line-manager' or the less used 'middle level line-manager'; then there is a debate about the role of 'supervisor' within this nomenclature. Clearly, different organizations use different terms to denote the same role. McConville and Holden (1999: 408–9) and Hales (2005: 473–4) present a useful summary of this debate. The specific nature of managers' roles and duties will also clearly vary from organization to organization. For our purposes, we were interested in understanding the experiences and perspectives of those managers in our case study organizations, who stand below senior levels within the organizational hierarchy and have some responsibility for the day-to-day management of employees. For us, Hales's (2005: 473) definition is useful: 'the term 'first-line manager' is conventionally taken to denote those positions representing the first level of management to whom non-managerial employees report'. This allows us to include those who are designated as supervisors in some organizational contexts (for example, in our case study organization ServiceCo), but also those who for some authors (such as Currie and Proctor 2001; and McConville and Holden ibid) would actually be considered to be part of the middle management layer. What is important is to note key distinguishing features of the line-management role. Line-managers hold a position that is removed from that of the non-managerial employee, and they are accountable for outcomes beyond that of detailed tasks, including responsibility for the 'people management' of their subordinates (McConville and Holden ibid), involving activities such as the direction, monitoring and control of operational work. On the other hand, while line-managers often have some level of authority to make decisions, they are unlikely to have any kind of upward influence on the development or formulation of strategy and thus have 'limited political power' (McConville and Holden ibid: 409) within the organization.

Looking at the involvement of line-managers is important because, first, the central place given to the role of line-managers within the discourse of HRM and consequently within the emerging discourse of DM. Second, as discussed in Chapter 2, line-managers have been assigned a particular responsibility for the dissemination and implementation of DM policy within organizations. Finally, the issue of line-management 'buy-in' (or lack of) to DM policy is seen as a key obstacle to effective DM. Utilizing empirical material from our research project, this chapter will provide an analysis of the nature of line-management involvement in DM. The focus is mainly within our two case study organizations—ServiceCo, a multi-divisional private sector company; and PSO, a government department (public sector). Where relevant, we also draw on findings from the wider set of interviews with diversity practitioners in a broad range of organizations, in order to gain a perspective on their views of line-managers and the line-management role.

It should be noted that our sample of line-managers was predominantly white (the sample of respondents at ServiceCo included six white women and three white men in Health, and nine white men in Transport; while at PSO, there were four white women, three white men, one black and minority ethnic (BME) woman and two BME men), in line with data that indicated under-representation of BME staff at managerial levels at both organizations and evidence of heavily gender and race segregated work in ServiceCo. Where relevant, we highlight any differences between the views of line-managers on the basis of gender and 'race'/ethnicity, and where quotes are used, the gender and 'race'/ethnicity of the respondent are shown in order to enable the reader to set the comments against the respondents' identity characteristics.

THE ROLE OF LINE-MANAGERS IN A CONTEXT OF DM

Kirton and Greene (2005: Chapter 9) discuss the way in which shifts towards DM followed on from, or at least occurred in parallel with, the emergence of the HRM paradigm. The way in which a clear role for line-managers is established within HRM is therefore of key relevance to a discussion of DM. Take a cursory glance at any of the mainstream HRM texts and there can be no doubt that one of the main themes in the literature on HRM has been the central role of line-managers (McConville and Holden 1999). For example, one of the earliest theorizations of HRM in the UK context was Guest (1987), who outlined four core tenets and established the role of line-managers as one of the central components. A key mantra of the HRM discourse (one of the features making it distinct from Personnel Management) (see Legge 1995; Storey 1995) has been the need to 'return HRM to the line' (Purcell and Hutchinson 2007: 5), so that the responsibility for people management issues was no longer simply that of the human resources (HR) function.

The significance of the role given to line-managers should not be underestimated. As Watson et al (2007) point out, the devolution of aspects of HRM to line-managers has received considerable attention from both academics and practitioners. A key issue has been the extent to which such devolution leads to improvements in organizational performance. A large scale multi-method research project involving twelve UK organizations (Purcell et al 2003; Hutchinson and Purcell 2003) aimed to try and illuminate this vexed question by looking specifically at the role of line-managers in delivering people management practices. The devolution of people management to the line within HRM is seen as having a significant influence on the way that employees perceive and experience HR practices. In turn the degree of line-management engagement with HRM influences non-management workers' views of, satisfaction with, commitment to and, ultimately, performance within the organization, because obviously the people that they will see as answerable for these practices will be those people who have direct responsibility for them—their line-managers. This has wider significance because,

> . . . taken together people management has a non-instrumental role of communicating to employees the nature of the firm, their value to it, and the type of behaviours expected. Thus the group or bundle of people management practices as perceived by employees constitutes an important element in overall organizational climate. (Purcell and Hutchinson 2007: 7)

DM issues are of specific relevance here because reflecting on research in the USA, Konrad and Linnehan (1995: 413) indicate the way in which the nature of the content of organizational equality and diversity policies have a heightened propensity to affect individual attitudes, interests and behaviours and thus have more potential impact on employee responses to the company and levels of organizational commitment.

In earlier literature on the proposed link between HRM and improved performance, there was much discussion about the type, number and mix of policies as the crucial factors. However, Purcell and Hutchinson's (2007) paper challenges this, crucially arguing that it is not the quality of HR practices per se that is important, but the behaviour of line-managers in translating and delivering those HR practices. They found that employees who were dissatisfied with the way HR policies were applied had more negative attitudes about the organization and organizational performance was weaker. This indicated that it is not the quality of HR practices per se, but the behaviour of the line-manager in implementing the policy which is the most important factor. They suggest therefore that the design of HR policies should include consideration of how line-managers can apply them (Purcell and Hutchinson 2007: 17).

The general discussion above has direct relevance to DM, because equality and diversity issues are a key responsibility of HR departments and concomitantly have become a key part of the HR tasks that are devolved to line-managers. In essence, the line-manager is supposed to move away from a purely supervisory role (i.e. 'the proximal and immediate direction, monitoring and control of operational work' (Hales 2005: 474))[1], to something broader, taking on the more generic managerial role at the heart of practices and processes that used to be controlled by the HR/personnel function, such as 'general administration, quality monitoring and people management of a unit, as well as greater authority to take decisions' (ibid: 476). Many of the HR activities that are viewed as needing to be devolved to line-managers have equality and diversity dimensions. For example, McGovern et al (1997) find that typical HR roles to be devolved to the line included the selection, appraisal and development of subordinates. Line-managers should 'own' these activities and would therefore ultimately be responsible for the performance of their staff. These activities relate to the key processes (recruitment, selection, induction and appraisal) that Kandola and Fullerton (1998: 110) within their prescriptive model deem as critical to the success of DM within organizations.

As stated in Chapter 2, Kandola and Fullerton (1994, 1998) are credited with the dissemination of the diversity concept in the UK, and in their introductory chapter the 'crucial' role of line-managers is specifically highlighted. Diversity has been described as the 'perfect litmus test for modern management capacity' (Schneider 2001: 13). Cornelius et al's (2000) research finds that DM is likely to be most effective when there is proactive line-management. Having DM at the heart of the line-management role is felt to overcome a significant criticism of the traditional EO approach that it was largely seen as a specialist, peripheral activity (largely the concern of personnel or HR functions), and had little to do with core business concerns (Ross and Schneider 1992; see summary discussion in Maxwell et al 2001). In much the same way as HRM is positioned as a central business concern within HRM, there is a similar emphasis on the business case within DM (see discussion in Chapter 2).

Extent of Devolution

However, the consequences and implications of devolving responsibility for DM to the line are obviously affected by the extent to which devolution has actually occurred, the debate about which is now quite long-standing, but for which evidence continues to be inconsistent and contested. Qualitative case study research conducted more than a decade ago led Storey (1992) to be doubtful about the extent to which the role of the line-manager had significantly changed, with any changes often amounting to little more than retitling, rhetoric or aspiration. Additionally, Hope-Hailey et al (1997) found that the HR function often retained responsibility for key operational people management issues such as recruitment and selection. Hoque and Noon's (2001) analysis of Workplace Employment Relations Survey (WERS) data from 1998 finds that in accordance with the model of HRM, where an 'HR' rather than a 'personnel' specialist is present in an organization, there is wider devolution of people management responsibilities. However, they also acknowledge that the results concerning the specific activities devolved are inconsistent across the sample. Moving forward into the 2000s does not seem to offer any more conclusive evidence of more significant devolution; indeed Currie and Proctor's (2001) review of the literature indicates that the extent of devolution in the UK at least is often greatly exaggerated and part of the rhetoric of HRM rather than the reality. Updating analysis to WERS 2004 data, the extent of delegation of people management away from HR departments still continues to be rather limited and restricted, with the more likely situation being that HR responsibilities within an organization are still predominantly characterized by centralized decision making (Kersley et al 2006). Larsen and Brewster, for example, note that the UK consistently comes near the 'least devolved' end of the European spectrum (2003: 240; Brewster 2007). While certain surveys indicate that line-management roles are expanding and taking on more people management aspects, traditional day-to-day operational responsibilities remain the norm, with broader HRM responsibilities being the exception rather than the rule (Hales 2005).

Looking more specifically at DM issues, a particularly interesting finding of WERS 2004 (Kersley et al 2006) is that what they term equal opportunities (EO) is the area that line-managers were less likely to have autonomy[2] over, with 72 per cent (75 per cent in 1998) of line-managers following centralized policy, 64 per cent (46 per cent in 1998) having to consult managers elsewhere before a decision was made and 22 per cent (21 per cent in 1998) having to regularly report to managers elsewhere. Indeed, while the HR responsibilities of line-managers remained largely unchanged between 1998 and 2004, the one notable change was that ironically EO was less likely to be part of their job in 2004 than in 1998 (ibid: 47), despite the DM discourse insisting on the central role of line-managers. This pattern is explained by the fact that that responsibility in this area might have fallen on managers located at a higher level in the organization, although no further information is given. Perhaps this could be due to the fact that EO is increasingly seen as a legal minefield within the ever rapidly changing legislative context of the UK, and so line-managers are not seen as having the knowledge and competency to deal properly with any issues that arise, or that (as is discussed later) there is a requirement to have a more centralized monitoring function in order to ensure compliance with legislation that might be undermined by local autonomous decisions.

This also does not appear to be a UK phenomenon, for example, the DM function was incorporated into the HRM department in eight of ten organizations in the Netherlands (Subeliani and Tsogas 2005), while in the USA, despite the need for DM to be seen as more than an HR issue, research seems to indicate the resilience of a model of DM led by and centrally controlled by the HR department (Wentling 2004; Wentling and Palma-Rivas 2000). So there appear to be some contradictory patterns emerging—while devolution of responsibility to the line is central to models of both HRM and DM, the picture of line-management responsibilities remains broadly traditional. Certainly, UK evidence indicates that there is a decline in the extent to which equality and diversity responsibilities are being devolved, at the same time that a diversity discourse that has devolution of responsibility at its centre appears to be gaining a more global hold. Some explanation of this gap is required, some of which relates to the difficulties of and the problems that line-managers experience with taking on the responsibilities of DM.

DIFFICULTIES OF DEVOLVING RESPONSIBILITY FOR DIVERSITY MANAGEMENT TO THE LINE

Part of the reason for the limited extent of devolution in practice could relate to the now steady stream of research that points to the problems of devolving DM to line-managers. Indeed Maxwell et al (2001) list the emphasis placed on the role of line-managers as one of the key criticisms of DM. Overall, research illustrates that there is a gap between espoused and enacted HR practices, and this gap is often explained by factors to do with line-managers themselves (Purcell and Hutchinson 2007). A commonly cited problem is lack of line-management 'buy-in' to DM; indeed, when asked what were common barriers to progress on equality and diversity issues, without fail the attitudes and behaviour of line-managers were mentioned by all other stakeholders in both of our case studies, reflecting a common characterization of line-managers as scapegoats for a variety of problems associated with the implementation of DM (see Opportunity Now 2005). With regard to the diversity practitioners we interviewed, some spoke of line-managers as the 'permafrost' or 'marzipan' level within their organizations; in other words, the ones they consistently failed to get on board.

However, there is no reason to view line-managers as deliberately obstructive around diversity issues any more than any other organizational stakeholder; indeed, only three per cent of line-managers in a recent report in the UK indicated that they did not think that diversity issues are important (Opportunity Now 2005: 10), so the issue is to try and unpick why line-managers have become the target of criticism for so many. In looking at the more generic devolution of HR roles to the line, Storey (1992, cited in Hope-Hailey et al 1997: 8) questioned assumptions underlying mainstream discourses of HRM that line-managers are capable of taking on HR responsibilities, that line-managers would want to take on this responsibility and that line-managers have the time to do so. We argue that similar questions can be asked of the assumption that DM issues can be devolved and look at a number of key areas: (i) line-management understandings of what concepts of equality and diversity actually mean and how this translates into meaningful roles for them in DM implementation; (ii) how line-managers are trained for taking on DM; (iii) the extent to which line-managers are involved in the development of DM policy; (iv) the extent to which line-managers are accountable for their own DM practice; and (v) the relative place of DM issues amongst their priority of tasks.

Line-Managers' Understandings Of DM

With regard to the devolution of generic HR tasks to the line, it has been argued that this is at best only a very vague and ill-defined assumption, with little clarification of what this actually means in everyday terms for line-managers themselves and how this would change what they do (Hope-Hailey et al 1997: 8; see also McGovern et al 1997: 13). A key finding from Hope-Hailey et al's (1997) study was that people management was not a definable workload that could easily be devolved to line-managers. If there is ambiguity about what broad people management roles line-managers are supposed to take on, this ambiguity is only exacerbated when considering DM aspects of these roles. In this regard, the DM paradigm at a theoretical level is seen as more amorphous than EO in terms of what it means for actual policy action. The 'do-ability' of DM is therefore called into question in the more critical literature (Foster and Harris 2005; Lorbiecki and Jack 2000; Prasad and Mills 1997; Zanoni and Janssens 2004). This deals with the difficulties of establishing workable policy interventions around individual differences, and the business case for individual differences which is discussed in more detail in Chapter 10.

A key difficulty is the balance between line-management autonomy over HR issues and centralized control from the HR department. As Hope-Hailey et al (1997: 8) point out, if HR issues are seen as central to business performance, then devolution does not necessarily carry more freedom for line-managers, but in fact their actions are likely to be more prescribed and monitored, because they are now held more accountable for their HR practice than ever before. This situation can be easily translated directly to DM. That is, there are bound to be contradictions between a wider organization and extra-organizational context that require a standardized approach to DM (for example, because of the need to comply with equality legislation), and a business-led approach to DM that calls for local autonomy and practices tailored to individual local circumstances that is necessarily more contingent (Dickens 1999). The 'same treatment' principles of the UK legislation have provided the foundations of organizational EO policies. Arguably, if organizations are to meet the 'same treatment' principle, some kind of centralized policy-making and certainly centralized monitoring are necessary. At the same time, DM calls for different treatment in order to recognize (and value) individual differences. As Foster and Harris state: 'Potentially this creates a confusing state of affairs for line managers accustomed to demonstrating [and we would add, required to *continue* demonstrating] fair treatment through their adherence to procedures designed to remove a consideration of social group characteristics' (2005: 6). Therefore, a key finding is that, faced with the choice between accountability of managerial practice on DM and potentially expensive litigation, line-managers tended to take a very traditional defensive and compliance-based approach to DM practice (or in Dass and Parker's (1999: 70) term, 'a defensive strategic response'), that does not necessarily tie in with rhetoric, nor the intention of business case led organizational policy (ibid: 11).

This confusing state of affairs is only made worse by the wider lack of understanding by line-managers about what is meant by equality and diversity and how this translates into everyday action. Foster and Harris' (2005) study of DM in the UK retail industry, ironically entitled 'Easy to say, difficult to do', identified the 'analytical muddle' faced by line-managers. The issue is that conceptual confusion can lead to policy confusion; for example, the difficulties of coming up with policy that responds to employees' needs and desires to be treated differently and the same as each other simultaneously. In her research also in the UK, Liff highlights the difficulties of having policy frameworks which simultaneously aim to ignore *and* respond to differences, because, she argues, there is little understanding of the basis for deciding when it is appropriate to recognize differences and when to ignore them (1999: 73). Foster and Harris (2005: 12) give the example of line-managers being confused by employees expecting to be treated *the same* during recruitment and selection, but yet also expecting *different* needs (for example, as a parent requiring flexible working) to be recognized. Different understandings of the rationale for and way in which policies should be approached led to significant problems in implementation. So for some line-managers in Foster and Harris' study (ibid), taking responsibility for DM meant adapting supervisory behaviours to perceptions of individual differences of each subordinate, while for others it meant recognizing the effects of social group differences (ibid: 9), while for others it meant ignoring differences and focusing much more on same treatment (ibid: 10). Foster and Harris (ibid: 10) conclude that the lack of a common understanding of what taking responsibility for DM meant, contributed to the difficulties in interpreting policy and led to inconsistency of practice, the weaknesses of which are reflected on later in this chapter. This lack of understanding is not something exclusive to the UK context either. Despite the longer history of the diversity discourse in the USA, Wentling (2004) finds a key barrier to DM within organizations to be line-managers not understanding the value of workforce diversity. Similarly, utilizing examples and research from a large number of USA firms, Dass and Parker (1999: 71) indicate that negative line-management attitudes and backlash to DM policies can emerge from a lack of understanding and confusion about what diversity means.

In our own case study research, like Foster and Harris (2005), we also found a wide variety of understandings held by line-managers about the meaning of DM and what it meant for their roles and responsibilities. Questions were raised around the extent to which line-managers' activities should concentrate on treating everyone the same in order to ensure legal compliance or whether they should attempt to recognize and respond to individual differences (which as discussed above is difficult to reconcile simultaneously). As discussed in Chapter 4, our analysis of policy in the public sector organization PSO indicated that both the traditional language of equality and newer language of diversity was used to describe its policy initiatives, and interviews specifically explored line-managers' understanding of these concepts. The official view that DM should be the responsibility of all staff was clear at PSO, and the policy detailed specific responsibilities for all employees of the organization from senior managers to non-managerial employees. However, while some respondents had more extensive answers than others, many revealed a distinct lack of awareness about the policy and the concepts. Those who were able to offer a definition generally made a clear distinction between equality and diversity. Equality was associated with discrimination, the law and certain groups (for example, women, BME, disabled people and lesbians and gay men were mentioned). Diversity was perceived to be about valuing and utilizing difference and about the individual, rather than groups. In policy terms, equality was understood to be driven by rules and procedures and diversity about organizational culture and people's behaviour. In addition, diversity was seen by many to be about organizational change, and some saw equality as old fashioned, while diversity was equated with progress. These views are captured by the following quote from one white woman manager:

> I think it [diversity] is really recognising people's differences. I think whereas, you know, 'equal opportunities' is all about not discriminating against people and is law, I think diversity is sort of taking that to another level. It is really recognising the fact that we are all different and that different people have different strengths which we can utilise to the best, you know, to get the most out of the organization.

Interestingly, trade union representatives at PSO believed that line-managers were the greatest barrier to equality and diversity precisely because they lacked understanding of the policy. Talking to the line-managers themselves, a variety of perspectives on equality and diversity were revealed. Some seemed to have quite jaded and cynical views, with little enthusiasm either for specific initiatives or for the aims and ideas within the policy. Some seemed quite disengaged, particularly the white men, believing that the policy had little to do with them. It should be noted too that, importantly, a small minority appeared quite excited by it and its potential to achieve culture change within PSO. The latter managers were the ones who were most actively involved in DM either via diversity employee groups or via the trade unions. It was noticeable also that those who seemed most engaged by and involved in DM were those who themselves shared identity characteristics with the diversity strands. For example, two line-managers commented that PSO was 'a good place to be gay'. In particular, one white woman manager who was a member of the LGBT employee group saw the group as pivotal to the progressing of a lesbian and gay agenda in PSO:

> We advise them on HR policies and things like this and sort of taking part in staff surveys, we are quite good on that. And we do sort of advise the department on things like does the staff survey ask the right kind of questions, do we need to include other questions, do we need to include a sexuality box along with the ethnicity section of the survey. So we have consulted with the department on that. We have consulted with the department on pensions, on same sex pensions which we didn't achieve at the time but you know our current Secretary did lobby Cabinet Office on our behalf which is an extraordinary step for him to take. And that shows that we do have high-level support but we need to make the most of that. And we need to reach out to staff a lot more, let them know that we are here.

At ServiceCo, it should be noted that the policy was at a very early stage of development when fieldwork began, unlike the long-established policy at PSO. As set out in Chapter 5, ServiceCo also used some elements of the newer language of diversity to describe its policy (for example, references to the need to value diversity and recognize the impact of individual differences), although the policy generally reflected a more traditional approach based around treating everyone the same and avoiding discrimination (for example, gender, race, disability). When asked to explain their understandings of the concepts, line-managers indicated a general awareness of the term 'equality' with a common understanding being that it meant treating people the same, with this resulting in treating people fairly. However, even here there were exceptions, with some indicating very little awareness; for example, one of the housekeeping managers at HealthSite (a white woman) stated: 'I heard of equality but no, I don't understand'. If awareness of equality was variable, there was much more limited awareness of the concept of 'diversity', with, for instance, some believing it related to the variety of work organization or job roles and one manager at RoadSite saying he 'didn't connect diversity and equality at all'.

One manager at HealthSite had a more developed understanding and included individual differences in her definition:

> You do need to appreciate and respect everybody as an individual and actually not show any difference because they may be black or white or old or young or, you know, it is important that you treat anybody the same. But be aware of differences so that you can train them adequately or make sure that health and safety is covered for whatever reason. If they are a young person and they are new to a working environment, cover it at that level. If they are an older person with possibly disabilities that they have accrued during their lifetime, that you are aware of those types of things.

However, if this last quote is an example of a manager with a much broader view of diversity than most at ServiceCo, it is also a perfect illustration of Foster and Harris' (2005) presentation of the confusion experienced by line-managers, with the paradoxical situation of needing to recognize difference at the same time as being adamant about treating everybody the same. In general, unlike at PSO, where there was overall a more nuanced understanding from most line-managers, most at ServiceCo seemed to believe that diversity was synonymous with equality, which in turn they saw as about managing people 'the same', i.e. effectively not treating them worse because they are 'different'. Therefore, DM was about resolving any issues or conflicts that come up between staff or in relation to grievances.

Understanding policy rationales is also clearly related to exposure to them in the first place. At ServiceCo, there was very little criticism of policy, and line-managers held positive perceptions of what they knew of the ServiceCo equality and diversity strategy. However, actual working knowledge of the policy became much more limited further down the managerial hierarchy, to the point where line-managers with direct, daily responsibility for staff were largely unaware of specific initiatives or even the general strategy in this area. Part of the lack of understanding undoubtedly relates to the lack of training given to line-managers as discussed in the next section.

Line-Management Training

McGovern et al (1997: 19) outline three key constraints on line-management practice of people management, one of which was what they call 'institutional reinforcement of HR practices'. This refers to the extent to which the espoused emphasis on devolution of HR responsibilities to the line is formally institutionalized and reinforced, partly by the training of line-managers for their people management tasks. Training is seen as a key mechanism to achieve line-management buy-in by ensuring that they understand the reasons why policies are being introduced and what they are supposed to achieve. Indeed, in their 5-year project involving in-depth, multi-method research in four USA firms, a key finding is the importance of training (and development-focused HR practices) in reducing the negative effects that increasing workforce diversity could have (Kochan et al 2003). Again in the USA, Konrad and Linnehan's (1995) research involving over 240 line-managers in four organizations highlights the importance of appropriate diversity training. Their findings indicate that managers tended to have neutral rather than negative attitudes to affirmative action (see Chapter 2) programmes per se, but it was the low levels of understanding that would potentially lead to negative attitudes and corresponding lack of buy-in (ibid: 428–9). Thus, it might be expected that attitudes and buy-in should improve when line-managers receive a proper explanation of the rationale and expectations of policy and clearly understand what the activities actually are. Recent research on UK line-managers found that training was ranked as the second most useful method of support from their employer around DM, and 78 per cent of line-managers see it as an important influence on DM decision making (Opportunity Now 2005: 9). The USA has seen the rapid development of a multi-dimensional, multi-million dollar 'diversity management industry' (Bergen et al 2002: 240) in which DM is 'sold' to organizations and managers through consultants, trainers and 'how-to-do' books (Prasad and Mills 1997), with the UK rapidly following suit (Kaler 2001).

However, getting diversity training 'right' is problematic. Indeed, research in the USA indicates that the existence of training may actually be correlated with negative effects on organizational performance (Ely 2004; see also Kochan et al 2003). Explanations for these findings include that training concentrates too much on communicating company values of diversity rather than giving people concrete skills on how to 'do' DM, leading to frustrated and cynical staff, and the negative impact of dealing with difficult issues such as prejudice and discrimination within groups and teams (Ely 2004: 776). The content of training must be carefully designed; indeed, Bergen et al (2002) similarly indicate that rather than fostering harmony amongst participants, diversity training can stress differences and exacerbate divisions between employees at least in the short-term (Bergen et al 2002: 246; see similar arguments from a UK perspective in Kandola and Fullerton 1998: 154). However, the problem is that there is little regulation of or standards for diversity trainers, and Bergen et al (2002: 246) provide many examples of diversity training in the USA, where the typical methods used are ethically questionable at best and where many diversity-approved stereotypes used within the training are noticeably close to racist and sexist theories. Similar experiences are noted in our case study research discussed below. Moreover, as stated above, many critical commentators have questioned whether DM is 'do-able' at all.

Furthermore, it appears that diversity training for line-managers is not often seen as a priority for organizations. Indeed, one research report on line-managers found that as many as 31 per cent had received no training on equality and diversity issues in the last two years (Opportunity Now 2005: 9). Of more concern was the fact that 59 per cent of line-managers under 29 years old reported having received no diversity training in the last 2 years, as these were likely to be newer managers (ibid) and arguably the ones that needed more assistance.

All of the organizations represented in our diversity practitioner interview set had some form of diversity training programme in place. The nature of this varied highly from organization to organization depending on whether it covered all employees or was only for management staff, whether the training was delivered centrally or by departments and sectors, whether it was face-to-face courses or individual online courses and whether it was mandatory or voluntary. The pattern for most organizations was of a limited amount of 'sheep dip' training for all, often as part of induction programmes, and then more targeted training for different levels of the organization, often on a voluntary basis. However there was no consensus about what was the most appropriate way to deliver training, with pros and cons of each reported.

At PSO, diversity training was part of every employee's induction programme, and other types of more specific training were also mandatory for some groups of managerial staff (for example, specific training for those managing disabled staff). One strand of criticism from line-managers related to the policy of making diversity awareness training compulsory for all managers. Some interviewees agreed that this was necessary to ensure that all managers understood their role and responsibilities, while others considered this inappropriate, as the following quote from a white male manager illustrates:

> It was decided from an organizational point of view that it [diversity] was a good thing and you know, effectively we weren't given the option of ignoring it ... I hesitate to say this, but it was rammed down our throats.

The above comment suggests that not everyone in the organization felt that they had something to gain from DM (contrary to the rhetoric that 'even white men' gain (Kandola and Fullerton 1998)). The issue of whether or not training should be compulsory was also something brought up by trade union representatives at PSO, but their view was that more extensive and specific issue-based training should be compulsory for line-managers, as they felt that there was little time to cover anything in much depth within the induction programme. Interestingly, in the period following our fieldwork at PSO, a new initiative was introduced across the Civil Service called *Delivering a Diverse Civil Service: A 10-Point Plan* (Crown

Copyright 2005) committing PSO to ten key areas for action on diversity and targets for progress in making the Civil Service more diverse. As part of meeting these targets, it was reported that a new programme of mandatory diversity training for all staff across PSO was to be rolled out in 2007–8.

At ServiceCo, it was quite a different story, and its training programme was in its infancy and at the time of fieldwork it had largely only been rolled out to senior managers. The only location where there had been some line-management training was in Transport, but this was only specifically as a response to a costly legal suit in this business sector. Our assessment of the training at ServiceCo at this early stage was that the coverage and quality of training delivered so far were somewhat problematic. For example, as part of our fieldwork, we attended a meeting of the staff forum—an employee involvement mechanism. We had the opportunity to ask those attending to indicate what 'diversity' meant to them. After a lengthy silence, one senior manager started to respond only to be met with an intervention from an HR officer to the effect that the senior managers present should not respond as they had recently attended the training seminar on these issues (and therefore should know the answer). The complete lack of response from staff who had not been through training indicated their lack of awareness of equality and diversity and arguably their need for training. However, some of the comments by senior managers also suggested that there were issues with the quality and content of the training and questions surrounding its effectiveness in conveying the company's message about the need to value diversity. For example, there was a series of comments by some white, male, senior managers present that suggested what had been taken from the training was the need to ensure legislative compliance and not the necessity for behavioural and cultural change throughout the organization. Generally, the short discussion on diversity in the forum we attended produced either (what seemed to be embarrassed) silence from the group or 'old-fashioned' sex/gender jokes from male senior management (see detailed discussion in Chapter 5). Whatever the intention of the speaker, these comments played on stereotypes and were unlikely to encourage the culture change that the HR managers regarded as important.

The content of the training (as evidenced by the course we attended), at the same time as being peppered with statements such as 'Equality and diversity are everyone's responsibility', also tended to support the typical line-management perception that the DM policy was first and foremost an area of HR expertise and responsibility, rather than something affecting their specific job roles, and second, primarily concerned with legislative compliance, meaning avoidance of discrimination. The training did not deal with the issue of what DM would mean for the everyday job of a manager, or how practice would need to change, beyond needing to ensure that they did not fall foul of the legislation. Thus, the following comment from a white, male line-manager at RailSite was therefore not surprising:

I think probably [the Diversity training was] to make us aware how if we do things wrong, the company can be prosecuted. I think that was the general impression I got when I left.

The perceived prioritizing of discrimination avoidance was borne out by the specific emphasis of one of the trainers in the Equality Training seminar. Legislative pitfalls were stressed, with illustration from a recent case where ServiceCo was found guilty of race discrimination, resulting in a large financial penalty. Accordingly, line-managers recalled the primary focus of the seminar as being equality legislation. Beyond this, we did not get the impression that the training helped them to understand what DM might mean for their own jobs; that is, how they might 'manage' or 'value' diversity.

Other weaknesses of the training were observed during the session for senior managers that we attended. This training was to be the template for the training being rolled out company-wide and so is of relevance to a discussion of line-managers. There were several positive dimensions, including use of case study material that provoked debate about whether equality meant same or different treatment; messages about the need for inclusivity and recognizing diversity issues are not always visible and could include issues beyond the workplace. However, the training was itself flawed in some important ways. Due, it appeared, to the inexperience of the trainers, our view as observers was that too much was addressed in too little time; the main aims of the training were unclear, which was compounded by a lack of appropriate facilitation. Perhaps of most concern given the emphasis on discrimination avoidance (legislative compliance), some inaccurate information relating to legislation was given.

Line-Management Involvement in Development of DM Policy

Clearly offering diversity training is not enough to generate line-management buy-in. Indeed, Kandola and Fullerton (1998: 68) explicitly state that many organizations make the mistake of thinking that the way to tackle DM is to offer training sessions, when it needs to encompass processes and systems and the culture and skills of managers. Part of this involves the need for shared ownership of DM (ibid: 83; see also Ross and Schneider 1992: 65). However, the evidence for such shared ownership is severely limited. For example, recent survey research in the UK finds that feelings of ownership of DM decline further down the organizational hierarchy. While 45 per cent of senior managers felt some degree of ownership of DM in their organizations, this declined to 22 per cent for junior (line) managers (CIPD 2007). As discussed in Chapter 2, the mainstream diversity paradigm positions DM as top-down, and certainly the key emphasis in most texts is on the need for senior management commitment. Indeed, looking across eight USA multinational companies,

Wentling and Palma-Rivas (2000) find that the most effort on diversity initiatives is expended on activities concerned with senior management commitment and leadership. Indeed, it is interesting that in their summary of diversity initiatives in these organizations, the role or involvement of line-managers is not mentioned at all, even though DM is clearly positioned as the responsibility of line-managers at the implementation stage by all the organizations they researched. Similarly, McConville and Holden's (1999) case study research in two National Health Service trusts in the UK found that line-managers were being held to answer for the outcomes of policies which have generally been made without their input.

Looking at the involvement of line-managers in our two case studies, we see some distinct differences, although concerns about the level of shared ownership existed at both. As discussed in Chapter 4 more fully, PSO had fairly comprehensive and wide-reaching employee involvement mechanisms, including a number of diversity employee groups and progressive relations with the trade unions. These groups had direct involvement in early drafts of the DM policy and were able to influence changes to initiatives (so, for example, as detailed in Greene and Kirton 2008, concerns regarding the potentially disproportionate effect of the restructuring programme on BME and women staff in lower grades led to specific changes being made to the way selections for redundancy were made). However, while line-managers at PSO are held accountable for DM implementation (including through their performance appraisals), it is notable that, according to documentary evidence, it appears that they would only be involved in the development of DM policy if they were members of the diversity employee groups or employee relations negotiating bodies, of which very few were. Paradoxically, then, it seems that non-managerial staff at PSO may have had more formal opportunities to be directly involved in the development of DM policy at PSO than line-managers. Overall, though, the model at PSO, like so many other organizations, was that the policy was top-down.

At ServiceCo, despite the senior HR manager responsible for the policy stating that DM should be owned by everyone in the organization, there was a distinct lack of wider stakeholder involvement beyond senior managers in the development of the policy and no indication of what taking responsibility for DM would actually mean at line-management level. Indeed, as discussed more fully in Chapter 5, the policy was largely developed in an ad hoc fashion by a small team of people, with little input from other senior managers and no input at all from other stakeholders in the organization.

Line-Management Accountability for DM

The other aspect of McGovern et al's (1997) 'institutional reinforcement of HR' relates to formal recognition of line-managers' role in HR activities in their own performance objectives. Overall the evidence for this is very limited. McGovern et al (1997) found that while five of the eight organizations involved in their study had HR activities formally stated within managers' performance objectives, fewer than half of the managers surveyed actually considered HR activities to be an 'important' or 'very important' factor in their jobs. Having DM objectives included as part of overall performance management is seen as crucial to gaining line-management buy-in (see, for example, Kandola and Fullerton 1998 in the UK or Cox and Blake 1991 in the USA). A review of research in the USA found that organizations that evaluated line-managers' competence in DM had more successful diversity outcomes (Konrad and Linnehan 1995: 430; see also Schneider and North-craft 1999). One report finds that diversity as performance criteria is only used in 19 per cent of organizations in the UK and is only included in the performance appraisals of managers in 16 per cent of organizations (CIPD 2006). More recently, research involving over 800 line-managers in 22 organizations in the UK found that only 26 per cent of line-managers have diversity-related objectives as part of their personal performance reviews, and this is linked to remuneration for only ten per cent (Opportunity Now 2005: 5). There were thus high levels of skepticism amongst line-managers that the organization viewed diversity objectives as important to their success as a manager (ibid: 41). Thus, there does not appear to be strong pressure for managers to give serious consideration to DM.

The issue of diversity objectives for line-managers was brought up by the diversity practitioners we interviewed. Most organizations represented had some form of diversity criteria in performance appraisals for managers, while a large number had diversity objectives for all staff. Some organizations had directly linked compensation to elements of diversity performance. Generally diversity practitioners were positive about the principle of this, although they did recognize the difficulties of establishing meaningful diversity objectives, viewed as more difficult than traditional EO targets, thus again supporting wider academic critiques of whether diversity is 'do-able'. For example, many interviewees spoke of the ways in which having a more diverse workforce made things more difficult for line-managers, but as this quote below illustrates, being able to assess a manager's performance or indicate an identifiable objective on the basis of the behaviours/actions/practices that were seen to comprise DM was seen as particularly problematic:

> [You're] asking them, to manage in a more complex way. Asking them to start managing more flexible working arrangements or virtual teams or home working, so you are asking them to change habits of a lifetime in how they communicate, you know, how they performance manage.

PSO had taken the step of having a specific diversity objective as part of every individual's performance appraisal. However, in practice, as discussed more fully in Chapter 4, a key finding was that line-managers experienced difficulty in working out how to demonstrate the diversity objective, and there were many examples of how it had become tokenistic. For most line-managers at PSO, the diversity objective was not as important as other operational objectives.

At ServiceCo, despite some managers indicating awareness of a business case for DM, diversity was not seen as related to their day-to-day work, as encapsulated by this quote from a white male manager at RoadSite:

> I think it's not going to affect me at all. Because apart from being aware of recent legislation I like to think that, you know, I am fair and I haven't got prejudices towards people. I like to think that I treat everybody as I like to be treated myself. And I think that with that underlying ethos if you like, I don't really think it's a problem.

The need for sub-contractors to comply with equality legislation in order to be able to secure public sector contracts was commented on and therefore the need for managers in charge of contracts to be on top of legislation. However, the widely held view was that in reality equality and diversity issues were not given high priority.

Another question impacting on the role of line-managers is whether diverse teams are easier or more difficult to manage than relatively homogeneous ones. Again, there is conflicting evidence in both the USA and UK literature (for example, Iles 1995; Kossek et al 2003). Even proponents of DM recognize that the likelihood that diversity will promote team creativity and innovation and improve problem solving and decision making is debatable (Kandola and Fullerton 1998). Some research has highlighted the way that diversity in work teams can (or be widely held to) lead to divisions, conflicts and poor interpersonal relations (Schneider and Northcraft 1999), potentially contributing to poor performance. The issue is that if (i) line-managers do not understand the reasons behind the DM policy or what it means for their jobs, and (ii) encouraging more diversity in their work teams or managing in a way which takes specific regard for diversity concerns is more difficult, then (as discussed in a previous section) managers may try and avoid it altogether, beyond the bare minimum they have to do to meet legislative requirements. Thus, this might result in line-managers having a preference for homogenous work groups in order to avoid the extra time and effort they might believe is necessary to manage diverse ones and thus limit damage to operational targets. Part of the reluctance to embrace DM implementation clearly relates to the balance of priorities within the workload of line-managers, where as discussed in the next section, equality and diversity concerns generally come out very low down.

At ServiceCo racialized divisions within workplaces were seen as difficult to manage, but to a large extent as self-imposed by the workers concerned. One white senior manager in Health spoke of his experience: 'You know, the Goan housekeepers, the white housekeepers . . . they separate themselves. And collectively they sit in different groups'. This divide was an established part of the Health culture, but regarded as outside the remit of management to 'manage', and certainly not connected with the DM policy in any way.

The relative place of DM within line-management priorities

The issue of short-term imperatives and heavy workloads is presented as another key constraint on the HR role of line-management (McGovern et al 1997). Gooch and Blackburn (2002: 145) summarize research that suggests that line-managers are selective about which aspects of HR they choose to be involved with and indeed tend to choose those related to short-term business targets (Leach 1995). At the same time as line-managers are being exhorted to take responsibility for HR and to see HR activities as a central concern, most research seems to indicate that the reality of their everyday work lives is that performance objectives are based around short-term and 'hard' targets, such as sales, rather than people management. Similarly, Whittaker and Marchington (2003) find that HR takes second place behind other business needs such as sales, marketing and finance. One would anticipate that as part of their HR responsibilities, DM would also suffer the same fate, and a short-term approach is unlikely to do much to advance the equality and diversity project (see also Dickens 1999). Foster and Harris (2005) clearly indicate how line-managers in their study saw the implementation of diversity initiatives as unattractive when faced with the monitoring of their own performance against operational targets which, as discussed above, usually do not include diversity dimensions. Thus, Schneider and Northcraft (1999: 1455), reflecting on research in the USA, talk about the 'dilemma of managerial participation' in DM. In other words, line-managers are reluctant to engage with DM because the costs and disadvantages appear certain and immediate, while benefits appear likely to take a long time to develop (what they call a 'temporal trap'), and, as individuals, they find it difficult to see what the specific benefits of DM would be for themselves, and thus face a 'collective fence', where they are unable to see past their own short-term interests for the longer term collective good of the organization. A wider, more structural issue is the way that other organizational policies and procedures conflict with DM principles. Indeed, recent research on line-managers in the UK finds that such conflict was seen as the most significant hurdle to applying diversity principles in their management role. In particular, rules about headcount and flexible working or job specifications and criteria for recruitment were seen to make applying good gender equality or diversity principles difficult (Opportunity Now 2005: 36).

The conflict faced by line-managers in terms of competing priorities came across very clearly in our case studies. In PSO, where there was a better understanding of what a business case for DM could look like, some respondents, typically those who were involved in the employee diversity groups, clearly believed that workforce diversity could enhance organizational effectiveness; however, there was some concern expressed that sometimes elements of the policy, such as flexibility, could conflict with organizational goals focused on getting the job done and providing a flexible service to 'customers'. Thus, even empathetic managers were wary of a conflict between DM goals and operational ones. There was an ironic conflict between an emphasis on giving attention to individuals' work–life balance and flexible working needs as part of line-managers' responsibilities for their subordinates, and a view that flexibility was not appropriate in their own jobs. Most line-managers, especially women, felt that to get on in PSO involved working long hours, showing commitment and dedication to their work through 'presenteeism'. This 'long hours culture' often meant that almost all line-managers, regardless of their own identity characteristics, felt under considerable pressure and were disinclined to take on anything that they saw as extra work, such as the diversity agenda. However, the pressure was considered greater for women managers, with some stating that the more senior a woman became the more necessary it was to 'behave like a man' by working long hours, not taking advantage of the flexibility policy and not mixing socially with or showing any concern for lower grades (disproportionately women). This they felt was a problem in terms of changing the culture of PSO to make it more 'woman friendly'. Concerns were voiced by participants at a women's group event where an external speaker talked extensively about her company's experiences of implementing a flexibility policy. The female speaker and many women in the audience expressed concerns about the possible negative effects on future career development if managers choose to work flexibly. In a 'Valuing Diversity' training course, two women managers talked extensively about the flexibility policy and their experience of some senior managers' negative view of it. These women highlighted the difficulties that mothers and other carers have in attending the residential training courses that form part of the management development programme. While within the flexibility policy individuals can be 'exempted' from the requirement to attend such courses, the concern of these women managers was that women in particular could be missing out on important networking and team bonding opportunities that could be significant for future career development. The fact we found that work–life balance issues were exacerbated for women managers at PSO supports wider survey data in the UK (Opportunity Now 2005: 44), that finds that while the need to balance work and family commitments is seen as a major barrier to women's progress in organizations by both male and female line-managers, there was a significant gender difference within this, with 73 per cent of women and 43 per cent of men agreeing with this, respectively.

These concerns also need to be seen within the wider context of threatened staff cuts as part of the restructuring of PSO (see discussion in Chapter 4) as one white woman line manager explained:

So you know it's hard to even get your job done, let alone think about what a lot of people consider to be peripheral issues. So I suppose that's the long way round of saying that diversity is not really mainstreamed. It's not part and parcel of everything you do . . . But people don't have time for the extras. So it's almost like a vicious circle, really.

Such short-termist attitudes are therefore only reinforced when a context of restructuring is added into the mix (McGovern et al 1997). Organizational restructuring, especially where there are potential redundancies within the management layers (so called 'delayering' or 'downsizing'), obviously can lead to larger workloads for the remaining line-managers. This clearly constrains their involvement in activities that do not produce an immediate return. Restructuring pressures thus lead to managers finding even less time to devote to DM activities, because often they are the ones who are expected to implement the restructuring changes (often involving difficult HR tasks and decisions relating to redundancy and job displacement). For this reason, McConville and Holden (1999) see the role of line-manager as exemplifying, like no other role in the organization, the tensions between different groups of staff and the role dissonance that can emerge for them in trying to balance all these different demands. At PSO, it was clear that many line-managers felt under considerable pressure and saw equality and diversity as something else they had to think about, but something of lower priority than their 'real' work, even if some of them showed considerable enthusiasm and support for the principles and aims of DM.

At ServiceCo, line-managers generally seemed to perceive their DM responsibilities as primarily about resolving conflicts and tensions between different groups of employees, usually 'majority' versus 'minority' groups, thus minimizing disruption to operational goals. This lends support to Dickens' (1999) claim of the partial and contingent nature of the business case for DM. There was general acceptance in ServiceCo of strongly gendered (and some racialized) occupational divisions by most staff members we spoke to, particularly line-managers (both male and female). For example, clear patterns of sex and race segregation in both Health and Transport Groups were framed largely as a fact of life and one that was not relevant to question or tackle if they did not pose any managerial problems. One white, male manager at RailSite where no women were employed in operational roles, when asked whether he thought more women could be recruited, commented:

I think there would be a lot of resistance within the workforce. But at the end of the day if they can do the job . . . I think one of the things that may be off-putting is there's a lot of physical, manual labour. Maybe that's off-putting from a female perspective. I think there will be problems but from my own point of view, I'd have to be certain that they were damn good and they could—this is going to be right out of the equality window—the girls who are really tomboys in effect, that can hold their own and take what they get, the jokes and the jaw. We couldn't have a timid sort of character. It would have to be quite a strong sort of character.

The gendered nature of the existing occupational culture is acknowledged, but accepted, here. In fact disrupting the culture by introducing 'different' people was seen as a potential hassle for the manager. A white, female line-manager at HealthSite, considering the possibility of recruiting a man to her all-woman team, presented a mirror image of gendered occupational culture to that given by the manager at RailSite:

It needs to be somebody who can communicate with all different types of people so it would need to be a female in that position anyway. But it's about, could they sit there and listen to them gossip all day long? Because let's face it, you've got a room full of women, they are going to be chatting about last night's *Eastenders* and what they are cooking for tea, as opposed to football or whatever it may be. It's not that you would discriminate but you'd have to be very careful [because it would upset the team].

Thus within the pressurized work demands of the line-manager, and the fact that these divisions did not seem to affect operational goals, it was not seen as something that should be dealt with. Certainly the declared impetus for the ServiceCo DM policy, becoming an employer of choice, was not being supported by managers' recruitment and selection practices.

Within DM, line-managers have often become the central conduit for deciding when, where and how workforce diversity and DM initiatives are important—in Dickens' (1999) terms, they decide when business needs and DM coincide. While in theory DM represents an opportunity for interested and committed managers to get involved in equality and diversity, as we have argued, in practice there is evidence of line-managers' reluctance to give priority to diversity issues (see also Cornelius et al 2000; Maxwell et al 2001). The freedom to manage and to exercise discretion that comes with devolution can also provide an opportunity for line-managers to ignore the equality and diversity agenda. As Cunningham (2000: 706) points out, DM policies clearly run the risk of marginalization or collapse during periods of cut backs. Considering the factors discussed in earlier sections—the lack of clarity surrounding the concept of DM, the range of contextual pressures, the lack of training and involvement and competing demands and workloads—it is not so surprising that for many line-managers, DM is about what is most expedient at the time, which as we have seen, in the case of ServiceCo, may mean that gender and race discrimination are not tackled. It also means that managerial practice is likely to vary highly from individual to individual, even within the same organization. This is not to say that we are arguing that the EO bureaucratic model of consistent practice and same treatment is to be advocated because this has been shown to not always advance equality for all. If there is to be a focus on the business case, then better to have a business case specific to the particular organizational context. As Kirton (2008) points out, the most common position taken by organizations is to put forward very generic, 'best practice' business case arguments for DM. However, there are now a number of writers who highlight the importance of contextualized approaches to diversity management (Janssens and Zanoni 2005; Benschop 2001; Kamenou and Fearfull 2006; Dass and Parker 1999). Those responsible for equality and diversity issues within organizations need to be aware of how the external and internal context affects policy, so that different kinds of difference are likely to have greater salience in some places and certain moments (Prasad et al 2006: 3). Dass and Parker (1999) claim that an organization's diversity approach will depend on the degree of pressure for diversity action, the types of diversity in question and managerial attitudes to diversity. Janssens and Zanoni (2005) identify the role of the customer and profile of customer service as a key determinant to the types of diversity policy and approach that are implemented.

However, it is when this variability of practice is considered to be unfair that it becomes the source of major criticism of line managers. Dickens (1999) alerts us to the fact that devolution to line-managers is not necessarily good news because it represents a shift away from expertise in equality issues within organizations. Recent survey research in the UK (CIPD 2007: 16) finds that 64 per cent of organizations do not have a specialist equality or diversity function and 70 per cent do not have a dedicated budget for equality or diversity activities. In their research into the race equality plan in two UK public sector organizations, Creegan et al (2003) found that devolution of HR and EO to line-managers was seen to have a significantly deleterious effect on the effectiveness of the race equality plan, in that devolution weakened and compromised the centralized monitoring role of the HR function. A key issue was the level of management discretion, leading to practice being highly uneven across the organization, meaning that, in the end, the perception was that responsibility for the tackling of discrimination was being left to the non-managerial staff themselves rather than the line-managers. This can hardly be regarded as effective implementation of DM.

Linking back to Purcell and Hutchinson (2007), if uneven practice is viewed as unfair, then this can have implications for the way that employees view line-managers and, by association, how they view the organization. Indeed, reviewing a number of psychological studies in the USA, Konrad and Linnehan (1995: 416) highlight that consistency of approach is key to employee perceptions of procedural justice, which is deemed to be a crucial determinant of satisfaction with the organization. McGovern et al (1997: 18) found that variations in line-management practice of such things as appraisal inevitably led to a sense of dissatisfaction about perceived fairness of the organization. There is no doubt that in the views of stakeholders in our research organizations, a high level of individual discretion within line-management practice of DM was seen as a considerable disadvantage. As discussed in more detail in Chapter 4, trade union representatives at PSO indicated that they had experienced cases where managers tended to give lower performance ratings to staff in lower grades, thus disproportionately affecting BME employees who were concentrated in these grades. Moreover, this situation was recognized officially as a problem by the organization, as demonstrated in the Diversity Impact Assessment on the Restructuring Process conducted in 2007 (produced in order to comply with the Department's statutory duty as a public sector body to assess and consult on the likely impact of proposed policies on the promotion of equality). Here, an assessment that performance appraisal markings tended to be lower in the lower grades led to a disregarding of these markings within decisions about jobs to be selected for redundancy so as not to unfairly discriminate against disabled and BME staff. This was of course exacerbated by the fact that BME people are under-represented among managers.

The perceived lack of central direction and enforcement meant that how the policy was implemented depended very much on the individual line-manager. Therefore, whether or not flexible working was offered or equality training needs met was the individual manager's decision, meaning that there was wide disparity between practices in different departments/groups. One male BME non-management employee explained:

> Some managers are really good in ensuring that they do keep track of staff. Make sure that their staff know what their rights are, you know, with the changes in the department and the changes within the department and what help is out there if they need it. But other areas, you know, you are basically an individual, isolated, people chucking their own rules in, you know, and that happens quite a lot.

Some non-management participants commented positively on their managers' attention to diversity issues while others reported more negative experiences. For example, consistent with the views of trade union representatives, flexible working hours were seen as possible for some employees but not others. One employee related how her current manager had a very progressive attitude towards flexible working and caring responsibilities, while only 2 years ago, a different manager had told her that in order to care for her sick father, she would have to use her lunch hour.

One clear example of uneven engagement with DM issues is illustrated by line-management views of the employee diversity groups at PSO. There was no overt disapproval of their existence, but it was clear that some managers knew little about them and displayed little interest in their activities. As discussed earlier, others considered that the groups had played and continued to play an important role in improving the situation of women, BME, disabled and lesbian and gay employees. Those with the latter view tended to be involved in an employee group themselves.

It was a similar story at ServiceCo, although it was more difficult to assess given the recent introduction of the policy and the lack of awareness of it by many managers. Trade union representatives and non-managerial employees frequently spoke about the way in which practice depended on the individual manager. For example, views from ServiceCo trade union representatives varied from the relatively positive, 'I think the spirit is there but it doesn't always—you know what I mean', to the more recognizably cynical:

> I think a lot of, like I said with managers and that, I think if the policies, I mean, sometimes they make their own rules up. Or they don't always carry out what they say they are going to do. (White woman, Unison representative at HealthSite)

DISCUSSION: THE REALITIES OF LINE-MANAGEMENT INVOLVEMENT IN DIVERSITY MANAGEMENT

There is no doubt that line-managers have become perhaps the most common scapegoat for why DM in practice does not meet the expectations of policy statements. However, rather than simply blaming line-managers and seeing them as the barrier to successful DM, there is a need to understand their perspectives—the pressures they are under and the views they hold—all of which could prevent line-management 'buy-in' and by extension prevent the policy from achieving its aims.

Many organizations are grappling with how to make DM a 'core competency' so that managers have to demonstrate how they build diversity into their own performance and goals (Schneider 2001). What comes out clearly from our case study research is that line-managers face many conflicting priorities, including heavy workloads and tight deadlines and that these difficulties (as discussed in Chapter 2) might lead them to opt out of actively 'managing diversity'. In a context where restructuring is a common and regular feature of organizational life, the pressures on line-managers are exacerbated. In the PSO case, as discussed in Chapter 4, the public sector has undergone such extensive changes over the last 20 years or so that the pressures that line-managers are under are magnified to the extent that they might even feel 'besieged' (Cunningham 2000). Further, reflecting the under-representation of women and BME people (and other 'minority' groups) among the ranks of managers, there are simply too few managers who genuinely feel that they have something to gain from DM. Our findings also support a view that line-managers' understanding of DM, its rationale and what practices are expected from them is extremely uneven and often very limited. However, for some line-managers, it might not simply be a question of lack of time or commitment, but rather that they might genuinely be at a loss to understand exactly what it is they are supposed to do to demonstrate that they value diversity (Foster and Harris 2005).

One issue is that while line-managers have responsibility for certain areas of HR practice, they have little influence upwards on the way in which policies are developed because they are so far removed from strategic planning. Indeed, rather than 'responsibility', McConville and Holden state that line-managers are given 'liability' for HR issues (essentially accountability without authority). Their overriding view is that the experience of line-managers was of being 'piggy in the middle: caught between the directives of their seniors and the exigencies of the service on the one hand, and the demands and the problems of their staff and the consumers of the service on the other' (1999: 421). Given the difficulties faced with devolution and the myriad of constraints on line-managers, it is not so surprising that the extent of devolution is limited. At the same time, attempts to devolve responsibility, or at least the aspiration (even if only in rhetoric) to do so, have made line-managers' jobs particularly difficult. 'The incumbents of the role are far from being power-hungry, self-serving individuals, seeking a means to justify their existence. Rather they are fulfilling a vital role in balancing tensions and mediating potential conflict, often at personal, emotional cost' (McConville and Holden 1999: 422).

Therefore, despite the hold of the diversity discourse, with its central focus on valuing and utilizing individual differences, the investigation of line-management involvement offers an explanation for why so much actual practice looks very similar to traditional EO. For Foster and Harris (2005: 14), despite the myriad of corporate diversity statements acknowledging the importance of employing and valuing a diverse workforce, line-managers reported that a standardized approach to dealing with employee differences (associated with an EO paradigm) was seen as more sustainable and workable. This is particularly the case within the recently fast changing UK legislative context, and, we would add, within HRM models that have line-management accountability at their centre. For Foster and Harris (2005: 14), coming back to fair procedures and standardized rules was a preferred comfort zone for line-managers: 'implementing innovative diversity practices that require the application of personal judgement and discretion may well seem unattractive to line managers preoccupied with their own performance against functional operational targets and concerned about the increasing complexity of employment law'. This is accentuated given the lack of equality and diversity training and expertise of many line-managers, thus meaning that falling back on the 'rule book' is a much safer option than risking innovation. This goes some way to explaining why most line-managers at both PSO and ServiceCo were unwilling to think beyond compliance with legal requirements, and why they continue to be perceived to be a key obstacle to DM within the organizations.

8 Employee Experiences of Diversity Management

By Chris Creegan

INTRODUCTION

This chapter focuses specifically on the perspectives and experiences of non-management employees on DM within our two case study organizations, government department PSO and multi-divisional private sector company ServiceCo. Just as with the HRM literature (Legge 1998), research on the implementation of equality and diversity policies has typically focused on the perspectives and experiences of managers and professionals within organizations, in particular those responsible for policy development. However, less attention has been paid specifically to those on the receiving end of HRM and DM initiatives—that is, lower level, non-management employees or those on the 'sticky floor' of organizations. Yet it is at this level that employees (the recipients of policy and amongst those intended to benefit from its implementation) have to deal with the messy reality that can derive from organizational rhetoric.

This organizational level has been referred to elsewhere as the 'stone floor' where the most pronounced inequalities prevail (Richards 2001), arguably as a result of the failure of top-down managerial initiatives and the absence of a 'transformative approach' to EO (Cockburn 1991). The lack of attention to the perceptions of those at this level of organizations is perhaps surprising. It could be argued that a key test of the effectiveness of any HR policy (including DM) may be the extent to which it resonates with employees and is perceived by them to be implemented effectively. Clark et al (1998) argue compellingly that it is important to examine the 'receiving end' of HRM for four reasons: (i) individuals are the primary recipients and 'consumers' of HRM initiatives; (ii) the individual is the prime arbiter of HRM; (iii) individuals are where the 'adjustment burden' is typically placed (i.e. they are expected to change); and (iv) individuals are the central, non-passive, co-creating actors in the conceiving, implementing and reconstructing of HR strategies. Clark et al argue that if we are to gain a full understanding of HRM, then the 'inside view' must become more prominent. Since DM is an integral component of HRM, these arguments apply equally to DM. Indeed the recognition within HRM of the importance of paying attention to the way in which employees are managed within organizations means that HRM itself offers potential advantages for promoting equality (Kirton and Greene 2005a), suggesting that the effective implementation of both is necessarily co-dependent.

We explore employee experiences and perspectives using a framework, which was developed during analysis of data concerning employee perceptions of the implementation of equality policy within organizations (Creegan et al 2003). This framework consists of four key elements: employee perceptions of the *culture* of organizations and of the *ownership, performance* and *efficacy* of policy. In other words, it is concerned with the context in which policy operates, the extent to which it is carried out, who is responsible for it and whether it achieves the desired result. Although the framework was originally developed analyzing perceptions of the implementation of a race equality policy, it provides a sufficiently broad lens through which to view equality and diversity policies more generally and in this instance of the development of *diversity management*.

In 1987, prior to the rise of DM in the UK, Jewson and Mason (1987) argued that there are four key dimensions to EO policies, each of which requires different procedures of investigation. These were the existence of a formal programme embodying procedures that can be demonstrated to be fair, the practical implementation of the programme, the effectiveness of the programme and workforce perceptions of the programme. Though distinct, these dimensions are clearly interconnected. Jewson and Mason (1987: 128) suggested that an investigation of workforce perceptions involves an examination of whether the policy is seen 'to be fair, to have been implemented and to be effective'. Yet in the succeeding 20 years, even where research about DM (and EO) policies and practices has discussed the employee context, it has rarely been with regard to their perceptions about such issues. It is of course important to make a distinction between DM and EO. However, as discussed in Chapter 2, whilst the distinction can be quite explicit amongst experts, both researchers and practitioners, in practice it is often far less so. Indeed, in the UK, the term 'equality and diversity' has become common, suggesting that though different EO and DM are not considered to be mutually exclusive (Kirton and Greene 2005a).

Indeed, the meaning of the term DM and what it implies for the management of employees is contested. Liff (1997, 1999) has identified four versions, two of which are particularly salient for our discussion. The 'dissolving differences' approach focuses on *individual* differences and recognizes the unique contribution of each employee and the need to maximize individual potential. In contrast, the 'valuing differences' approach recognizes the different contributions that employees might make because of their *social group* membership (for instance, ethnic group). This difference in interpretation has real implications for those managing employees and for employee perceptions of the fairness of policy. With regard to how managers manage employees, Foster and Harris (2005) have suggested that while the business benefits attributed to DM may be appealing to employers, it is an approach that may lack clarity for line-managers both in terms of what it is and how it should be implemented within the legal framework of EO. They found that line-managers were familiar with the value of demonstrating a consistent approach to decision making, i.e. treating people in the same way as the key means of avoiding accusations of discrimination. As a consequence, they regarded a DM approach, concerned with recognizing and being responsive to individual differences amongst employees, as more likely to lead to feelings of unfairness and claims of unequal treatment. They conclude that, in the implementation of DM within organizations, employers need to take greater account of the tensions facing line-managers, the way in which they interpret DM and perceptions of fair treatment amongst the workforce as well as the operational context. This is discussed in more detail in Chapter 7.

Similar tensions surrounding manager–employee relations within the DM paradigm have been explored elsewhere, for example by Zanoni and Janssens (2004) who found that managers they interviewed tended to resort to stereotypes to explain differences and were interested only in how such differences could be deployed in relation to organizational goals. In some cases, differences were interpreted by managers as deficiencies (of skills, competencies, dispositions, attitudes etc). This could provide a managerial rationale for not appointing, promoting or rewarding employees. Alternatively, differences were interpreted as vulnerabilities, and consequently such employees were considered to be more compliant and malleable to managerial demands. They conclude that 'diversity is conceived in a very selective and instrumental way with reference to the productive process in the specific organizational context. In this way, these diversity discourses clearly reflect existing power relations between management and employees in the organization' (Zanoni and Janssens 2004: 71). This is all bound to influence employee perceptions of DM.

Before turning to a brief review of further relevant literature in the field, it is worth reflecting on why employee perceptions of DM have largely been neglected by diversity research. There are three possible explanations for this. First, DM is essentially a managerial concept. It denotes and even advocates an approach to equality and diversity that is driven from the top down within organizations by managers. This provides a strong incentive for enquiry to focus on managers as the actors most centrally involved in its delivery and implementation within organizations. Second, because DM embodies such a top-down approach, insofar as it points researchers towards employees, it does so in terms of the ways in which they are managed and the effect of that approach on issues such as organizational performance and workplace relations. In this sense, it encourages researchers to focus on employees as the *passive recipients* of policy rather than *active participants* in shaping it. Third, as we found ourselves in the course of this research, conducting research with employees poses significant challenges in terms of research design, practice and ethics. It requires intensive resources to achieve robust purposive sampling of employees within organizations; a sensitive approach to data collection which creates walls of confidentiality within the organizations being studied and extensive negotiations with gatekeepers within organizations over the nature and level of access to employees.

A brief review of recent literature on DM and EO soon reveals that, insofar as attention has been paid to the employee context, consideration of employee perceptions of the *impact of policy* on them as individuals or on the culture of the in which they work is largely absent. Brandling and Mistral (2005) note that much DM literature may be seen as implying that diverse workforces are potentially problematic and that the model has concentrated on the perspective of the employer, i.e. those with the power to implement DM in practice, rather than focusing on those subject to such practices at the level of the workplace. Similarly, other authors (Prasad and Mills 1997; Lorbiecki and Jack 2000) have criticized the way that DM is often presented as something that 'is done' to employees by managers and in which employees themselves have no active part to play.

More commonly, DM and EO literature has focused on the employee context in relation to *organizational performance, culture, employee performance and motivation* or *employee attitudes and behaviours*. Literature has, for example, explored the relationship between employee perceptions of diversity within the senior management team and other management levels of their organizations and their perceptions of performance (Allen et al 2008), the relationship between diversity and business performance (Human Resource International Management Digest 2005) and the encouragement of innovation within organizations (Trevan and Mulej 2007). Consideration of the cultural dimension has included examining the challenges of managing a culturally diverse workforce in a specific context (Devine et al 2007; Hunt 2007) and an investigation of the perceived similarity in cultural values for identification with work team and organization (Luijters et al 2008). Examples of an employee performance and motivation focus include consideration of the relationship between specific employee groups such as black and minority ethnic (BME) workers and issues such as absenteeism (Avery et al 2007) or retention (McKay et al 2007). Finally, employee attitudes and behaviours have provided a further focus, for example, the relationship between diversity attitudes and norms and workplace diversity initiatives (Linnehan et al 2006) and the relationship between DM and the way in which employees engage with control in organizations (Zanoni and Janssens 2007). There is also a lot of talk about DM being the responsibility of everyone, non-management employees included (Kandola and Fullerton 1994). However, what is largely missing is any discussion of employee *rights* and the extent to which employees regard DM as addressing their rights and interests.

Where research has focused on employee perceptions of the impact of DM or EO policy, a number of issues emerge. These include concerns about implementation, the quality of management delivery, the role of line-managers, the focus of policy and variations in perspective amongst different groups of employees. Concerns about implementation have centred on the rhetoric and the reality of policies, whether in fact such policies have had sufficient impact on a culture of (in)equality within organizations despite a formal commitment to do so (Liff and Cameron 1997). Research has shown that though senior managers within organizations may believe that policies are being actively implemented and are not an 'empty shell' (Hoque & Noon 2004), employee perceptions may differ (Deem and Morely 2006). In Creegan et al's (2003) study of the implementation of policy within a local authority, employee perceptions of the rhetoric and reality of policy delivery were linked to concerns about strategy and operation. First, there was the question of whether strategy was sufficiently robust given the deeply embedded culture of discrimination it was designed to challenge. Second, there was the question of whether the operational implementation of strategy was successful particularly in terms of the role and responsibilities of line-managers, an issue we will turn to in a moment.

Elsewhere research has revealed that employees do not necessarily have confidence in the delivery of policy by managers. For example, Heer and Atherton (2008) point to a lack of confidence amongst Asian employees in the probation service about the way in which their managers have addressed diversity issues. Such concerns can of course contribute to a sense that inequalities are not being tackled even if organizations are actively attempting to address equality and diversity issues. Responding to such concerns within one section of the health service, Bogg et al (2006) have argued that employees at all grades and levels must be empowered to feel motivated and make policy a reality, to ensure that policies and guidelines link to employee perceptions of workplace reality.

Creegan et al's (2003) research also raised employee concerns about the role of line-managers. It was felt by employees that the devolution of responsibility for policy implementation from HR specialists to line-managers had diluted the effectiveness of policy implementation and resulted in line-managers making decisions unchecked. These concerns echo arguments raised previously about the expertise and commitment of line-managers to equality issues (Dickens 1998; GLEA 2000). This touches on the issue of the extent to which mainstreaming the delivery of DM and EO policies is effective. Lawrence's (2000) findings based on a study of equal opportunities officers' perspectives suggests that mainstreaming may have both advantages and disadvantages, but that there are other factors which impact on the value of specialist officers shouldering the responsibility for policy implementation, including the support they receive from senior managers and their own level of seniority. Arguably these are both issues that could be applicable to line-managers.

Deem and Morely's (2006) research about staff perceptions of EO policies in higher education institutions raises the issue of the focus of policy and who is intended to benefit from its implementation. There was a sense amongst employees that student equality was ultimately accorded a higher priority than staff equality. This was combined with a view that the implementation of policy tended to rely on a recognitional and cultural approach to inequality rather than a redistributive one. In other words, employees felt that it would do little to address material inequalities such as pay gaps, lack of access to training and development opportunities. It could be argued that such an approach results in differences being dissolved rather than valued within organizations (Liff 1997, 1999). Or even if differences are valued, it is at a rhetorical level, rather than rooted in practical action to tackle inequalities.

Those affected by discriminatory practices within organizations may inevitably be more aware of the existence of such practices (Acker 2000), and this has been shown to be an important factor in shaping their perceptions of the implementation of policy. For example, in Creegan et al's (2003) study, a notable feature of workforce perceptions was the extent to which they were racialized and gendered. The perceptions of BME women were firmly rooted at the more critical end of a spectrum of opinion, while those of white men were at the other. It is also worth bearing in mind that attitudes towards different groups at work are not necessarily uniform (Creegan and Robinson 2008) and that perceptions of the existence of inequality within organizations may also vary. For example, Deem and Morely's (2006) research revealed that respondents were mostly likely to focus on occupational inequalities and inequality relating to gender or race. Those reporting other types of discrimination, such as discrimination based on sexual orientation, disability and religion, were thinner on the ground.

PERCEPTIONS OF ORGANIZATIONAL CULTURE

Before turning directly to employee experiences of DM in the case study organizations, it is worth setting the scene with a mention of employee perceptions of organizational culture. Previous equality and diversity research suggests that perceptions of the rhetoric and reality of policy need to be considered within the 'appreciative context' of organizations—that is, the 'constellation of images, beliefs, judgements and values', which contribute to the prevailing culture within organizations (Young 1992: 259). Indeed, it has been argued that EO policies and practices are unlikely to secure equal treatment on their own unless employers are able to develop an environment and culture that enables equality of opportunity to flourish (Hoque and Noon 2004). Arguably, this is particularly relevant when considering the impact of DM, since it is an approach that is supposed to seek to incorporate equal opportunities considerations into the design and delivery of organizational strategy and performance.

Our research with employees within the two case study organizations reveals very different perceptions of organizational culture amongst employees both within and between the organizations. In ServiceCo, there was a perception, at least amongst some white male employees in RoadSite, of an open culture where people were encouraged to share their views.

> They are on the ball with anything that relates to the workforce. Very quick on getting anything out and either discuss it or, we have meetings, there are more chats about different things and we're given the opportunity to talk very freely.

It was argued that opinions could be given to senior managers without fear of criticism or repercussion, and there was a view that openness and fairness were instilled into people. In this part of the company, there was an overwhelmingly male workforce, but this gender segregation was seen as inevitable due to the nature of the work and men perceived women as being fairly represented within the workforce. The lack of female operatives was not seen as connected to equality and diversity, but rather a natural reflection that such jobs appealed more to men. The physical nature of the work undertaken, for example on the roads, was seen as a barrier to employing disabled people as well as women. This reflects a view expressed in previous research that gender segregation in employment is often perceived as relating to 'individual choices and natural gender differences' rather than inequalities in society (Howard and Tibballs 2003: 8). However, while there was an implicit assumption in the responses of some male operatives that their work was 'men's work', others appeared to take a broader view:

> I am happy to work with anybody to do the job properly. It doesn't bother me, you know, if it's a woman or you know whatever race. Workers are workers aren't they? It wouldn't affect me at all.

Elsewhere in the company at HealthSite, BME female employees seemed to feel valued in a variety of ways. For example, one said that '[Co-workers and managers] talk to us very nicely and if there is anything, they make us understand. It's nice that they talk to us'. Their responses suggested that they did not see any difficulties arising from their 'difference', including in relation to language, which was in general something mentioned as problematic amongst white employees. It was suggested by white co-workers that they 'kept themselves to themselves', talking in their own language in their own 'little group', and that they could be difficult to understand. For the BME staff themselves, although it was acknowledged that there could be difficulties because of language barriers, it was suggested that this was also a positive reason for staff speaking a minority language to work together in the same area. There was even an implicit suggestion that they were more likely to understand the situations and be supportive of each other. Like gender segregation, then, segregation of the workforce by race was not generally perceived as a problem or issue to be tackled.

At HealthSite, the general feeling amongst employees was that, because the composition of the workforce was mixed in terms of age and ethnicity, ServiceCo *de facto* had a positive attitude towards equality, and that everyone was treated the same—a good thing. There was also evidence of positive feelings about their experiences of the company's attitude to people with caring responsibilities:

> [My manager] is very in touch with people who have got children and if there is a problem, he is very good about that. You could go to him and apologise and say I've got a little one and I can't . . . he's got children of his own, so he understands the problem.

However, it is worth noting that there is no awareness or expectation of policy here. The manager's flexibility in relation to diverse needs was credited to his personal empathy. This could of course be interpreted in a variety of ways. On the one hand, it could be taken to mean that the delivery of DM is really mainstreamed in everyday management handling of different employees' needs. On the other hand, it could be that managers in practice exercise discretion in ways that are influenced by their personal circumstances rather than by any policy requirement. Either way it is not clear that the existence or the role of policy is transparent to the employee, and it could of course result in inconsistent treatment of staff in similar situations. Indeed, as is discussed later in this chapter, there was variable understanding and awareness of the policy and its initiatives by employees. At HealthSite, in a more negative vein, there was also a sense that the culture of the organization had changed with outsourcing, although it should be noted that the link between this and specific diversity issues was not made. A perception of a 'real division' had arisen between lower paid clerical and ancillary employees whose jobs had been outsourced and health professionals such as nurses remained NHS employees. It was argued that previously it had been 'friendlier', like 'one big family, all pulling in the same direction, but that now there was a sense of 'them and us'.

There were differences in the perceptions of culture at RailSite. In some instances, contradictions were apparent within the perceptions of an individual employee. For example, a woman administrative worker at RailSite was initially very positive about her workplace, but on reflection acknowledged that there were problems:

> I mean, as you see, you've had a walk around the office, it's quite a mixed organization . . . But I mean, pretty much gels together, everybody just gets on with everybody really. There's not been any discrimination of any kind at all, really. Whether it's gender, race or religion. So I mean, it's probably, it's not a bad environment to work for . . . you do get, I tell you the truth, some men are really rude to women. Seriously. Seeing is believing, trust me. One guy has like PMT everyday. All the guys laughed about it because it was one of the things that was expected from him . . . he's been off sick now. So that makes it a bit easier for me.

Here at RailSite, therefore, workplace culture is underpinned by gendered norms found in society at large and that generally go unquestioned. Further, what appeared to be an ongoing culture of harassment seems to be accepted by management, in that no intervention seems to have been made. The contradictory perception of equality and diversity within the workplace is manifest in the assertion of no gendered discrimination, followed immediately by the acknowledgement that some men are routinely rude to women. However, this was not construed by employees as a form of sexual harassment or gender-based discrimination. Such behaviour seems to fall into the category of 'sex-role spillover' identified by Gutek (1985) in single gender-dominated workplaces. This suggests that people's perceptions of equality and diversity are of something formal and institutionally driven, rather than in relation to the 'normal' continuum of day-to-day behaviour. The organization and the actors within it are separated in the minds of employees when assessing the efficacy of equality and diversity policy. So in fact gendered discrimination may be commonplace with the organization, but this does not render the organization guilty of gender discrimination in the eyes of employees or by implication in breach of its policy. This is an example of the 'space between words' that in practice exists within an organization, which has adopted a formal policy but not transformed the workplace culture(s) within it (Young 1987).

Within the government department PSO, a more homogenous picture emerged. Here there was a general sense that what mattered was whether your face fitted and who you knew rather than what you knew. Gradism was seen as widespread and meant that junior employees felt overlooked and undervalued. Gradism is a term that is commonly used in the Civil Service and describes the discrimination people can feel is used against them just because they are in a lower grade or the threat people of higher grades can feel when their status is undermined. It has a strong bearing on how communication occurs inside and between central government organizations (National Audit Office 2006). Examples of gradist practices in the Civil Service cited in previous research conducted for the National Audit Office (NAO) include people not being allowed to communicate directly with more senior ranked people in other divisions or other organizations, but having instead to route communication upwards to someone in their own division of the same rank as the 'target' person to be contacted. In our research, it is important to note that there is a clear intersection with race and gradism since BME workers are under-represented in the higher grades and over-represented in the lower grades (see Chapter 4). However, it should be noted that employees we talked to rarely articulated this link explicitly. Comments about gradism also fitted in with fears for jobs more generally as well, and interestingly, here, explicit links were made between downsizing and the potentially disproportionate effect on BME employees which is discussed in much greater detail in Chapter 4.

As is discussed in more detail later, while the knowledge of the policy document was more widespread amongst employees at PSO than at ServiceCo, the prevailing equality culture tended to be described as a 'file it and forget it' or a 'tick box' approach. The diversity objective contained within the performance appraisal system was frequently alluded to in this respect. One research participant did not think this was looked at seriously by managers:

> Diversity is a prominent issue like you say but I only fill it out once a year and then it doesn't get reviewed until the next year when I do it again. Management just aren't concerned about anything to do with the [performance appraisal].

Even positive messages could have a de-motivating effect because they were seen as hollow, creating an underlying sense of contradiction. This experience appears to run counter to the findings of previous research on UK employers and equality policies. It has been suggested that public service organizations, once they develop equality policies, are more likely to make efforts to implement them than private sector employers and therefore less likely to have 'empty shell' policies (Hoque & Noon 2004).

One view was that the workforce was increasingly diverse, though it was acknowledged that this was not necessarily reflected across the organization or at all levels. There was an understanding that the intention was to achieve a mixed workforce in terms of gender and race, something our respondents valued highly.

> Diversity is increasing. Where I work I was the only ethnic minority out of seventy for a number of years, but now more Asians and Blacks [sic] are coming in.

> In recent years, there has been an awareness of cultural diversity [here]. How long it will take to achieve I don't know . . . I can see quite a few young ethnic minorities have been promoted, so you could say that it's going in the right direction.

In addition, employees shared the view of other stakeholders (line-managers and trade union representatives in particular) that there had been substantial improvement in terms of promotion and visibility in senior jobs of women (something confirmed by demographic statistics; see Chapter 4). However, this was not viewed to be the case for BME employees. Indeed, there was a perceived lack of promotion opportunities for BME staff and even a suggestion that the way to progress was to 'bow down' to management.

The attitude of management in PSO was characterized as conservative coupled with an atmosphere of caution. It was suggested that they did not like 'pushy people' and that it was therefore best to 'keep your head down'. The consequence for some was that people were quiet at meetings in part because they were concerned about being labelled as trouble-makers. Overall, a picture emerged of low morale and despondency, sometimes combined with a sense of insecurity. Employees sometimes felt ground down and not valued. The result was that they felt they were 'just coming into work and doing a job'.

> Are junior staff valued? It's difficult to say. I think we're still overlooked and taken for granted . . . we are just the little man.

To emphasize, this perspective has to be set against the fact that women and BME people are over-represented in the lower, non-management, non-career track grades.

PERCEPTIONS OF THE OWNERSHIP
OF DIVERSITY MANAGEMENT

It has been suggested that the discourse of DM is primarily aimed at managers rather than employees, particularly those who are sceptical about a more traditional EO approach (Noon 2007). It tends to encourage managers to take ownership of diversity with the result that its identity in the workplace is associated with a top-down management agenda. The effect is arguably that employees at the sticky floor of organizations do not or are given little space to own diversity. This has even been seen as an advantage of a DM approach over an EO approach because it 'depoliticizes' the issues. This is a major paradox because even the strongest advocates of DM argue that it is everyone's responsibility (e.g. Kandola and Fullerton 1994).

Amongst employees a key starting point when considering ownership of the policy is to establish the level of understanding and awareness within the workforce. This provides an indication of whether policy has been communicated effectively by management, whether by senior or middle managers.

Within PSO there was a varied level of awareness of policy. In general employees were for example aware that a policy document could be viewed on and downloaded from the intranet. However, typically they had not read the document, clearly indicating their perceptions of its lack of applicability to their working lives. There was some awareness of the different employee diversity groups that had been established within the department. And here there was some evidence of a greater degree of shared ownership, through the participation of employees in those groups, suggesting some employee involvement in policy implementation. This was limited, however, and the prevailing message was that communication about the existence of the groups was not reaching all employees. Various reasons were advanced for this, including information overload and difficulties getting time off to attend events. These difficulties appeared in part to be related to the fact that the perception was that, in general, managers did not value diversity events sufficiently, perhaps a refection of the wider problem of paying 'lip-service' to diversity, while in fact being more focused on the bottom line. As a consequence, employees may have felt reluctant to attend the groups either because it might lead to them being labelled as 'trouble makers' or because they were for career-minded individuals who did not wish to damage their promotion prospects.

In ServiceCo, there was widespread lack of awareness of the policy, and the overall impression was that DM was something that was done to employees rather than something they were actively involved in. Indeed, there was little evidence at all of bottom-up pressure for diversity initiatives. The clearest indication of this was the lack of understanding of the meaning of diversity itself or of its connection to equality. At HealthSite, non-management employees were largely ignorant of the concept of diversity, but there was generally some understanding of the concept of equality, albeit that this was conveyed in very basic terms and did not appear to emanate from policy communicated by the company, but from everyday, commonsense understanding. For example, an employee at HealthSite suggested that as all employees worked for the same company and put in the same degree of effort, they should all be treated in the same way.

At both transport sites within ServiceCo, there was a similar range of reactions. As with managers, equality was equated to fairness and diversity was either stated as not understood or connected to work organization, for example, being allowed to do different jobs or job sharing. At RoadSite, while the notion of equality resonated with respondents, for example, as being related to fairness or equal treatment, understanding of the concept of diversity was more patchy and only understood in exceptional cases, for example, by a graduate trainee:

> I think it just means that there is a range of people, everybody is different and even though there might be groups of people who are different to another group, recognizing the fact that there are distinct groups there, it's probably mostly to do with diversity, and then I suppose the equality bit comes into it. Recognizing that even though there are these distinct groups, we are equal anyway.

In contrast, the lack of understanding was particularly pronounced amongst white male manual employees for whom it did not resonate in the same way as the concept of equality:

> [Diversity and equality] are big words, they are. . . . Can you explain what those words mean? [Diversity] is still a word that I don't understand. [Equality is] you know, everybody is treated the same and no matter what colour, the same and everybody is treated properly. The diversity, I ain't up on that word, I have been in a gang [work group] now for [a long time]. I don't read many books.

This general lack of understanding suggested a failure on the part of the company to communicate and explain the basis of DM policy to non-management employees, what the aims were and what employees could expect from it. At RoadSite, there was some awareness amongst operatives that meetings about equality had taken place, but no evidence of direct communication or involvement.

> I haven't seen a great deal as such, but they bombard you with that much paperwork sometimes, and you know, it's hard to, most of it's safety and everything. I can't remember seeing anything specific about it but I might be wrong.

Administrative staff similarly reported that they could not recall equality and diversity coming up at team briefings or being asked for their views.

> I mean, we have team briefings every month so I am sure there must have been something within that, that's come up, but I couldn't put my finger on anything.

As at PSO, there was some awareness that the equality policy was on the intranet, but the impression was that the articulation of policy was remote and not particularly accessible:

> Yes, but I am sure it is in paper form somewhere. I don't think it's in this office stuck on a notice board saying "This is the equality policy or this is the rules". There is nothing in this office that is stuck on a wall like that. Yes, I am sure if you rang, if you haven't got a computer and you rang to head office "I can't get on the intranet site will you print it off and send it to me", or somebody sat next to you could print it off from their computer.

A further noticeable aspect of the level and nature of employee awareness of equality and diversity in both organizations related to the perceived coverage or possible relevance of policy to different diversity strands within the workforce. Observations tended to focus on race, gender and, to a lesser extent, disability, with little mention of the other more recently recognized equality strands, sexual orientation, age and religion. This was also true of references to the type and extent of discrimination within the respective workforces. This mirrors both the findings (see, for example, Deem and Morely 2006 above) and indeed the focus previous research and is particularly interesting in the context of a shift from EO to DM.

Arguably, DM should facilitate greater awareness of other strands because of its focus on differences across the whole workforce. However, in practice, this may depend on the extent to which differences are 'valued' or 'dissolved' in the formulation and implementation of policy (Liff 1997, 1999). Where differences are not proactively valued through the explicit promotion of policy, they may in effect become dissolved. Differences that are often less visible anyway, including disability, sexual orientation and religion, may be particularly vulnerable here. Amongst employees in these organizations, acknowledgement of the significance of race and gender threaded through the perspectives of all employees. In contrast, references to disability and sexual orientation, for example, tended largely to be confined to workers belonging to those groups.

More generally, the low level of understanding could also suggest that DM, like other contemporary management practices such as quality management, is a 'slippery concept' (Wilkinson et al 1998), which for employees contains terminology that is nebulous and open to interpretation (Glover and Noon 2005). It also suggests a very large gap between the discourse of managers and that of employees. It is interesting to reflect on the parallels with The Future Foundation's suggestion that the public is comprehensively not 'on board' with current approaches of equality professionals (Howard and Tibballs 2003). These 'equality professionals'—'policy makers, academic sociologists, think tanks and women's representative groups' (2003: 42)—operate with an analysis of structural inequality that simply is not shared by the British public. In this context, The Future Foundation suggest that:

> A new vision of equality needs to be set out that makes clear the social, organizational and individual benefits of a more equal society. . . . A new language needs to be developed, based on people's current understandings and perceptions, to help make the connections between recognition of prejudice and the need for societal change. (2003: 10)

PERCEPTIONS OF THE PERFORMANCE OF DIVERSITY MANAGEMENT

We turn now to perceptions of performance, that is to say the extent to which employees felt that DM was being put into effect. The dominant story across both employers was of an 'implementation gap' (Young 1992;

Creegan et al 2003). However, the narrative about this was more explicit in the accounts of PSO respondents.

At PSO, the implementation gap was described in terms of both a failure to implement altogether and uneven implementation. Perceptions of a failure to implement policy were conveyed by a strong sense of a gulf between paper and practice:

> There is a cynicism, you read it and it's just management speak, lip service, they don't really mean it. So many things don't happen.

Diversity employee groups established to facilitate the involvement of employees from particular groups with the workforce (including women, BME workers, disabled workers and lesbian, gay, bisexual and transgender workers) in the implementation of policy were largely seen as 'talking shops' and 'toothless'. This was ironic given that the motivations of those involved in such groups typically included a desire to bring about policy change and challenge discriminatory practices. While some participants had been involved and spoke positively of initiatives their groups had taken, there was widespread ignorance of the existence of the groups. It was clear that communication about the existence of the groups and their activities was not reaching all employees. Concern was expressed that meetings were not well publicized and lacked the necessary attendance and input from senior staff. As one participant commented on finding out that four out of six people in his focus group did not know about the diversity groups:

> You see, they should know about it, they do some very high profile events. Sometimes they can't see the relevance because it's nothing to do with their job. They think 'why should we come here?

The overall impression given was that intentions were well placed, but lacked the impetus of implementation. There was a sense of a lot of 'talk the talk' but not a lot actually being done.

> It's just on the surface, it's just words. It's easy to write things down but the people who are going to put into practice are indifferent to it.

This suggests perceptions of a lack of organizational drive to implement policy, though how far this could be attributed to a lack of management commitment or to 'circumvention by manipulation' was a moot point (Jewson and Mason 1986).

In PSO, there were also recurrent accounts of uneven implementation that was associated with devolution to line-management. Managers were felt to differ considerably in the way they approached equality and diversity issues. A key indicator of managerial attitudes was the extent to which they were associated with a progressive attitude towards flexible working. For example, one employee reported both positive and negative experiences with different managers. In practice, the policy of flexibility was not necessarily considered to be available to everyone, which could result in a feeling of poor work–life balance. The discretion of individual managers played a large part in whether or not employees could work flexibly. This is an example of the dangers of devolution working against equality objectives that have been highlighted in much earlier research (e.g. Collinson et al 1990).

Thus, a further key aspect of unevenness was the extent to which managers were seen to exercise discretion in relation to the implementation of policy. Concern was expressed that managers failed to prioritize equality and diversity issues and that they were insufficiently challenged and made accountable for the implementation of policy by senior managers.

> Line managers can read something but do what they want. If they are not that way inclined they are difficult to change. . . .it needs to come from the top.

The above is an interesting point because in principle the policy does 'come from the top', but the problem is that managers are given discretion in terms of how they interpret and apply it locally. If a manager argues that allowing an employee to work flexibly would hinder operational goals, then the request can be denied. Associated with this was a concern that the human resources function had insufficient authority. The implication here was that traditionally, the central personnel department had exerted greater control, but that line-managers were now able to exercise greater discretion in the operation of policy with limited interference.

In ServiceCo, there was generally a qualified response to the 'realities' of management practice. Like PSO, there was, for example, a perception that high-profile events on diversity were not necessarily connected to day-to-day practice and a sense that managers were not sufficiently committed. The implicit message in the responses of employees was that, insofar as policy was being implemented, this was driven by an emphasis on legislative compliance. For example, when asked about experience of the company's equality and diversity policy, one employee commented:

> I've never heard of a policy towards that. But I would imagine that it is . . . there would be equal opportunities for anybody. I don't know if that is the policy but I would imagine, given the age that we're in and the time we live in, I would imagine that anything other than that wouldn't be accepted would it?

In relation to the implementation of policy, an interesting comparison with health and safety emerged at RoadSite. While there was some evidence from the responses of employees that the company regarded equality and diversity as important, safety was very much seen as the top priority because of the potentially hazardous nature of road maintenance work. Perceptions of the performance of health and safety policy suggested that it was driven by managers, which contrasted sharply with the backseat approach taken in relation to equality and diversity. One employee spoke of the way in which the importance of health and safety was 'drilled' into you at ServiceCo. This perceived difference could also relate to the greater resonance of safety messages with the day-to-day working practices of employees. That is, health and safety matter for employees in an everyday sense, whereas equality and diversity are seen as largely irrelevant.

In contrast, the lack of awareness of equality and diversity policy amongst employees reflected a management perspective that it was not necessarily seen as something that people needed to be reminded of constantly. Nor was it always seen as directly relevant to the job performance of managers on a day-to-day basis or rooted in their performance objectives. Rather, it was HR, which was perceived as being in the driving seat by both managers and employees, holding the expertise in relation to diversity and equality. Indeed, there was a low level of awareness of employee rights under the law in relation to discrimination.

PERCEPTIONS OF THE EFFICACY OF DIVERSITY MANAGEMENT

To what extent then was policy perceived as achieving the desired result in either organization? How far employees were really in a position to make informed judgements on this is a moot point, particularly in ServiceCo, where awareness of equality issues was low. That is, it was unclear what employees expected from the policy. However, an exploration of the barriers to equality and diversity cited by employees is revealing.

As indicated above, within PSO, the difficulty of being promoted from the lower grades was seen as a significant problem. A range of reasons was cited for this. First, concern was expressed that 'subjective' judgements were made about staff and that the appraisal system was affected by a quota system or forced distribution, which meant that only a limited number of employees could actually obtain a high performance ranking. There was a sense that you had to be proactive to get your voice heard, suggesting that advancement was based on individual agency and initiative, rather than being nurtured by management. Second, promotion was seen to occur if 'your face fitted', as is evident from respondents' descriptions of the culture of the organization. Third, it was suggested that the availability of training was variable. Opportunities for training apparently differed from section to section depending on the manager's approach. Some participants said that while there was some training related to their specific job, they were not given adequate training opportunities to allow them to progress beyond this, and because of their grade they had limited choices about courses:

You can't as a [grade x] apply for any management course, I have applied for many courses and they said it's not related to my job.

There were exceptional examples of participants who felt they had been given adequate opportunities to progress, but that there needed to be effort on the part of the individual to take up these opportunities. Similarly, flexible working practices were seen to be possible for some employees, an issue which has been shown elsewhere to be at the heart of employee (male as much as female) aspirations in relation to equality and diversity (Human Resource International Management Digest 2003). Employee perceptions suggested that the variability in practice referred to earlier related not only to the discretion of managers, but also the status of employees.

It works for certain people, but not for all . . . Sometimes the people in charge don't allow it.

The lawyers have one set of policies for them, but for everyone else, they get dumped on. Lawyers automatically get promoted after so many years, while everyone else has to fight for it.

Such concerns resonate with Hoque and Noon's (2004) findings regarding the 'empty shell' phenomenon referred to earlier. This could relate not only to workplaces that have an EO policy with no supporting practices, but also workplaces within which EO practices are in place, but only a minority of employees have access to them. These factors were seen as related to the notion of gradism referred to earlier. Whereas open racism and sexism were generally not witnessed, covert discrimination in the form of gradism was felt to exist. It was acknowledged that there had been some changes, but concern was expressed that it still existed.

Against this backdrop, it is perhaps not surprising that when asked whether the equality and diversity policy was beneficial to employees, a degree of scepticism about its impact and sustainability was expressed.

It's a bit like a lollipop in the desert. (It) stops you being thirsty for ten minutes but is no good in the long term.

The role of the diversity groups referred to earlier in delivering policy was called into question conveying a perception of truncated implementation. The initiative to establish the groups was seen as positive, and it was acknowledged that the groups themselves did some useful work. However, there was a sense that this did not translate to change in the workplace, in part because of a lack of corporate drive:

It's not like years ago when we had a central personnel department and they had goals to be implemented, but now it's not like that. I'm a member of the race action group and it does some good work, but when I go back to my work it's different, efforts dissipate and they're wasted.

A range of suggestions was put forward by employees at PSO for ways in which the efficacy of policy could be enhanced. These ranged from a change in the grading structure to positive discrimination. It is perhaps worth noting here that both positive discrimination and positive action measures have attracted criticism for giving people unfair advantages (Johns 2005) and that such measures have proved no more popular with the supposed recipients of them than with managers (Cockburn 1991). It was argued that a safety net was needed to keep people and behaviours in check. More critically, it was argued that bad managers needed to be exposed. Both these factors point towards an underlying perception of the need for policy to be better regulated through both monitoring and where necessary enforcement.

Within ServiceCo, there was very little evidence that employees were in a position to assess the efficacy of policy. Ultimately, this appeared to be rooted in a lack of understanding as expressed by an employee who, when asked about implementation, said, 'if I knew what it did I might be able to give you an accurate answer'. As at PSO, however, the extent to which policy was delivering equality in practice was called into question by employee concerns about internal mobility and recruitment to jobs. The charge was that managers acted as a barrier to internal promotion because of the potential impact on performance in their areas. The view was that managers preferred to keep reliable employees with a proven track record where they were in order to keep things running smoothly. The company leadership programme was also criticized for at the time having a cut off recruitment age of 35, which appeared contradictory to employees in the context of equality training.

Even more tellingly, it was suggested that recruitment practices were in effect discriminatory, perpetuating a lack of ethnic diversity in the workforce in certain areas:

> The jobs are like managed by word of mouth. It doesn't always get advertised. It doesn't always go that far to the job centre. There's probably 300 lads who will say "I know some decent guy". If you are a company that are white orientated anyway, you are going to get their brothers, cousins, sisters and wives and everybody. I mean, it's just human nature.

When asked at a company employee involvement event whether they expected anything to be done about such issues, the overwhelming majority (88 per cent) of those present said they did not. This underlined a lack of confidence on the part of employees in the willingness and ability of the company to ensure that policy delivered substantive change.

EMPLOYEE EXPERIENCES AT THE STICKY FLOOR

Since DM is about embedding equality and diversity policy in organizational practice, it can be argued that the ultimate test of its efficacy is the extent to which it is perceived to be having an impact at the sticky floor of organizations. The findings from this study underline how surprising it is that relatively little attention has been paid to the experiences and perspectives of non-managerial employees in previous accounts of the implementation and impact of DM. As indicated earlier, there may be a number of explanations for this which are inherently related to the managerial focus of DM itself and the kind of focus this encourages researchers to take, as well as the practical and ethical issues associated with talking to employees. However, in this instance, the employee perspective was an integral part of the research design, and, notwithstanding the challenges that presented, the findings vindicate the value of this approach. In eliciting the 'insider' perspective that Clarke et al (1998) argue is so important to understanding the implementation of HRM properly, it allows the research to shed light on the relationship between policy and practice in a way that managers might be unable or unwilling to do. As a consequence, a different dimension to the organization is revealed. Whatever the intentions of adopting a DM approach were in these two organizations, the message about the efficacy of policy from employees is at best mixed. Analysis of the research data creates an impression of a vicious circle in which a problematic organizational culture is perpetuated by the flawed implementation of DM rather than transformed by its success. There is a very real sense that the everyday experiences of employees are far messier than the rhetoric or the demographic statistics of either organization might suggest.

It is therefore important to ask the question, to what can the perceived gap between rhetoric and reality be attributed? From the perceptions and experiences of employees, three key dimensions emerge. First, there is a lack of shared ownership of policy and practice, most clearly evidenced by a lack of understanding and awareness amongst employees, particularly in ServiceCo. This may relate to the 'slipperiness' of the concept of DM itself, as well as to a failure of communication resulting in the absence of a shared discourse between managerial and non-managerial employees. The fact that this resonates strongly with concerns referred to earlier about DM being something that 'is done' to employees (Prasad and Mills 1997; Lorbiecki and Jack 2000) suggests that there is a need to refocus DM to enable employees to be *active participants* rather than *passive recipients*. As we have suggested, this is something that can be illuminated and encouraged by a researcher focus on the employee voice.

Second, even where policy is understood and efforts have been made to involve employees in its delivery, an impression of tokenism emerges, even though this is sometimes seen as well placed. Policy may be underpinned by good intention but not efficacious in practice. The extent to which such an impression was explicit in the accounts of employees varied both within and between the two organizations. In PSO, it was explicitly articulated, particularly by those who might be expected to benefit from the implementation of DM. In ServiceCo, on the other hand, where policy was less clearly understood and employee involvement very limited, such an impression can only be inferred from the accounts of employees.

Third, there is a perceived lack of management buy-in and commitment sometimes because of the way in which discretion is exercised by line-managers and sometimes because of the lack of emphasis on equality and diversity in day-to-day management practice. Thus, within these organizations, the familiar narrative of an implementation gap (Young 1992; Creegan et al 2003) in the delivery of equality and diversity policy can be seen. In these organizations, the implementation gap appears to be underpinned by gaps in ownership between managerial and non-managerial employees, the commitment of those responsible for implementation, consistency of implementation by mangers both individually and collectively and enforcement of the policy by senior management and HR.

The consequence of these gaps is the sticky floor at which employees operate. The messy reality can be one where employees believe that a number of fault lines exist in the management of diversity. First, the composition of the workforce is not perceived to fully reflect the population from which it is drawn, particularly at certain levels, e.g. more senior positions and in particular types of jobs, e.g. those seen to be 'men's work'. Employee perceptions about this within the two case study organizations varied in the extent to which this was seen a problem which in itself calls into question the efficacy of DM. Second, in the absence of a proactive DM approach, the emphasis of policy may be (or give the appearance of being) skewed towards valuing some differences rather than others, particularly those in respect of which legislation is more established or where differences are more visible within the workforce. Third, workplace relations may not be sufficiently harmonious or integrated for example in terms of ethnicity or gender. This suggests a policy, which is insufficiently embedded in organizations to the extent that racialized or gendered clustering within the workforce may reinforce normative behaviours and cultural differences. Fourth, flexible working policies may be seen to benefit some and not others, and there may be perceptions of unfair treatment. However, this appeared to relate more to 'privileged access' that renders EO policies 'empty shells for non-managerial employees (Noon and Hoque 2004) than to some of the practices associated with EO policies. Thus, the emphasis on being responsive to individual employees that is associated with a DM approach (Foster and Harris 2005) was not realized. The overarching fault line is that employees may feel that, despite a rhetorical commitment to DM, there is in reality an absence of equality of opportunity on the sticky floor, underlining the crucial importance of non-managerial employees being empowered to share ownership of the policy and responsibility for its implementation. In this sense, the efficacy of the policy depends on realignment within organizations so that a top-down commitment to valuing diversity is reinforced by a bottom-up demand for equality, with the checks and balances in place to ensure that policy implementation does not intentionally or otherwise prioritize the interests of some groups over others.

9 Trade Union Experiences of Diversity

INTRODUCTION

With any management practice, it is important to address the question of whether different national employment and legal systems, political discourses or cultural values have an impact on its development. This is certainly the case with diversity management (DM). As discussed in Chapter 2, DM emanates from the USA, where it was developed within a specific political, economic, social and legal context as a business-friendly alternative to the controversial legally driven 'affirmative action' approach that had provoked much backlash. In the UK, DM entered a less proactive and more minimalist legal environment to which such an intense backlash had not been seen. Apart from DM emerging in a very different legal context in the UK, for the purposes of this chapter's discussion of trade union experiences of diversity, it is important to note that the industrial relations system of the USA was and is very different from that of the UK where our research was conducted. We concur with the argument that the 'success or otherwise of diversity policies . . . either at a national or at firm level, will be determined by the prevailing employment system' (Hunter 2003: 88), which includes the processes that govern relations between employers and employees. The law is one aspect of these processes, but another is trade union–employer relations.

As outlined in Chapter 3, against a backdrop of enormous union membership decline in both the UK and USA since the 1980s, one significant historical difference in the regulation of work and employer–employee relations remains: higher union density in the UK than in the USA. Today, approximately 29 per cent of UK employees belong to a union, compared with just 12 per cent in the USA. Arguably, the USA situation of low levels of unionization (especially in the private sector) is one of the defining features of the context of DM, which in turn has led to a strong emphasis in DM on the management role. With regard to similarities, union membership in both countries is heavily concentrated in the public sector, and there is increasingly less union presence in the private sector, meaning that joint employer-union regulation of industrial relations in the private sector is patchy and overall weaker. Further, union membership in both the UK and USA has become increasingly feminized since the 1970s, so that the historic gender membership gap has more or less closed. Black and minority ethnic (BME) people are also an increasingly important source of members for unions in the UK, USA and most other developed countries. Arguably, then, increased membership diversity has changed the agenda for unions in the UK, USA and elsewhere, and unions can no longer afford to ignore equality and diversity issues even if they stand accused of doing so in the past. However, perhaps reflecting the very low level of union membership in the private sector in the USA, together with the fact that DM is primarily a private sector phenomenon there, the American DM literature rarely even mentions the role that trade unions are playing or might/should play in the design, development and implementation of DM. In contrast, European authors have addressed this question (Dickens 1999, 2006; Greene et al 2005; Kirton and Greene 2006; Wrench 2005).

Specifically in regard to the UK, we made the point in Chapter 3 that, despite the current low union membership levels and the consequent constraints on unions to have an influence at workplace level, unionized workforces are still generally characterized by less pronounced inequalities than non-union ones (Colling and Dickens 2001; Walsh 2007). Further, Colling and Dickens (ibid) argue that the political and policy context post-1997 under a Labour Government has held out new opportunities for joint engagement on equality issues. They link this not only to the Labour Government's somewhat more favourable orientation to unions, but also to the promotion of joint engagement that is part of the European agenda. They argue that this has resulted in a renewed legitimacy granted to unions by current public policy (ibid: 150). Thus, in our view, it remains relevant, even within the context of relatively low union membership in the UK, to consider the role that unions might play in advancing workplace equality.

This chapter examines the role that trade unions have traditionally played and continue to play in bargaining for equality and considers what the advent of DM has meant for the unions both theoretically and in practice. The chapter discusses UK trade union experiences of DM, drawing on interviews with workplace representatives conducted in our two case study organizations—PSO and ServiceCo, interviews with a group of union negotiators in the banking and finance industry and interviews with national trade union equality officers.

TRADE UNIONS BARGAINING FOR EQUALITY

In order to provide some context for the discussion of what DM means for trade unions, this section considers the role that trade unions have traditionally played in the equality project, focusing on the UK. Taking an international perspective for a moment, the stark reality is that globally only a minority of workers benefit from free and fair representation of their rights, needs and interests via trade unionism and collective bargaining. Even in contexts where collective bargaining does exist, trade unions have not consistently taken up equality issues (see, for example, Colling and Dickens 2001 on the UK; Cobble and Bielski Michal 2002 on the USA; Mahon 2002 on Sweden). Yet, as Blackett and Sheppard (2003: 419) note, the International Labour Organization (ILO) Declaration on Fundamental Principles and Rights at Work adopted in 1998 could not be clearer when it declares 'the effective recognition of the right to collective bargaining' and 'the elimination of discrimination' as central to the ILO social justice agenda, which most unions in theory endorse.

The unions' reluctance (historically at least) to bargain on equality might be explained, in part at least, by the common understanding of collective bargaining as concerned with industrial and economic issues and of equality with social issues. This means that the potential to advance equality through collective bargaining may be limited because of its traditionally restricted scope. Certainly, there is plenty of evidence that workers excluded from the scope of collective bargaining globally have often been from marginalized groups, including, for example, women, BME and the disabled (Blackett and Sheppard 2003). This is despite the fact that so-called social issues, such as family-related leave or protection from discrimination and harassment, have economic implications and that so-called economic issues, such as pay, working conditions and job security, have equality implications. The charge that unions have faced is that collective bargaining usually reflects the priorities and needs of the dominant workers (usually taken as white men), again meaning that issues of particular concern to women or BME workers, for example, have not been and in many instances still are not consistently included in the agenda. One of the reasons for the absence of women, BME workers and other marginalized groups on the bargaining agenda is that unions are primarily class-based organizations. The notion of common interests based on class, occupation and employer has been used to build worker solidarity, but the downside has been lack of attention to membership diversity and a narrow bargaining agenda. Nevertheless, the conclusion drawn by many authors (including Blackett and Sheppard 2003; Colling and Dickens 2001) is that collective bargaining has considerable potential to enhance equality. Indeed, more recently unions in the UK and other countries have begun to recognize the need to represent a plurality of interests within diverse groups (Greene et al 2005; Colgan and Ledwith 2002). Another factor is that women and BME workers are under-represented among the ranks of union representatives and officials. Whilst over time improvements have occurred, this remains a much debated problem (Kirton and Greene 2002).

However, despite the considerable potential for unions to have a positive impact, in many industrialized countries, unions now operate in a hostile context, not least because of significant membership decline and dwindling presence at organizational and workplace levels. This context has allowed 'new' management techniques, such as human resource management (HRM)—the 'parent' concept of DM—to emerge and take hold without significant challenge or resistance as the dominant organizational paradigm. It is argued that whereas HRM entered the scene in the USA primarily as an *anti-union* device, in the UK, the experience has been quite different (Hunter 2003). At least in the early days of HRM in the UK, it existed alongside traditional collective bargaining and did not seem to be employed as a substitute for collective bargaining (Cully et al 1999). However, that is not to say that HRM has had no effect on employment relations in the UK or that DM as a sub-policy of HRM has none (as we discuss below).

Turning to equality bargaining, Colling and Dickens (2001) chart its evolution and the changing context in the UK. They describe the period between 1979 and 1997 as a 'cold climate'—a difficult period for equality measures, trade unions and joint regulation, when the state, under the Conservative Government, saw collective bargaining as imposing undesirable labour market rigidities. Management in many organizations seized the opportunity to reclaim equality policy-making within managerial prerogative and joint management-union equality committees and the like largely became a thing of the past (Colling and Dickens 1998). Yet, a counter pressure was that, during this period of massive male membership loss, it was female membership that remained relatively stable, and therefore women became a larger and stronger force within the unions. Persuaded by the changed context, by feminist demands and pressures from other minority groups and of the necessity to develop renewal strategies, the unions began to adjust their bargaining agendas to reflect membership diversity (Kirton and Healy 1999). In contrast, post-1997 following the election of a European Union (EU)-friendly Labour Government, the climate for the severely weakened trade unions and their more developed equality agenda became somewhat warmer. Two important aspects of the EU social agenda are the (i) promotion of joint engagement in the form of social partnership and social dialogue, and (ii) promotion and strengthening of equality. In theory, these two factors create a stronger platform for equality bargaining, and there is certainly evidence of union activity, especially at the national level. The TUC and most unions now routinely include equality and diversity issues on workplace bargaining agendas, and when bargaining fails there are examples of unions using the law to fight for improved conditions. The most high-profile example, stretching over 15 years, is the major union for skilled workers and professionals, MSF's (now part of super union Unite), use of the law when bargaining failed, to mount and win an equal pay claim against the NHS on behalf of around 1,500 speech therapists.

Thinking about the workplace level, it is clear that diminished union presence (and power) has meant that employers are now more able than formerly to set the bargaining agenda unilaterally. Therefore, it is relevant to consider briefly what employers might gain or lose from equality bargaining. One question that is particularly apposite presently is whether union decline makes it harder or easier for employers to tackle DM issues (Hunter 2003). On the positive side, it is argued (Perotin and Robinson 2000) that the joint existence of employee participation (including representative forms) and equal opportunities (EO) policies is generally associated with a productivity advantage over and above the separate effects of the two types of policy. One possible explanation, according to the researchers, is that EO policies are better designed and more effective in a participatory environment. Certainly, evidence from WERS 2004 suggests that unions positively influence the availability of some EO initiatives and that unionized workplaces are more likely to have EO policies. This indicates a business case for union involvement in equality policy-making. In other words, it could be argued that employers have nothing to lose, but potentially much to gain from involving unions in the design and implementation of DM. On the other hand, participation schemes inevitably involve levels of time commitment that employers might not be prepared to give over to DM, particularly if in the context of union decline they have got used to sidelining, ignoring or simply operating without the unions. Further, it would be naïve not to acknowledge that if unions are involved in designing the EO (or DM) policy, their agenda is likely to, and should, extend beyond business benefits to enhancing employee rights (beyond minimum legal requirements). Management might prefer to avoid the rights-based agenda associated with EO and focus instead on bottom-line business benefits (we return to this point below). Again, WERS 2004 data indicates that management normally negotiated about EO matters in only a tiny minority of workplaces (5 per cent) with the presence of recognized unions. In the majority of workplaces (72 per cent), managers neither negotiated, consulted or informed union representatives about EO issues (Walsh 2007), indicating a very low level of equality bargaining activity in the UK.

DIVERSITY MANAGEMENT AND TRADE UNIONS

Against the context described above, this section develops a brief critical analysis of what DM means for trade unions in theory (for more detailed discussion of DM theory, see Chapter 2). Using existing research, it then considers trade union responses to DM in different countries.

The Problems with Diversity Management— A Trade Union Standpoint

We have argued previously (Kirton and Greene 2006) that three of the distinguishing features of DM are potentially problematic for unions if employers follow it as their policy-making paradigm: (i) the business case,

(ii) the focus on the individual, and (iii) the positioning of DM as a top-down managerial activity. In order to explain why in more detail, we return briefly to the discussion of the differences between EO and DM contained in Chapter 2, with emphasis on the potential implications of employers' DM policies for trade unions.

(i) The Business Case

The first point is that the business case as the primary rationale for DM does not sit well with trade union objectives, particularly when contrasted with the social justice impetus for EO. The EO policy focus on employee rights and workplace measures to eliminate discrimination, and disadvantage obviously resonates with the trade union 'sword of justice' orientation; that is, trade unions exist to defend, protect and promote employee rights, not to worry about employers' performance. However, from a management point of view, this social justice rationale is one of the main criticisms of EO, and rights-based discourses have less of a place within managerial DM. Although advocates of DM do not propose abandoning the moral principles of EO altogether, the cornerstone of DM is that it will deliver business benefits (Kirton and Greene 2005; Maxwell et al 2001). Unions are likely to be concerned about the commodification of labour that using workers as a resource for organizational objectives ultimately implies. However, it is important to stress that unions frequently marshal the business case to argue for EO/DM initiatives—but, as a means to a social justice end, which is a rather different position from that taken by managerialist advocates of DM. Further, as discussed in Chapter 2, it is by no means certain that a strong business case can be made for all types of organizations and workers in all places at all times. Overall, unions are likely to have more sympathy with critics of DM who argue that the business case is selective, partial, contingent and, therefore, a less robust way of tackling inequalities (Dickens 1999; Kaler 2001).

(ii) The Focus on the Individual

DM emphasizes individual difference, rather than social group difference as in EO. This is problematic for unions for several reasons. First and fundamentally, a greater emphasis on individual difference distracts from and might dilute efforts to tackle the considerable discrimination and structural disadvantage experienced by certain social groups (Kersten 2000). For example, within DM, there is less emphasis on standardized procedures to eliminate discrimination (such as job evaluation) and more on individualized techniques such as performance appraisal and performance pay (the latter are supposed to result in the valuing of all individuals). The problem is that the individualized DM approach fails to even recognize the patterned, historic disadvantage that unions seek to combat. In contrast to valuing individualized management techniques, unions see strong collective agreements on pay and conditions as the vehicle for eliminating discrimination and disadvantage. Another unwelcome policy implication is the lack of space for positive action measures within DM; measures such as recruitment initiatives or training courses targeting specific under-represented and marginalized groups. Unions now favour the principle of positive action as they see it as a way of redressing historic disadvantage of certain social groups (Kirton and Greene 2002, 2005).

(iii) The Positioning of Diversity as a Top-Down, Managerial Activity

The DM literature typically emphasizes organizational vision, top management commitment and downwards communication. Where employee involvement does appear in models of DM, it is usually in individualized forms, such as suggestion schemes or attitude surveys (Kandola and Fullerton 1994). Even the more critical literature says little about the possible role of representative, organized forms of employee involvement, nor is their absence generally remarked upon. Again, this arguably *over-*strong emphasis on management within DM reflects the USA situation of low levels of unionization (Wrench 2005). Extending this critique, we argue that theoretically at least DM threatens to marginalize the union role even in contexts where unions are stronger. This stands in contrast to the widely held ideal model of EO, where at least in the UK context, the role of trade unions is seen as a vital piece of the 'jigsaw' making up the campaign for equality in the workplace (Dickens 1997). This has echoes of the debate about the marginal role of unions within an HRM framework (for example, Guest 1987).

   Thus, in summary, our argument is that as a model the distinguishing features of DM (as compared to EO) have the potential to weaken the union role and the union campaign for equality. DM is a paradigm that, like its parent concept HRM also imported from the USA, theoretically fits best within non-union organizations (Webb 1997; Kirton and Greene 2005). Moreover, we cannot escape the fact that organizations held up as exemplars of diversity are predominantly non-union (Kandola and Fullerton 1994; Liff 1999). Indeed, Miller states that 'managing diversity can arguably be classed as the HRM approach to equality initiatives in the workplace' (1996: 206). However, as stated above, this does not mean that unionized organizations have not adopted DM.

Trade Union Responses to DM

So, having established that theoretically DM presents challenges and dilemmas for trade unionism, how have trade unions themselves in different countries responded to the spread of DM? It is fair to state that trade unions and their role or perspective have not been at the centre of DM research, so the evidence is rather thin. As stated above, the American DM research rarely even mentions trade unions, so it is particularly difficult to ascertain how or if USA trade unions have responded to employers' DM policies. Certainly, in the early days, there is evidence that the UK unions were not convinced that DM was a positive development in the fight against discrimination in employment (Wrench 2005). Wrench (ibid: 74) notes, for example, that at the 1997 Trades Union Congress (TUC) Black Workers Conference, a motion was passed deploring and opposing the spread of DM. Indeed, John Wrench's and our own previous research (Kirton and Greene 2006) has revealed strong trade union resistance to DM in the UK, with attitudes ranging from skepticism to outright hostility based on the problems we outline above. Essentially, the UK unions have regarded DM as a retrograde step that threatens to undermine previous efforts made to tackle discrimination and disadvantage within an EO paradigm (Kirton and Greene 2006). The reported response to DM of trade unionists in some other countries is not dissimilar. For example, in research conducted in New Zealand (Jones 2004), it was found that trade unionists felt that the placement of DM within HRM tended to take it out of the domain of industrial relations (with scope for bottom-up demands and action) and into the domain of (top-down) organizational strategy where the unions have less or no influence. One trade unionist interviewed by Jones (ibid) coined the expression 'screwing diversity out of the workers' to describe the exploitation of minority cultural skills in organizations that forms part of DM practices. Trade unionists in New Zealand saw DM as going against workers' interests, quite contrary to the unitary message embedded in DM that 'everyone benefits' if the business does. In contrast, and underlining the importance of context in understanding DM, the response of trade unions in Scandinavian countries has been more positive. According to De los Reyes (2000: 257), in Sweden the term 'diversity' seems to be viewed 'as an instrument and goal for the integration process of migrant people in society and working life', something that the unions see as positive. This also mirrors research on Denmark where the unions have been slower (than UK unions) to develop responses to immigrant and minority ethnic members and where the more recently developed DM is seen as a way forward (Greene et al 2005). Unlike their UK counterparts, the Danish trade unionists were also firmly in favour of the business case for diversity, seeing this argument as a way of encouraging employers to recruit previously excluded immigrant and minority ethnic groups. This position is explained as fitting well with the Nordic industrial relations tradition of consensus and union cooperation with employers (ibid: 189). It is also important to note that in Scandinavian countries unionization remains high (at 80–90 per cent), and as Wrench (2005) argues it is therefore difficult to imagine the development of DM policies without union participation. In summary, although the evidence on trade union responses to DM is thin, the evidence that does exist indicates that the broader industrial relations system and context impact to the extent that we cannot expect to see a uniform response internationally.

TRADE UNION EXPERIENCES OF DIVERSITY MANAGEMENT IN THE UK

This section presents and discusses findings from our research project, drawing on interviews with: (i) trade union representatives at our two case study organizations—PSO and ServiceCo, (ii) trade union negotiating officers in the banking and finance industry and (iii) national trade union equality officers. The union representatives we talked to at PSO belonged to PCS (Public and Commercial Services Union), the fifth largest trade union in the UK and the largest Civil Service union with over 300,000 members. They comprised five white women and three white men. The three union representatives from ServiceCo (two white men and one white woman) were members of Amicus—now part of Unite, the UK's largest union with over 2 million members—and from Unison (public services union with 1.3 million members). The trade union officers from the banking and finance industry—three white men and two white women—worked for the then 140,000 member-strong UNIFI, also now part of Unite. The national trade union equality officers worked for AUT (representing academic and academic related staff in universities—now part of UCU), CWU (telecoms and postal services union), GMB (general trade union), GPMU (print workers' union, now part of Unite), PCS (Civil Service Union), Connect (represents managers and professionals in the communications industry), TUC (Trades Union Congress) and Unison (public services union). Among the latter group were two BME men and nine white women. More information on research methods is presented in Chapter 1. At this point, it is relevant to underscore the fact that every effort was made to gain the views of a diverse group of trade union representatives and officers. The lack of BME workplace representatives included in our sample is unsurprising in the UK context.

Trade Union Engagement with Critiques Of DM

Our theoretical critique of DM, briefly outlined above, reveals potential challenges and dilemmas for trade unions. What evidence did we find of trade union engagement with critiques of DM? The national equality officers' work involved supporting and advising union negotiators and workplace representatives on equality and diversity issues; some also got directly involved in negotiations and consultation with employers; they therefore had a wealth of experience of a range of employers' DM policies. As we have argued in more detail elsewhere (Kirton and Greene 2006), it was quite clear that the national equality officers were in agreement with many aspects of the critique of DM describing it as 'diluting' traditional EO strategies, lacking focus on group-based discrimination and disadvantage, another example of individualization of employment relations and potentially marginalizing the role of unions. The dangers in privileging the business case were also remarked upon, particularly if the business case is foregrounded at the expense of the social justice case. However, the caveat is that it was also evident that as pragmatic organizations the unions were prepared (and always had been) to summon business case arguments to support their equality and diversity demands. One equality officer's comments sum up the general view of the impact of DM:

> We have to start putting issues of discrimination back on the agenda. If employers want to do this diversity stuff, then we can't stop them, but we've got to make sure that they really understand that there is much more to be done as well. They can do the diversity stuff, like celebrating multi-culturalism, as long as they understand that there's another agenda to be addressed too, whereas I think a lot of employers will think the diversity agenda is enough. It's not threatening, whereas tackling discrimination is threatening to some people, particularly those who are being discriminatory—they have to be removed, but I don't think diversity will do that. (BME man)

The trade union equality officers demonstrated a high level of awareness of the potential challenges and dilemmas of DM for trade unions, which is perhaps to be expected among those whose jobs are dedicated to equality. But, is the same true of union negotiators and workplace representatives? Are they alert to the critiques of DM? The answer is both yes and no, as their experiences at workplace level clearly shaped their positions within the debate about the rights and wrongs of the DM paradigm. The UNIFI negotiators were dealing with companies that were shifting from an EO to a DM policy-making paradigm, and the negotiators saw this in a positive light as an opportunity to refresh the 'tired' equality agenda:

> I think managing diversity has got something new to offer. We need to make sure that it looks new and that we make sure people understand what's new about it and it's not just another, you know, politically correct phrase for something that's completely empty and meaningless. (White woman)

They all remarked that in the past companies' EO policies had neglected issues of sexual orientation and age, but that these issues were now beginning to be addressed as part of an expanded diversity agenda. The individualizing aspect of DM was also cautiously welcomed as a means of ensuring that everyone is valued regardless of, for example, their gender, race, age, sexual orientation or disability. One UNIFI negotiator gave the example of one bank's handling of the needs of a group of visually impaired telephonists—she felt that the DM paradigm meant that attention was paid to their individual needs. In terms of a more critical perspective, there was some concern about the idea of 'managing' workforce diversity as an organizational resource and the potential for conflict if people's talents and abilities do not contribute to organizational goals. Related to this, there was mild criticism of the business case, but overall respondents felt that the tightness of the labour market, combined with the banking industry's dependency on female labour, meant that the business case was fairly strong. It is notable that the partial and contingent nature of this business case was not acknowledged.

We now turn to workplace union representatives' interpretations of DM in the context of our public and private sector case study organizations. In the Civil Service, bargaining and consultation take place at both national and departmental (local) levels; similarly in ServiceCo, there are both national and local bargaining and consultation arrangements. Our argument is that how workplace representatives interpret DM is bound to have a bearing on the equality agenda that unions pursue locally. In our public sector case study organization (PSO), union representatives agreed that there is a distinction between the concepts of EO and DM. Following a textbook definition DM was seen as concerned with issues of difference between individuals and with utilizing difference for organizational benefit. In contrast, EO was regarded as treating everyone the same and to do mainly with compliance with legislation. In terms of which paradigm was better or worse, one union representative expressed it like this:

> I think we needed something like equal opportunities law to make a difference and to get people actually responsible for their actions and you know, the fact that if they didn't abide by that, then they could be prosecuted or whatever . . . I think now maybe it's changing in the fact that that is embedded . . . into everybody's way of thinking, so the natural progression from that is 'Okay, everybody is equal but actually when you look at us as individuals we are a diverse group of people. There are people from all walks of life, from all experiences, from all backgrounds, working for an organization, so how can we best utilize the experience and the knowledge that exists here?' . . . I suppose it is all about getting the most out of your staff. (White woman)

In other words, the PSO workplace representatives generally saw value in both the EO and DM approaches, but like the UNIFI negotiators saw DM as broadening the EO agenda—a good thing. The relatively sophisticated awareness of the conceptual turn from EO to DM is partly explained by the fact that their union—PCS—had been very active at the national level in engaging with and disseminating information and critique on new management techniques such as DM. Nevertheless, as indicated by the quote above, some of the representatives saw diversity as a positive concept—unlike their national union officials—believing that it was time to move on from the negative orientation of EO. However, two workplace representatives held a more critical view of the shift from EO to DM. One saw DM as a more superficial approach that did not deal with fundamental issues of discrimination. Significantly, this respondent reported that this concern had led to a demand (that was conceded) from the trade union side that PSO's policy should be entitled 'Equality and Diversity' rather than just 'Diversity' in order to send a very clear signal about the need to continue to tackle discrimination. The other more critical union representative felt that the term 'diversity' was used because it was less offensive and less likely to cause backlash, but that in reality it was just a new label for the same initiatives:

> Because they often use diversity to mean equality, because they think it's less offensive. So they very much refer to diversity policies, diversity initiatives, rather than equality, even when the initiatives are about equality and not diversity . . . If they start talking about equality and breaking it down into race and gender and sexual orientation, it may offend white men. I think that's the thinking behind it. (White man)

Their interpretations reflected some of the points we made above in our theoretical critique of DM. In the private sector case study—ServiceCo—trade union representatives' interpretations of DM were far less developed and more uncertain:

> It covers a lot of things. It covers, I don't know, I might say, is it like harassment or jobs for everybody? It covers a wide range, doesn't it, diversity? (White woman)

> Racial understanding; I don't really know. I presume it's something to do with how the managers and the workforce get on. (White man)

However, ServiceCo union representatives were a little more familiar with the EO label:

> . . . no matter what race or anything. That's what it means, equal for everybody. I presume that's what it means, equal for everybody, no matter where you come from. (White man)

There was a sense that the ServiceCo union representatives had less contact with their national unions and were more wholly focused on day-to-day local issues. Given the highly transient nature of the workforce and the dependency of the company on winning contracts, the pressures they faced were quite different than the more stable environment of the Civil Service.

There was also less generous facilities time (time off for trade union duties) for trade union representatives in ServiceCo compared with PSO, meaning that the ServiceCo representatives were more pushed for time. The very different industrial relations contexts of the two organizations (discussed in more detail later) inevitably played a part in their engagement with DM. In turn, lower levels of awareness of concepts of DM and EO in ServiceCo signaled lesser engagement with an equality and diversity agenda, mitigating the potentiality for bottom-up action on equality and leaving management to design DM initiatives without challenge or even input from the unions (discussed below).

Joint Regulation of Equality and Diversity?

As discussed above, collective bargaining is no longer as extensive as it once was, and the available evidence indicates that the joint regulation of EO/DM matters appears to be rare in UK workplaces (Walsh 2007). Against this background, one of our areas of research enquiry was how involved the trade unions were in the development and implementation of DM at the workplace level. Dickens (1999) argues for a three-pronged approach to equality action, in which one of the 'prongs' is social (joint) regulation, usually meaning trade union involvement. From the point of view of the national union equality officers in our study, experience of involvement in DM was mixed. The officers representing single employer/industry and public sector unions generally felt that they were able to shape the development of central DM policies. They were typically involved in central, senior level policy forums. The problem they identified was more one of how to get those central policies implemented at the workplace level (discussed further below). The national equality officers dealing with multiple employers/industries took the role of supporting and advising negotiating officers and workplace representatives as best they could, although resources were enormously stretched. The experience of the UNIFI negotiators we talked to was generally positive. They reported that the companies they worked with involved them in the development and implementation of DM often as part of partnership agreements. They reported largely constructive relationships with senior management. Indeed, one of the UNIFI negotiators remarked that senior and HR management in the bank he mainly worked with had more trouble with line-managers (i.e. convincing them to buy into DM) than with the union. In several banks, UNIFI negotiators had successfully negotiated with management to conduct equal pay audits, in which they subsequently participated via working groups. One of the female negotiators, involved with a major bank's equality and diversity team, along with others, firmly believed that DM created opportunities for trade unions to share their expertise on equality and diversity issues. She described the bank she dealt with as having been 'very open and transparent with us' with a 'constructive dialogue' established throughout the whole process of developing a new DM policy. She also felt that union involvement was positive for union-member relations 'in terms of saying to the members, well look what we've done for you'. Another stated that the union was a 'centre of knowledge' on equality and diversity issues and that there was an opportunity to offer a real benefit to employers as well as employees. In contrast, another (female) UNIFI negotiator was more circumspect about union–management relations:

> Under the nature of the recognition [agreement] they have to present us with the policies, but if I'm honest they pay lip-service to negotiating with us. I've spent hours going over their policies and coming back to them with comments as to what I think they should be doing and it's a heart-breaking exercise. They make their own minds up and their policies with us having, if I'm honest, a marginal influence on that rather than an in-depth influence.

The same negotiator also criticized the major bank that she dealt with for refusing to share workforce monitoring data with the union and for refusing to recognize the importance of data-gathering:

> You cannot . . . manage diversity without knowing where you're starting from and having some idea of where you want to go and [the bank] refuses to share all the monitoring data with us.

As might be expected, within the public sector case study—PSO—industrial relations were described by union representatives as good, and all the respondents were generally positive about the level of union involvement. Most felt that the unions were consulted adequately on equality and diversity issues and that the union had an opportunity to shape DM policy (see discussion in Chapter 4). However, this view was challenged by a national official from PCS who had this to say:

> Departments were told to go away and develop their own diversity action plans. There was no consultation with the unions on what was in those plans, so there was a complete lack of shared understanding and common goals. There were some elements that were compulsory, but departments had huge scope to set their own goals and priorities. (White woman)

What the above quote highlights is variability in local industrial relations practices within the Civil Service. Within PSO, union representatives told us that they were asked to comment upon drafts of any new policy initiatives before implementation. However, even in PSO, management–union relations had not always been so positive. The union had initially opposed the establishment of employee diversity groups (women's group, disability group, race equality group and lesbian and gay group) set up to discuss and advise management on equality and diversity issues. The unions interpreted this direct channel of communication between management and employees as an assault on trade union involvement. For example, there had been some early problems with new policies going to the advisory groups for comment before the unions had seen them, but these had been resolved, and the view now was that both bodies were consulted on equal terms. Therefore, over time, the union hostility had waned, and now these groups were seen as useful to unions in gauging employee opinion:

> I think in the very early days . . . all levels of our organization were hostile to what was seen as an attempt to kind of undermine the position of the unions and undermine the Whitley committee system. Which of course is meant to be the system for consultation between the management and the representatives of the staff . . . we've long lost that hostility. And now in fact . . . we have . . . membership of all the advisory groups. On the basis that it's extremely useful to get feedback from people on their concerns direct. (White man)

How proactive were trade union representatives in raising equality and diversity issues with management? The PSO branch secretary, who worked full-time on union duties, had in-depth knowledge of the policy document and spoke about its various provisions and initiatives and how the union might use it to defend or promote employees' interests. He had also got himself onto various committees where workplace equality and diversity issues were dealt with. Other workplace representatives had a more defensive orientation. They consulted the policy when necessary for their own personal case work, but they had not identified an equality and diversity agenda for change.

In the private sector case study company—ServiceCo—the industrial relations climate was very different. Union–management relations were described in less positive terms by union representatives who felt that the company did not value union presence and indeed that even being a union member may have negative consequences:

> Sometimes some people are frightened to join because you know, they might not get promoted. (White woman)

Even at workplace level, union representatives in ServiceCo felt that management support for and willingness to engage with unions was variable. Some described managers at their workplace as supportive, others as actively hostile. In the transport section, where union–management relations were described as positive, managers were reported as frequently stating, 'I am there, speak to me . . .' Reflecting the broader situation depicted by the latest WERS survey (Walsh 2007), there was no formal union input into

ServiceCo's equality and diversity policy. However, an absence of formal bargaining or even formal consultation arrangements need not necessarily mean complete exclusion from policy development and implementation as informal relations between union representatives and HR and other managers at workplace level could have an influence, particularly on implementation. At the time of our research, however, communication of the equality and diversity policy to union representatives was almost non-existent with very few even aware that a policy existed. Nevertheless, some union representatives believed that the company's efforts to value workforce diversity were genuine, 'I think the spirit is there but it doesn't always—you know what I mean', while others were more cynical:

> I think a lot of, like I said with managers and that, I think if the policies, I mean, sometimes they make their own rules up. Or they don't always carry out what they say they are going to do. (White woman)

Trade Union Perceptions of Workplace Equality and Diversity Culture

As discussed in Chapter 2, within DM, a positive, inclusive workplace culture is seen as essential, and indeed organizational culture is a primary concern of DM (Kandola and Fullerton 1994). However, beyond the rhetoric of valuing diversity often lie conflicts and divisions that cross gender, race, ethnic and other boundaries (Prasad and Mills 1997). It is also the case that the culture of an organization can be experienced and interpreted differently by different stakeholders. In this section, we explore trade union perceptions of workplace equality and diversity culture.

The UNIFI negotiators working within the banking sector reported that they were aware of few complaints and grievances from employees. At the same time, they felt that employees typically had low levels of awareness of inequalities. For example, it was reported that equal pay audits had exposed gendered pay differentials in more than one major bank, but that employees were unaware because of the secrecy surrounding pay in the sector:

> We've not had any big issues around equality and diversity. I mean I guess the thing that most people would pick up on would be around pay, you know, if they thought they were being paid differently to their male counterpart. Looking at the stats there are a significant number of people in that position, but they don't realize it. Other than that, I'm certainly not inundated by equality or diversity issues. Either that means that [the bank] is managing quite well or it means people perhaps just aren't as aware as they should be of what the issues are. (White man)

Equal pay was identified as a major project for the union to work on. Generally, though, the banking sector was described as having relatively good terms and conditions and a number of DM policies going beyond the legal minimum requirement (for example, enhanced maternity leave and pay, accommodation of religious dress).

Within the public sector case study (PSO), union representatives commented that various policy initiatives had created more opportunities for a wider range of employees and had led to positive culture change:

> I think when you really look at equal opps, I think there has been a major change in people's perception. And I think the department has done some good work in ensuring that people were given the opportunity. . . to ensure fairness for all who are applying for jobs. And I think that has had a positive effect on the department. (White woman)

Some trade union representatives felt that opportunities for women in particular had improved:

> The position of women is better . . . There does tend to be a sort of glass ceiling, but not an absolute one . . . And in many grades faring better than men, in the same grade . . . I don't think there are any problems, any significant problems, for women in terms of their position at different levels in the organization up to and including Director General. (White woman)

Indeed, one respondent believed that women were treated more favourably than men in terms of promotion opportunities:

> . . . one year, I think 250 men applied for promotion and 100 women. You would expect, you know, all things being equal, that 60 per cent of the people passed by the board would be men and 40 per cent women. But ironically 100 per cent almost were women, there were just two men out of whatever it was. (White man)

However, despite women's progress, respondents talked about the continued existence of an 'old boys' network':

> I think there is also very much a sort of Oxbridge culture in PSO and if you don't fit into that, then you are sort of looked down on. There is some class discrimination in PSO, I believe. And I think it is quite 'gradist', as well. (White man)

The culture was regarded as less positive when it came to race and ethnicity issues. The under-representation of BME people, especially women, in senior positions was perceived by trade union representatives as a significant problem in PSO. Whilst respondents agreed that there were very few cases of overt race discrimination, it was clear that they believed that BME employees were still facing significant barriers within PSO. The trade union representatives commented on the extremely low numbers of BME employees in senior positions and their concentration in the lowest grades in the organization:

> . . . [government minister X] . . . she wants changes in the department because most of the government departments seem to be stuck in the old school, you know, the bowler hat and the umbrella, you know, the pinstripe suit sort of thing. And she wants to come away from that. She said at one of the seminars that, you know, it's nice to come to a meeting, a high profile meeting with directors, to see that there's female faces in there. Because when she started, she was literally on her own, you know, maybe one or two dotted around. But from that she said it would be nice to see some ethnic minorities at the DG [director general] level, you know, which you don't get. You don't get it in the Civil Service. It's very, very hard to get there. (White woman)

Relating to recent government measures to cut staff numbers, BME employees were also believed to be concentrated in the 'holding pool', the register of employees waiting to be relocated to other parts of the organization following restructuring. Two trade union representatives claimed:

> . . . most of the people on the 'project working team' [holding pool] . . .they tend to be from ethnic minorities . . . at the lower grade bands . . . they try and make us believe that it is not a dumping ground for the people that they don't particularly want in the department anymore. But it really is . . . the project team is literally there as a holding station so that you can start looking and applying for jobs within the department or outside. (White man)

> There's quite a lot of work to do on the position of minority ethnic staff. The trouble is of course is that a lot of the initiatives, in terms of cutting staff, in the Department generally and relocating staff from London, will impact more on minority ethnic staff than it does other . . . the percentage of minority ethnic staff in London is higher than outside London and since the cuts and the relocations are aimed at posts in London, minority ethnic staff will suffer more than white staff. (White woman)

The trade union respondents also claimed that there was evidence of BME employees being given lower performance rankings compared to white employees, and some were dealing with personal cases relating to treatment of BME employees. In fact, most of the union representatives' case work involved BME women employees. These cases concern a number of different issues, such as disciplinary matters, dismissal, bullying and harassment:

I think particularly with race issues, harassment and bullying. I think there is also multiple discrimination, particularly against black and Asian women. So that obviously is twice as bad, because it is a mix of gender and race . . . I did a study last year on appraisal and I looked at all the cases I had and they were all from black and Asian members. I think one or two were men, nearly all of them were women. (White man)

In ServiceCo, we detected fairly low levels of awareness of and sensitivity to equality and diversity issues among union representatives. However, it was evident that there were racialized divisions and tensions in the workplace. Talking about the group of Goan staff at a hospital, one commented:

They haven't come to me to say that they have been [discriminated against], because it does work both ways because sometimes when we first started here they would only work in their own community. They didn't want to work with 'us whites' as they once put it. Which is squashed out now I am glad to say. (White woman)

Another union representative summed up the gendered and racialized culture of the rail division:

There's a crew room over there and there's probably fifteen, twenty blokes in there and they will be swearing; there's nude photographs, there's calendars, there's stuff like that. If you take the letter of the law, a lot of that is wrong because they are discriminating against women, foul language. There's two Asian lads who work over there, so there are probably Pakistani jokes or Indian jokes, things like that. You've got to be careful because you want communication but in a sense you are saying 'Watch what you are saying, watch what you are doing, don't do this, don't do that'. So you've got, you know, you are almost sort of capping them . . . you've got to present it in a way that they'll understand that they are not being watched, they are not being targeted and that, one sentence that was said yesterday [in equality training], 'It's not what you say, it's how the other person interprets it. (White man)

This representative's account illustrates the embedded character of organizational culture shaped around a dominant group (see, for example, Watts 2007; Collinson 1988). Further, he did not see it as his responsibility to intervene to change things. This account also points to the limitations of (employer) diversity training (which the representative had had) as a mechanism for change (see further discussion in Chapter 7) and also to an absence of national union engagement with workplace representatives around these issues. Certainly none of the representatives reported having received any information, advice or training on equality and diversity issues from their unions at the regional or national level. Of course this did not necessarily mean that such information was not available (it is in both the unions our respondents belonged to), but that for whatever reason it had not reached this workplace or had not been sought out by representatives.

Trade Union Perceptions of Diversity Management Implementation

DM is regarded as the responsibility of everyone in the organization (rather than simply HR), but the role of line-managers is seen as critical (Kandola and Fullerton 1994, 1998). However, while senior management support for DM is often taken-for-granted, critics have argued that gaining line-management buy-in is also the greatest challenge that organizations face (Cornelius et al 2001; Foster and Harris 2005). This is discussed further in Chapter 7. Here we are concerned with union perceptions of the line-management role. The national union equality officers we interviewed agreed with the view that line-managers are the greatest barrier to implementation of DM. They underlined the difficulties organizations experienced in 'rolling out' DM to line-managers who reportedly faced other pressures and were often simply not progressive enough to really care about diversity. The UNIFI union negotiators in our study between them worked with some of the UK's largest banks, and whilst they did not hesitate to confirm senior management commitment to DM, they too often expressed severe criticisms of implementation at the workplace level. However, they did not simply vilify line-managers; their criticisms related more to the pressures that line-managers are often under and the lack of resources ploughed into DM initiatives:

> I think the senior management team has committed to it, but I don't think there's enough resources behind it . . . so I think an awful lot of managers ignore it . . . and a lot of that relates to the messages they get from senior management. If they're not strong enough and they're not backed with resources, then a lot of these high level policies fall flat. (White woman)

Similarly, among PSO trade union representatives, there was little criticism of the objectives of the DM policy and senior level commitment to it, but more negative views about implementation. Trade union representatives here also identified line-managers as a key barrier to successful DM, commenting that the organization had encountered problems in getting them to buy into DM:

> I would need a bit more convincing as to whether or not line-managers really understand it [the DM policy] . . . You know, I think . . . unless you are that way inclined anyway and unless you are interested in that as a subject, you are not going to really pass it on to your staff, to be honest. (White woman)

When asked to discuss why they thought managers did not buy into the policy, the PSO trade union representatives raised a number of issues, one of the most significant of which was problems with the way policy objectives were communicated to line-managers:

> It's not been explained to them well enough. If they don't really understand it then they are not going to buy into it. So I think it's sort of like it has a knock-on effect, if they don't understand it, then how can you expect them to be really that committed to implementing it? (White man)

> ... you break it down and explain it to them, then they tend to back off or understand it at least, even if they don't really accept the idea. So I don't think PSO does enough of that. You know, there is more that they could do to make people understand why it is important. (White woman)

As these quotes suggest, reflecting previous research (Foster and Harris 2005), the trade union representatives felt that line-managers did not understand what their role in implementing DM was meant to be. This was also perceived to be partly because of the lack of a clear steer from the centre:

> But it's not joined up or consistent a lot of the time ... So you can have one group championing one element of equality, for example, doing some sort of awareness events and seminar, and another group doing absolutely nothing ... You know, even though there is sort of an overarching HR unit and within that there is an Equality and Diversity Unit ... not every idea or policy that they come up with is enforceable in every group and it does not necessarily get filtered down the line of the management chain in the same way within different groups. (White man)

> The centre should be doing things and the process of delegation and fragmentation has meant that to a certain extent the centre does not regard it as their [responsibility] to intervene. (White man)

Again, according to trade union representatives, this resulted in uneven practices by managers, indicating that devolution to the line is not always good for equality:

> ... some managers are really good in ensuring that ... their staff know what their rights are, you know, with the changes in the department and what help is out there if they need it. But other areas, you know, you are basically an individual, isolated, people chucking their own rules in, you know, and that happens quite a lot. (White woman)

Another example of uneven treatment was implementation of the flexible working policy, under which individuals had to gain the agreement of their line-manager. Most trade union representatives felt that it was more difficult for lower grade employees to get their mangers' agreement because such employees were widely seen as easily replaceable. However, the pressure was now on for managers to accommodate requests for flexible working for operational efficiency reasons (the business case):

> . . . there is a conflict between the efficiency of the unit and . . . the needs of the staff on the other hand. But I suppose because of the Department's strategy and the need to encourage flexible working, this is going to have to change anyway, because there won't be enough desks for people to be in. And certainly the pressure for everyone to accept that this is the new culture is quite intense and intensifying. So yes there will be people who will be reluctant to allow people to work flexibly and obviously there is already [hypocrisy] in the sense in which it's always been easy for people at range 10, which is the Civil Service principal grade and above, you know, to work flexibly. And they've always been trusted to deliver. (White man)

Another initiative criticized by PSO representatives was the diversity objective within the performance appraisal system. This had been introduced in an attempt to make DM everyone's responsibility, but according to the trade union representatives it had become another bureaucratic, 'tick box' exercise:

> . . . people found that really difficult, that diversity objective. That was quite interesting. They didn't think 'Oh great, I have a diversity objective here but my problem is which things shall I put in there because I do fifteen things on diversity', you know? (White man)

The problem was that many people, particularly in lower grades with no management responsibilities, found it hard to know how to engage with the diversity agenda, and again they were given little help by the centre.

Devolution also meant that there was a lack of communication at the workplace level about certain central policy initiatives that PSO had introduced. For example, trade union representatives spoke of Diversity Champions—senior people responsible for championing DM—as being 'invisible' at workplace level, claiming that most people would not even know the name of the Champion in their section. Another significant criticism from PSO representatives concerned workforce monitoring—frequently cited by academics and practitioners as an important step in DM implementation—which was described as incomplete, particularly on ethnicity. While data was readily given to trade union representatives when they asked for it, the problem was often that the data was not available:

And certainly we know it is one problem the Department faces that, response to ethnic minority monitoring requests is very low. And in fact lower than it was in previous years. So we don't necessarily know precisely how many minority ethnic staff the Department employs. And certainly we don't know what grade they're [in]. (White man)

PSO was criticized for not making sufficient effort to address this problem. In addition, the trade union representatives criticized the delivery and content of diversity training. Some felt diversity training was not widely available enough; they felt that a basic course should be compulsory and part of induction for new starters:

> There is an introductory course when people start in PSO and there's like a snippet in there on equality, I think . . . So they touch on equality. Can you imagine, they have three days on everything to do with being a civil servant and the department, that equality doesn't get much of a look-in. (White man)

As explained in Chapter 5, ServiceCo was at a relatively early stage in developing and disseminating its DM policy and in rolling out training to managers and employees. Therefore, it was unsurprising that trade union representatives had little comment to make about policy implementation within the company and whether or not it matched the policy's aspirational statements. However, they did remark on the extent of the company's sincerity in its aim to value diversity and become an EO employer and on its practical ability to implement DM. There was a cautiously optimistic view, for example, 'I think the spirit is there but it doesn't always—you know what I mean'; but at the same time a more cynical one: 'I think a lot of, like I said with managers and that . . . I mean, sometimes they make their own rules up. Or they don't always carry out what they say they are going to do'. These comments by ServiceCo trade union representatives hint at the possibility of the by now familiar problem of how to ensure that line-managers buy into DM.

CONCLUSION

As part of a stakeholder perspective, this chapter has explored trade union experiences of DM. We have argued previously (Kirton and Greene 2006) that the theoretical model of DM presents various challenges and dilemmas to trade unions and ultimately threatens to undermine, if not exclude altogether, their involvement in equality policy-making. Taking Dickens' (1999) argument that a 'three-pronged' strategy of the business case, legal regulation and social (joint) regulation is likely to make the greatest headway in tackling inequalities, then the exclusion of trade unions from DM can only be a retrograde step. In the research presented in this chapter, we attempted to gauge trade union responses to DM and tried to get behind the theory to reveal the realities of the trade union experience.

In terms of engagement with critiques of DM, we found considerable disparity between the views of the national trade union equality officers and the trade unionists working at the grassroots level. As we have noted here and previously (Kirton and Greene 2006), we found considerable skepticism and some hostility towards DM among the national equality officers who had a sophisticated and politicized understanding of equality and diversity. However, at the same time as pragmatists they signaled their preparedness to 'talk DM' if this seemed the most expedient way to keep equality and discrimination on the organizational agenda. The union negotiators and workplace representatives generally expressed more qualified approval for the principles of DM, but naturally the potential for union exclusion from policy development was a matter of serious concern. Their experiences suggested that their exclusion could result in a narrowing of the equality and diversity agenda and in a reinforcement of the perception of non-management staff that DM policy offered few benefits to those on the 'sticky floor' (see Chapter 8). Reflecting the traditional class-based nature of UK trade unionism and perhaps the fact that they were mostly white men, the workplace representatives tended to be more concerned about basic trade union issues than specifically with equality and diversity issues.

So, what kind of input into DM development and implementation were the unions having? Unlike in Scandinavian countries, where it is argued that it is difficult to imagine the development of DM policies without union participation (Wrench 2005), in the UK, this prospect is all too real. WERS 2004 found that in a majority of UK workplaces (72 per cent), managers did not negotiate, consult or even inform union representatives about EO matters (Walsh 2007). Our research confirms the findings of the latest WERS survey indicating low levels of *bargaining* activity on equality and diversity. However, that is not to say that the unions in our research had no influence on DM, or that they were not consulted or informed. Our research demonstrates that it is possible for unions to exercise influence that falls short of collective bargaining, with discussions (consultation) often occurring outside of the formal bargaining arrangements, sometimes between individuals on the union and management sides. In the banking sector and in our public sector case study, we did find evidence of union input into the design and implementation of DM policies. This occurred via various formal and informal channels. For example, in our public sector case study, PSO, the senior branch officer got himself onto various working groups dealing with equality and diversity issues. Even though he was not formally representing the union, he was able to bring to bear a union perspective. Similarly, one of the female UNIFI negotiators in particular reported a very strong working relationship with a major bank's diversity manager. This had enabled the union to have considerable informal influence on a new DM policy, highlighting the fact that key individuals on the union side can act as agents (of change) in organizations, if they press do so, even if employers are unwilling in the present era to institutionalize union involvement. In conclusion, our research revealed a *degree* of joint regulation of equality and diversity, but the relative failure to institutionalize bargaining and consultation with unions in this area renders trade union influence fragile.

10 Experiencing Diversity Management
The Value of a Stakeholder Perspective

This chapter provides a reflexive conclusion to the book, summarizing the key themes and debates to emerge from the research findings. The chapter begins by considering the general picture of diversity management (DM) in the UK revealed by our research, before moving on to discuss the explanations for the picture we present. We then discuss the prospects for DM as a paradigm to advance the equality project within UK organizations. In reflecting on these aspects, we explore the different stakeholder experiences of DM and highlight the tensions and dilemmas that these multiple experiences reveal. We aim to critically appraise the value of a stakeholder perspective for equality and diversity research within the wider field of industrial relations.

Overall, we are aware that as critical researchers within the field, while we believe it is important to provide an antidote to the 'upbeat naivety' of many practitioner representations of DM, it is also important to recognize that our accounts can sometimes be overly negative and can often offer a disappointingly pessimistic view of the state of things. In some ways, this can sometimes belie our own philosophical and practical commitment to upholding the importance of action on equality and diversity within organizations. We often come across this dilemma in our teaching or in our work with organizations, where as researchers in the field we are often called upon to contribute to company diversity days or training events. While we want to present a critical account, we do not want to give the impression that we think all policy and practice is pointless or without effect. In this chapter, we try to highlight the positive experiences and examples we found in our research, and we hope that our critical analysis will indicate possibilities of thinking about and practicing DM in a different way, reflecting on both our own research and other recent research in the field.

THE STATE OF DM PRACTICE IN THE UK

What's happened in the past number of years is that . . . I've seen equality policies go from about a paragraph and a half, to twelve glossy pages. I've seen things move from the odd committee to a committee structure

> ... I've seen a whole equality industry develop ... and they're making millions out of producing packages which appear to be radical in theory and in the text, but actually provide a very safe tick-in-the-box solution for the organisations that they work for. (White, female diversity consultant)

There is no doubt that DM is a policy paradigm that has firmly come of age in the UK in that it seems to have become an ubiquitous part of organizational life and of the wider public discourse (such as government documents and campaigns, and media representations). We did not find a single organization where the term 'diversity' was not used in some way or another (albeit a relatively recent development in some, especially in the public sector), and usually the term 'diversity management', 'managing diversity' or some variant of this has replaced (particularly in the private sector) or is at least in addition to the more traditional terminology of 'equal opportunities' (EO) or 'equality'. In parallel to developments in terminology (and arguably approach) in the broader field of HRM—from personnel managers to human resource managers—equality units have often been renamed 'diversity', and almost all diversity practitioners in our research had 'diversity' somewhere in their job title. The question, however, is whether all this retitling and 'talking the talk' of DM has really had any effect on policy and practice, and it is here where we can really begin to question whether DM as a policy paradigm has really gained a hold on practice within the UK.

Continuity of Practice with Traditional EO

> Just because people use the word diversity, doesn't mean they're not still talking about the same old things, and if you say the agenda has broadened, well that's just part of the way that we've all begun to look at work in a different way, um, and we talk more about the hours that people work and the way that work is organised, but that doesn't mean that you're moving away from any notion of equality, in fact when you're talking about flexible working and people's hours of work, it's all bound up with concepts of equality ... So I'm still not convinced that there have been great changes out there. (White, female, trade union equality officer)

Reflecting on the discussion in Chapter 2 and leaving aside the critique of the DM paradigm or of the potential detrimental effects of aspects of it for a moment, what practices might we expect to see that would fit within a DM paradigm? While we would obviously expect that organizations would still take action to ensure that their basic legal responsibilities were covered, we would expect that the *emphasis* on legal compliance as the primary driver of policy and practice would diminish. We would also expect to see a range of policies that demonstrated the central tenets of the DM paradigm. This might include policies that focus on individual differences, and therefore processes, procedures and initiatives that related to individual employees and their individual contracts, rather than initiatives or policies that targeted particular groups of employees (for example, women, black and minority ethnic (BME), disabled etc). Indeed, we might expect that such policies, procedures and initiatives would also be inclusive of all employees, emphasizing individual differences. We would not expect to see positive action initiatives or targets or collective agreements encompassing diversity issues. Indeed, taking the viewpoint of DM advocates Kandola and Fullerton (1998), they are more than clear on this point, for example: 'We believe that such [positive action] approaches do not fit in with a managing diversity approach and need to be rethought if an organization truly wishes to become diversity-oriented' (ibid: 5) and in an amusingly colourful turn of phrase: 'positive action in our view is no better than applying a sticking plaster to a festering wound' (ibid: 134). We would definitely expect to see a central focus on the business case for diversity, such that public rationales (for example, company communications, written policy documents, campaigns) for DM within the organization would stress the importance of diversity for business objectives. In terms of ownership and responsibility for DM within the organization, we would expect to see significant senior managerial commitment to DM, through taking on roles as diversity champions, making regular public statements about the importance of attention to diversity within the organization, and also demonstrating this commitment through behaviours (for example, taking time to attend diversity events, groups, consultative activities, as well as demonstrating commitment to things such as work–life balance through their own work patterns). Senior commitment would also involve considerable and significant resourcing of DM within the organization through (depending on the size of the organization) specialist roles and departments, and well-resourced programmes of training and other initiatives. We would also expect to see the responsibility for DM devolved through the organization, particularly to line-managers, who are seen as the crucial implementers of policy. Overall, the commitment to the DM paradigm would see policy that led to initiatives that required organizational cultures to be transformed so that differences, in DM rhetorical terms, could be valued, and everybody regardless of their social group or individual background would feel able to contribute to their fullest potential in the organization.

Bearing this in mind, reflecting on our findings in our two case study organizations (ServiceCo and PSO) and on viewpoints gathered from the interviews with diversity practitioners in a broad range of public and private sector organizations, we do not believe that we are seeing much of what we would expect to find if organizations were working within the DM paradigm beyond a lot of talk and use of the rhetoric of DM. As discussed in Chapters 4 and 5, the DM policies of both PSO and ServiceCo contain various aspects that reflect the central tenets of the DM paradigm. Our findings would confirm that there has been, as stated in Chapter 2, a significant shift in the way policies are formulated, and the way that stakeholders talk about policy, away from the need to dissolve or simply accommodate differences towards recognizing the value of individual differences and the way in which these individual differences can make a difference to the organization and its business objectives. Both PSO and ServiceCo's policies specifically mention 'valuing differences', and this term, perhaps more than anything within the DM paradigm, seems to have become the mantra of organizations in this policy arena.

For the diversity practitioners, the managers and even the more critical trade union national officers we spoke to, this broadened conceptualization of difference and the recognition of intersectionality facilitated by it was seen as a particularly positive aspect of the DM discourse. We can also see some evidence of how this broader understanding of what difference is and how it should be dealt with impacts upon the types of interventions introduced. For example, PSO has more recently established a cross diversity strand employee group within one part of its organization (indicating a desire to be more inclusive), and we see examples of policies being made inclusive of all staff, such as the time off and flexible working arrangements. As discussed in Chapter 6, exploring the perspectives of diversity practitioners, perhaps the area that appeared to most clearly encompass aspects of the DM paradigm across the majority of organizations, were policies relating to work–life balance. This was seen as an area that could cross-cut group identities, allowing individuals to participate to the best of their ability in line with their individual requirements.

However, in the main, we did not see anything fundamentally radical in any of the policies of any of the organizations involved in our research. The core components of the policy at all of the organizations were still fundamentally based around social groups (namely women, BME, disabled, lesbian and gay, with some looking also at age), with associated initiatives that would not have looked out of place in a traditional EO paradigm. Indeed, the traditional focus on gender and race as a priority amongst these equality strands is still commonplace in most organizations. The focus is therefore still very much on those groups covered by legislation. Despite exhortations from professional bodies such as the Chartered Institute for Personnel and Development (CIPD 2007) and comments from the majority of senior managers and diversity practitioners of the need to move away from legal compliance-based policy approaches, there can be no doubt that the need to comply with legislation still retains a key prominence within the policy framework and direction of organizations. In fact, in the case of the public sector in the UK, the need to comply with legislation around diversity issues has arguably become even more prominent with the addition of statutory duties to promote equality and concomitantly its place within the policy arena. Our interviews with stakeholders in both PSO and

ServiceCo further down the organizational hierarchy confirm that often what is understood as the rationale for DM policy (although issues about stakeholder understanding of DM rationales or lack of will be discussed in more detail later) is closely connected to the need to comply with legislation, some of which can be seen to have been reinforced by the nature of diversity training (especially in ServiceCo). Moreover, organizations tended to set group-based targets for the diversity of their workforce, something practitioner writers like Kandola and Fullerton (1998: 136) would not deem part of the DM paradigm at all. For example, the benchmark targets set for the future and the evaluation of how these targets are being met in PSO (as discussed in Chapter 4) are a case in point.

Continuity of Limited Stakeholder Involvement

[We need] policies that actually mean something . . . It's no good developing a strategy or policy unless you've consulted the people who are actually going to be doing it . . . and got some ownership from them. So that whole issue around leadership and strategy is very much about involvement and inclusivity and consultation. So for example if I want to change my patrol policy on the Division, then there are a whole group of people that I need to get involved in that. Including people outside the organisation, so who are the key stakeholders? Community representative, partnership representatives, but most of all the actual officers who are going to be doing this. (White, female, public sector diversity champion)

As already established, within a DM paradigm, we might expect to see considerable shared ownership of DM as manifested by stakeholder involvement. As discussed in Chapter 2 (and in relation to trade union critiques of DM in Chapter 9), on the one hand, DM is often positioned as a top-down, managerial approach. Certainly we would expect to see considerable levels of senior commitment and resourcing at an organization working within a DM paradigm, and it is the vision and commitment of top management that is seen as critical to the success of DM initiatives, rather than the involvement of other stakeholders. On the other hand, there is also a lot of emphasis within the DM paradigm for shared ownership and responsibility for DM (see Kandola and Fullerton 1998: 83). 'Taking diversity out of HR' was something that was frequently mentioned by the diversity practitioners we interviewed. However, it is interesting to note, however, that responsibility for equality and diversity, and reporting lines of both diversity champions and specialists tended to be most frequently based within HR. At PSO, where there was a designated Diversity Unit, the link with HR was not so tangible; however, DM was firmly situated in the HR department at ServiceCo.

In terms of senior commitment, the vast majority of people we interviewed as part of our research attested to the importance of support and leadership from key senior management figures (often including the CEO). Commitment and involvement at the senior level did not appear to be problematic for most respondents; indeed, most diversity practitioners stated very clearly that they believed they had the personal support of senior management, perhaps because (as discussed in Chapter 6) they were mostly senior people themselves and therefore able to engage with senior managers as peers, but also because they believed there was genuine support for the diversity agenda from the top. Even those at a more junior managerial level believed that they had the personal backing of key senior people. However, this support did not always translate into necessary resources. For example, at ServiceCo, the team tasked with developing the DM policy was small, with one senior manager and two junior colleagues. The senior manager was not exclusively employed on DM issues, also being the Head of Employee Relations. The profile of diversity practitioners in Chapter 6 reveals the extent to which it was often the case that DM responsibilities were taken on along with a myriad of other business and operational responsibilities by the specialists and/or champions. Evidence from other recent research in the UK supports our finding of the fairly limited level of resourcing for DM. EO/diversity practitioners are most often at middle management level, work only part-time on equality and diversity issues and have relatively limited resources; indeed, less than a third of respondent organisations in a recent survey even had a designated budget (CIPD 2006).

Now in some respects, the multi-tasking manager taking on DM, alongside other key business and operational responsibilities, would seem to sit comfortably within a DM paradigm that stresses the need for shared ownership of DM, that it should not just be the responsibility of the HR or the diversity specialist, and that DM should be seen as a mainstream business activity. However, unfortunately, our research seems to point to the fact that ownership for DM is still largely limited to a small number of individuals, and overall there exist very low levels of wider stakeholder involvement. A prime example of this is the way in which line-managers were commonly seen by other stakeholders to be the biggest obstacle to the success of DM within organizations at the same time as they are also seen to be the key implementers of policy. As discussed in Chapter 7, other stakeholders involved in our research saw line-managers as lacking understanding of the rationale for DM, as lacking the competencies and skills to implement DM and as key conduits of unfair practices within organizations. For example, with regard to work–life balance initiatives, non-management employee and trade union experience of their implementation was often extremely inconsistent, with much left to individual line-management discretion resulting in perceptions of unfairness. Our interviews with line-managers at PSO and to a greater extent at ServiceCo illustrated the extent to which dissemination of the rationale for DM policy to them and their awareness of what it meant for their jobs was extremely limited. While most had an understanding of what 'equality' and EO meant, far fewer understood 'diversity' or DM. At ServiceCo, line-managers had no involvement in policy development. At PSO, line-managers did have the opportunity to be involved in the development of policies and initiatives, but notably only if they were part of employee diversity groups or were explicitly involved in negotiating bodies. Diversity training is seen within the practitioner literature and by stakeholders themselves as a key mechanism to help achieve understanding and buy-in. However, training for line-managers was also extremely variable within organizations, although vastly greater in quantity and quality at an organization like PSO, with a long-established history of policy-making and action on equality and diversity issues compared to one at the very beginning of its policy development such as ServiceCo.

If line-managers, seen as the central implementers of policy, are only engaged and involved in DM policy development and implementation in a very limited way, then this situation is exacerbated for stakeholders further down the organizational hierarchy. In principle, the diversity practitioners we interviewed all agreed that it was important to involve non-management employees in policy-making, but how organizations conducted employee involvement differed. Only a minority of interviewees indicated active commitment to involving the recognised trade unions. In other organizations, trade unions played only a marginal role, even though there appeared to be no in principle opposition to their involvement. Across the organisations, there was evidence of a variety of direct forms of employee involvement including surveys, focus groups, and employee network groups. ServiceCo represented one end of the employee involvement spectrum, where there was no stakeholder involvement at all beyond senior management, with the union seen as benign and supportive, but not necessary to involve. PSO had fairly sophisticated employee involvement mechanisms, including designated employee groups around diversity strands and proactive involvement of the recognised trade unions. Chapter 4 provided examples of the way that these groups at PSO were able to have some kind of constructive impact on the policy itself, while Chapter 9 provided further examples of proactive trade union involvement and joint working in this area both in PSO and in other organisations. However, even at PSO, the number of non-management employees involved in employee groups was extremely small, and it was clear from our research that non-management employees typically perceived a representation and communication gap. This was particularly the case for those at lower grade levels, indicating the extent to which there is still more work to do in engaging stakeholders in DM. In general, non-management employees at PSO were aware of the policy being on the intranet, but typically they had not read it, clearly indicating that they saw it as unimportant or inapplicable to their working lives. At ServiceCo, most people were unaware of the policy.

Therefore, despite the majority of managers we spoke to, whatever their level, believing that DM should be everyone's responsibility, coupled with this being a central mantra of the practitioner writing on the DM paradigm, only a very small group of organizations in our research appeared to have the kind of integrated, supported and multi-channel forms of employee involvement that could potentially lead to significant input by non-management employees. The need to generate buy-in of a variety of internal stakeholders is clearly a challenge that organisations and their diversity specialists and champions still need to address.

Continuity of the Generic Business Case

I think one large problem with the [line management] group is that they don't really know what they're *meant* to do. What actually as a manager am I meant to do to do this diversity stuff? They don't know, therefore it means they get very defensive. I think there are some who are very deliberately obstructive and don't give a toss what's being said from above or anywhere else, they're gonna do it their way. And, but at the end of the day you could have great top level buy-in and you can have real champions amongst whatever group whether it's, ethnic minorities or whether it's women. But if you don't tackle that [middle] group that operationalize stuff, nothing really does change . . . And there were clear examples of men who, were known bulliers, known misogynists, known to really, to be really offensive, but they bring the money in and they get the big bonuses. And that, you know, you speak to the people in the organisation and they just say until *that* changes, until they challenge *his* bonus, we know [nothing will change]. (White, female private sector diversity specialist)

As someone at the very bottom of the ladder I don't see where there is any application of diversity. (White, male, non management employee at PSO)

As discussed in Chapter 2, a key tenet of the DM paradigm is the establishment of the business case as the *primary* rationale for policy, distinguishing it from the EO paradigm, where the social justice or moral case is more prominent than the business case (Noon and Ogbonna 2001; Kaler 2001). Our research confirms that UK organizations are employing the business case as a prominent feature of the rhetorical rationale for DM, although as discussed later not necessarily to the exclusion of the moral/social justice or legislative case. The business benefits that diversity practitioners within our research cited closely resembled those advocated in management literature (see Chapter 2). Wanting to be an 'employer of choice' was a frequently cited benefit. However, the most commonly cited business case for diversity was to gain a workforce that was better reflective of the customer base, with the assumption that this would improve customer service.

Like Kirton (2008), we found in our research that the most common position taken by organizations was to put forward generic, 'best practice' business case arguments. This is supported by recent research specifically involving line-managers that found that only 46 per cent of managers believe that their organization has made the case for diversity to the effectiveness and success of their organization (Opportunity Now 2005). This is despite the fact that the dominant view in mainstream HRM writing (the 'parent' concept of DM) is that the focus should be on 'best fit' (see Boxall and Purcell 2000 for a useful international review). The problem is that most of the organizations had difficulty operationalizing this generic business case. If, as was discussed in Chapter 2, there is only limited 'bottom-line' evidence for the benefits of DM, this is made even more difficult when diversity specialists and champions are trying to persuade stakeholders of the benefit of a business case that may have very tenuous links to their own organizational objectives. A few of our diversity practitioners were more able to quantify the benefits in terms of direct 'bottom-line' effects depending on the nature of the business; however, the vast majority recognised that benefits were largely qualitative, intangible and had to be seen as long-term. Out of the two case studies, it was the diversity specialist at ServiceCo that seemed to be able to articulate the tangible bottom-line benefits of DM to her organization, although, with its reference to legal compliance, it was not in terms that usually fit within a DM paradigm. As discussed in detail in Chapter 5, the diversity specialist saw the need to avoid the experience of recent costly law suits around diversity issues as a key part of the business case for why ServiceCo needed to take DM seriously. In addition, there was a further need to be able to demonstrate formal policy relating to DM, because this had recently become a central part of recent requirements to win key business contracts. What this indicates is the complexity of separating out the legal and business cases, and why there cannot be a strict delineation between the EO and DM paradigms. Even though there is an analytical distinction often made (for example, see Liff and Dickens 2000), in reality organisations often conflate the two, not only because of the financial penalties involved in employment tribunal cases, but also because of the damage to organizational reputation if the general public becomes aware of legal action.

As discussed in Chapter 5, the ServiceCo example also provides a demonstration of the way that diversity practitioners can fall into the trap of basing policy initiatives on generic best practice (i.e. recruitment and retention of graduates), without really considering whether this fits properly with the specific organizational context (i.e. that the problems around recruitment and retention at ServiceCo were not at the graduate level but at the low-skilled, low-grade levels). This essentially indicates the isomorphic tendencies around DM issues, when organizations start to follow certain best practice principles (or doing what other companies are doing) without any proper analysis of whether this fits the specific context of the organization or is likely to yield any benefits.

The problem is that it is very hard to apply a generic business case to the everyday work of organisational stakeholders, particularly line-managers. Chapter 7 highlighted the difficulty that line-managers found in operationalizing DM and in understanding what the policy actually meant for them as individuals in terms of their management style, behaviours and practices. A case in point was the universal diversity performance objective at PSO. Making DM a key (measurable) performance objective is seen as important to encourage shared ownership and responsibility of DM (for example, see Opportunity Now 2005: 12; Kandola and Fullerton 1998: 120–2). However, at PSO, a key finding was the difficulty that line-managers (and non-management employees) had in working out how to demonstrate the diversity objective in their work. Also, most line-managers believed that senior management did not see it as important compared with operational objectives. At ServiceCo, it was obvious that diversity issues had not even crossed the radar of many line-managers with regard to their own work. Overall, it was clear that many stakeholders could not identify the business case for DM in relation to their own organization. Thus, it is not surprising that our research reveals that line-managers' practice of DM was widely seen by other stakeholders as uneven and inconsistent. Equally, it is not surprising that DM issues were not a priority for line-managers, particularly given a context of competing demands on their time and resources.

Chapter 8 provided a picture of the extent to which non-management employees also found extreme difficulty understanding what the business case meant for them. In terms of shared ownership, there was little evidence of this apparent at ServiceCo, where the vast majority of employees had no knowledge of the policy at all and very limited understanding of the concept of diversity. At PSO, where there was greater understanding and awareness amongst non-management employees of both the concept of diversity and the policy, it was clear that they found even greater difficulty than line-managers in meeting the diversity objective (i.e. how to make DM meaningful to their own work). At both organizations, it was also apparent that there was pessimism that diversity initiatives would hold any tangible benefits for them.

Summary

We certainly have evidence of some (sometimes considerable) tinkering around at the margins of the DM paradigm, with organizations taking on some limited aspects of it, but nothing we could describe as a coherent, consistent DM strategy that epitomized the paradigm. What is emphasised overall is that, in practice, the move to DM in rhetoric often really represents little change from traditional EO, so that any new initiatives that we might see as fitting more with a DM paradigm become more of a supplement to EO, rather than posing a new and radical challenge to organisational structures and cultures. The findings also reveal real problems in gaining buy-in to DM and in operationalizing the business case at the organizational level, issues that we now go on to discuss in more detail.

IS THE DM PARADIGM 'DO-ABLE'?

> Because it covers, diversity seems to cover everything, you know what I mean? Where would you end diversity, it's never ending. (White, female trade union equality officer)

> It's not like years ago when we had a central personnel department and they had goals to be implemented, but now it's not like that. I'm a member of the race employee group and it does some good work, but when I go back to my work it's different, efforts dissipate and they're wasted. (Black, male, non-management employee at PSO)

One of the most obvious explanations for why so much policy remains within a more traditional EO paradigm concerns the difficulty in operationalizing the DM paradigm. Part of this links to the foregoing section dealing with the failure of most organizations to develop and articulate an organization-specific business case. However, above and beyond this, there is a broader theoretical question of whether 'diversity [the DM paradigm] is do-able' at all (Prasad and Mills 1997). Clearly, our research indicates that many stakeholders, at least outside of senior management level, have trouble understanding what DM policies are for and how to implement them. Overall, DM is a far more 'slippery concept' than EO; for instance, while EO involves explicit attention to legislative requirements, setting targets for improving the diversity of the workforce and concrete action to try to ensure fair and meritocratic treatment regardless of group identity, the attention to valuing the myriad of individual differences is much more difficult to get a grasp on in terms of what this means policy would actually involve. Woodhams and Danieli's (2000) research illustrates the difficulty of making the business case for diversity when looking at the case of disabled employees, perhaps the area where individual differences (in terms of every impairment being different) are most salient. It would be hard to justify diversity policies in purely business case terms because of this level of individuality, which would inevitably lead to increased costs. Therefore, their argument follows that policy has to have some underpinning collective group focus imperative (here supported by law). If the approach within the DM paradigm is conceptualised solely as concerned with individual differences, identified and dealt with on an individual basis, then it becomes very difficult to make a viable business case, and therefore it is not surprising that we do not find clear examples of its operationalization in practice. Senior managers, diversity practitioners and some line-managers in our research stated that diversity was about valuing individuals' differences and engendering a place of work where people felt able to make a contribution, but what this actually meant in terms of concrete policy-making and managerial action was much more vague and amorphous. This explains why, in their study of line-managers in the UK retail industry in much the same way as in our research, Foster and Harris' (2005) found that managers tended to fall back on the EO paradigm of fair procedures and standardized rules as a safer and more easily understood way of dealing with equality and diversity issues.

Conflict Between Context and DM Paradigm

> We're talking about culture and values, but we're also having to say to our managers and by the way you've got to do this, this, this and this. I'm giving them two messages now. I'm giving them a culture reason and then I am saying they have got to do this and they start getting very very nervous about anything to do with [the law]. (White, female, HR manager at ServiceCo)

Linked to the foregoing discussion, we reflect on the conflict that potentially exists between the DM paradigm and the wider legislative (and arguably the social and political contexts), as well as the organizational context. How 'do-able' is the DM paradigm, with its emphasis on an internally driven organization-specific business case, when organizations function within an external legislative context? There was some discussion of this in Chapter 7, looking at the potential confusion and difficulty experienced by line-managers when faced with an extra-organizational context that requires a standardized approach to treatment of social groups in order to comply with anti-discrimination legislation and an internal business led approach to DM that calls for practices tailored to local circumstances and attention to individual differences. Organizational stakeholders still identify various social *groups* as the recipients and beneficiaries of DM, even if there are the wider changes in direction towards individual differences within formal DM rhetoric. For example, at PSO, policies regularly refer to social group issues (for example, the recognition in the 2007 Equality Scheme of the problem of women's over representation in lower grades), while trade union representatives were concerned about the disproportionate effects of the restructuring specifically on BME employees. At ServiceCo, policy targets were still based around specifically increasing women's and BME representation in middle and senior management levels because the workforce was clearly segregated along gender and race lines. As discussed in Chapters 6 and 9 (see also Kirton and Greene 2006, 2007), we have indicated the way in which diversity practitioners and trade union officers have often commented that EO represents the 'building blocks' of DM or that DM needs the foundations of EO, questioning the ability or need to separate the two paradigms. This is unsurprising given that the greater available evidence suggests that there is still much work to be done around group-based EO issues at the vast majority (if not all) organizations. However, many diversity practitioner and senior management stakeholders believed that DM was possible once basic EO work was done. This just indicates how out of touch with organizational 'reality' are practitioner-based texts such as Kandola and Fullerton (1998), who start from the point of view of saying that DM should not be viewed as resting on EO, it requires a complete rethink about how difference is viewed and how organizations respond to these differences within their cultures, structures and policies. Our research indicates just how far from this radical transformation of thinking are the vast majority of organizations (even if such a transformation was 'do-able' in theory anyway).

Vacuum of Responsibility for DM

> I'm asked to go into an organisation very often because they want the business case to be explored and developed. So the first person I meet is the equality specialist. Now, you tell me . . . if they believe that it makes business and organisation sense to develop that talent, who should I be meeting? Who should be driving this? The chief executive, the chief officer, the managing director, the finance director and so on. (White, female diversity consultant)

There is a lot of 'talk' within the DM paradigm around the need for DM to be everyone's responsibility and that there should be shared ownership throughout the organization. However, as discussed earlier, there was fairly limited evidence for this in practice within our participating organizations. As established in Chapter 2, one consequence of the emergence and dissemination of the DM paradigm has been that many organizations have seen the decline of specialist equality units in favour of appointing diversity specialists and champions within the core business areas. However, there are many commentators (for example, Dickens 1999; Creegan et al 2003) who point to problems with the devolution of responsibility for DM away from specialists within HR and equality units, because then what group, individual or department is left taking on the central monitoring function and overseeing policy implementation? As we have just argued, consistency of implementation may be particularly important in order to comply with the requirements of legislation. However, as discussed in Chapter 4, trade union respondents at PSO specifically commented on the difficulties caused by weaker steer now given to line-managers from the centre, meaning that how DM policy was implemented depended very much on the discretion of the individual manager, with all the problems that then ensued with regard to inconsistency of practice and feelings from employees of unfair treatment. Arguably, it is inevitable that a paradigm that emphasizes individual differences leaves policy implementation to managerial discretion. The problem is that it is likely that this will only exacerbate feelings of felt unfairness due to uneven managerial practice. In turn, this might leave the manager/organization vulnerable to legal challenges.

With regard to whether responsibility for DM is shared amongst line-managers and non-management employees, our research findings really do not confirm that this is happening. The greatest obstacle to DM implementation is still widely seen as line-managers, but at the same time our findings point clearly to the difficulties that line-managers find in making DM a priority. As stated, our findings also point to the limited understanding of DM amongst non-management employees and the extremely limited opportunities for non-management employees to be involved in DM policy development and implementation in the vast majority of organizations.

In essence, what we tend to find is that there are lots of people saying that DM should be everybody's responsibility without the structures and accountability in place for it to be taken on proactively by any of the stakeholders. There is thus a conflict between the DM paradigm requirement for devolution and shared responsibility and existing structures, hierarchies and processes within organizations. What this results in is a serious vacuum of responsibility for DM in UK organizations. This can only exacerbate the difficulties of making DM 'doable'. As Creegan usefully states in Chapter 8, analysis of our research data 'creates an impression of a vicious circle in which a problematic organizational culture is perpetuated by the flawed implementation of DM rather than transformed by its success' (Chapter 8: 183). The implications of this for the prospects for the DM paradigm to advance equality are discussed in the next section.

DOES THE DM PARADIGM OFFER PROSPECTS FOR ADVANCING THE EQUALITY AGENDA WITHIN ORGANISATIONS?

I think it's more in the hands of the human resources people, that there's a kind of diversity industry springing up and therefore it's the next big thing, which wouldn't be so bad, if we had already achieved some of the building blocks, and I guess that's where my . . . what's the word . . . scepticism kicks in. Well I think, we're moving onto this, which is great, but by moving onto that, there's all sorts of stuff which hasn't been addressed, like the pay gap, right like the glass ceiling, well the concrete ceiling and the sticky floor. Those issues seem to be . . . well they do seem to be as if they're permanent features, so until we start to really dismantle those, and really make some movement, . . . we really shouldn't be moving on to broadening the debate, we should stick to some of the key issues. (White, female, trade union equality officer)

The reason why there has been so much debate around the implications of the shift from EO to DM is related to the question of whether DM offers anything that has the potential for progress on equality issues within organizations. Chapter 3 posed the question of whether DM can make progress on what are seen as key equality and diversity issues and challenges— namely, discrimination, labour market segregation, pay gaps and under-valuation of skills, and flexible working and work–life balance. If we are at the point now where the DM paradigm has become ubiquitous (at least in rhetoric) in organizations in the UK, then we would have to say that on a very general level, there does not seem to have been any radical improvement on these key issues. A major conclusion of our earlier critical review (Kirton and Greene 2005a) was the continued patterns of inequality faced by many social groups within the UK labour market and the tenacity of the 'standard worker' norm (white, male, non-disabled, heterosexual, 25–40 years). Overall, the evidence presented indicates that policy and practice at both the national and organisational levels pose little challenge to the existing status quo, existing social attitudes or the existing norm of work, which is gendered, racialised and sexualised. Whichever way the statistics are looked at, the UK labour market is characterised by continued segregation, disadvantage and discrimination, which disproportionately affects some groups more than others. Moving this to the organizational level, clear patterns of gendered and racialised job segregation, and examples of sexism and racism are found within our two case studies. Respondents commonly talked about the continuing work to be done on traditional equality issues, particularly in relation to women and BME employees.

This is not to say that there were not examples of good practice or of improvements. For example, as discussed in Chapter 4, at PSO, despite the persistence of gender inequalities, there had been progress for women in the organization. However, it is likely that these improvements had come about as a consequence of more long-standing EO policies, rather than as a consequence of the relatively recent emergence of the 'valuing differences' perspective to the policy. On the other hand, there is no doubt that, in some circumstances, the emergence of DM has provided an opportunity to reinvigorate and re-energize tired EO policies within organizations. Perhaps we should not underestimate the value of being able to couch what are effectively EO initiatives within the DM rhetoric of valuing differences and being inclusive which possibly causes less backlash and less theoretical opposition (see discussion in Chapter 2). This will be discussed in more detail below.

This leads us back to the consideration of whether there are more fundamental theoretical problems with the DM paradigm, however. Indeed, aspects of this are touched upon in a number of chapters in the book, particularly Chapters 2 and 9. Key elements which may pose a greater theoretical challenge to progress on equality and diversity from a critical perspective include the business case focus, the primacy of individual differences and the top-down nature of DM. Thus, we have reflected on the contingent and partial nature of the purely business case-led approach, the negative implications of the emphasis on individual differences in reinforcing stereotypes and ignoring similarities between groups and the individualising of the policy approach which can be seen as a challenge to the role of collective groups such as trade unions. However, in some ways, much of this discussion becomes somewhat redundant if we find that, in practice, as we have done, there are very few, if any, examples of organizations developing a coherent strategy within the DM paradigm. We have already established that whilst policies might be entitled 'diversity' and might be sprinkled with expressions such as 'valuing difference', actual initiatives tend to look more like traditional EO with a strong focus on certain social groups. We have also discussed the way that a pure business case-led approach is hard to operationalize, particularly in the context of the wider legislative and social policy contexts. One possible area where we may question whether a move to DM has led to negative consequences is around the area of the involvement of trade unions and other collective groups and correspondingly, non-management employees. As discussed earlier, despite exhortations within the rhetoric of DM for shared ownership and accountability, we found evidence of a real responsibility vacuum within the organizations that were part of our research. Line managers had difficulty understanding or implementing DM; trade unions, where they existed, were not routinely seen as partners in the DM policy arena; and there were very few examples of anything more than superficial involvement of non-management employees. Chapter 6 also indicated that a change from traditional EO included the fact that diversity specialists now typically did not come from activist backgrounds, a change which clearly fits with a DM paradigm (see Kirton and Greene 2009; Kirton et al 2007). However, the move away from the activist-oriented EO paradigm, that arguably would have routinely involved trade unions or other employee groups, has led to or has happened in parallel with a situation of very limited employee involvement in DM. This is the area where we found most evidence of DM as a retrograde step in practice.

VALUE OF A STAKEHOLDER APPROACH

Because in my experience, most organisations *don't* know what people do on the ground . . . what happens is policies get written, procedures get formulated, nobody has a clue what's going on, what unfairness feels like if you're working . . . So actually, coming up with mechanisms to find out how people are feeling on the ground and what their experience is, is quite important. (Black, male, trade union equality officer)

As outlined in Chapter 1, a stakeholder perspective was an integral part of our research design, and therefore it shaped the approach to the analysis of our research data and the presentation of its key themes. This approach required that as wide a group of stakeholders as possible within the organizations were participants in our research, with a particular importance placed on gaining the views of those usually missed from DM research, including non-management employees and trade union representatives. It also required qualitative research methods that facilitated the capturing of stakeholder voices in context. Overall, we believe such an approach has offered a valuable level of sensitizing detail to our research and provided a much richer, more rounded and more contextualized picture of DM in theory and practice.

A key value of this approach has been in realizing the nuanced way in which people understand and take on the DM concept and therefore has uncovered the complexity of its implementation. For example, many of our taken-for-granted assumptions about how a particular stakeholder would or would not respond to aspects of the DM paradigm, and concomitantly how it was then implemented, were often challenged by actually speaking to the different stakeholders themselves.

Our research uncovered strong levels of senior commitment to DM within organizations, which bodes well at least for a continuing platform of DM. As an example, the senior commitment to DM within PSO itself and that coming from central government as the overarching employer did mean that resources for and attention to DM did seem to have been sustained even through the period of restructuring and downsizing, when, in line with a lot of research literature, we might have expected it to fall by the wayside. There were also many examples of committed and enthusiastic diversity practitioners, which offer a positive note for the future sustainability of a focus on DM within organizations. However, what our approach presents is a clear sense of the complexity of their positions and orientations, providing some explanation for why policy developed by these stakeholders does tend to reflect a real mix of the old and the new. All the diversity practitioners indicated commitment to equality and diversity, and some were also passionate about the issues, but they also saw their wider transformative goals as not necessarily in contradiction with business goals. They were prepared to talk in the language of both the business and social justice cases to make progress. This for us was interesting because, when compared to our previous analysis of the views of trade union equality officers (Kirton and Greene 2006), we found the organizational diversity practitioners' orientations to be more complex and nuanced, with much more genuine commitment to social justice principles than we had originally anticipated. Most interviewees talked unprompted about equality, social justice or inclusion when giving a definition of what diversity was about, and some interviewees were clearly using the language of diversity as a means of capturing the attention and gaining the support of significant others in their organizations, something we had also noted that trade unionists alluded to. However, most diversity practitioners also seemed to have a genuine belief in the business case for equality and diversity, rather than simply using it as a discursive tool with which to disguise their goals. Overall, our approach allowed us a perspective from which it is possible to avoid assuming that diversity practitioners are not progressive, simply because they are willing to talk in the language of the business, or to genuinely have a belief that a business case was important, and/or could be made (see further discussion in Chapter 6 and Kirton and Greene 2007).

However, what of course is interesting is that had we only gathered the senior management and/or diversity practitioner perspective (which is often the case with research in the field), then we would have developed a very different picture of the state of DM than we have done by being able to explore other stakeholder viewpoints. Certainly, it is possible that the overall picture of DM would have seemed more positive and more radical a departure from EO, being largely based as it would have been on those responsible for the public and formal rhetoric of DM within their organizations. As has been commented upon many times throughout this book, line-managers are cited as the most common obstacle to DM implementation and its success within organisations. However, being able to explore the viewpoints of the line-managers themselves offered an insight into why they are viewed like this by other stakeholders and the difficulty they face in operationalizing DM. The line-managers we spoke to were not deliberately obstructive, belligerent opponents of DM, and indeed many of them were open to the idea of DM, or at least they may have been had they been given the opportunity to understand its rationale and be involved in its development. What comes out clearly from our research is support for McConville and Holden's (1999) characterization of line-managers as 'piggy in the middle', where they are given the theoretical responsibility for DM implementation, without any of the authority, and for policies in which they have had no input. Our findings flag up time and time again the weakness of current resourcing and provision for line-management training, dissemination of policies and rationales and the way in which the structures and processes of the organisation are not supportive of making line-managers accountable for DM (such as through properly integrated performance management around diversity issues). The experience of line-managers in our case studies also clearly highlights the difficulty of making the DM paradigm 'do-able' in terms of what it means for their everyday roles and responsibilities. When you begin to reflect on how you could make aspects of the theoretical DM paradigm relevant to line-managers, you immediately realise how difficult this is to articulate in concrete policy terms, especially when the various aspects of organizational and wider context are also brought into play.

The access to the employee perspective on DM has been one of the most important contributions of our approach as it is an area that has been and is still a significant gap in the field. For example, in their conclusion to their *Handbook of Workplace Diversity*, Pringle et al (2006: 533) establish one of the continuing existing lacuna in the field as the privileging of management views over employee experiences which they describe as a 'glaring omission' (ibid). One of the explanations for such an omission relates to difficulties of research access, where they find managers hesitant to allow access to study employees for fear of the legal culpability that the organization might face when 'hostile environments'(ibid: 534) are documented. This in itself is interesting, because it indicates that managers are aware of the existence of problems around diversity issues in their organizations but are too afraid to have them exposed. In Chapter 1, we outlined the difficulties that we experienced ourselves in persuading organizations to be involved in our study, and the further difficulties we encountered when trying to arrange access to non-management employees, leading to us deciding to conduct focus group interviews. However, we would argue that it is worth persisting with organizations in order to gain the employee perspective, and we found that once organizations had agreed to participate as case studies, it was not necessarily fear of what may be found that led to us having to adapt our methods slightly for the non-management employee respondents, but logistical issues with regard to time off and work organization.

Non-management employees are arguably the crucial litmus test of whether DM policies work, and whether the DM paradigm offers anything new or progressive, because they are the key stakeholders at the receiving end of policy, and they are the ones who are supposed to benefit most from it. So it becomes even more inexplicable why they are the stakeholder so often missing from the account. It is through the interviews with non-management employees and trade union representatives that we are able to put flesh on the bones of what organizational demographic data actually means. What does it mean to experience the over-representation of women and BME employees at lower grades, how does this feel, how does this affect how individuals view the organization and how does this affect views of DM policy and practice? As Chapter 8 establishes, our research reveals the very messy existence of the 'sticky floor', where employee understandings of patterns of inequality can vary highly from organization to organization. For instance, at both PSO and ServiceCo, there was evidence of heavily entrenched structures of gendered and racialised job segregation. However, this was often not recognized as unfair or as inequality. So at PSO, employees would talk often of 'gradism', which had obvious gendered and racialized characteristics, but this was only mentioned by some individuals. At ServiceCo, the occupational divisions were accepted as a fact of life, and it was clear that individuals had not connected the recent activity around DM as connected to these aspects of their work life. What came across clearly in the research was that non-management employees were not simply passive victims or waiting recipients of policy. Particularly at PSO, there was palpable frustration at their lack of involvement in the policy arena and at not understanding what was going on.

FINAL DISCUSSION POINTS

We have argued elsewhere (Kirton and Greene 2005a) that the debate about whether DM is something better does not necessarily appear particularly useful and may actually be counter-productive. Why should we think of new policies and approaches as necessarily eclipsing the old? Not only is this often detrimental, but it is also quite obvious that this does not happen in reality. From an ideological point of view (in terms of Healy et al 2006, where research is conducted with the purpose of hopefully having some kind of intention to achieve material and political outcomes), we are pleased to find that so much of traditional EO policy-making continues as we believe that it is crucially important for progress. Both the EO and DM paradigms have weaknesses and strengths, and we have elsewhere developed a collectivist framework for DM that tries to integrate them (Kirton and Greene 2005a: 183). The DM approach, for example, suffers from its focus on individual differences, but also is much more forward-looking than EO in its view of difference and diversity as positive features which should be valued and utilised and is therefore more inclusive generally, and cognisant of intersectionality between social group identities. We believe that it is crucially important that, in taking up some aspects of DM, there is recognition of the support and protection offered by legislation, and formalised procedures and initiatives based around social groups in line with a group-based 'politics of difference' (Young 1990). The DM paradigm offers challenges to organisational cultures, but particularly given the reluctance, or inability of organizations to respond to these challenges proactively in practice, policy needs to be underpinned by more positive action policies and increased legislative protection.

Finally, taking a stakeholder approach has for us confirmed Dickens' (1999) call for the joint regulation of equality in the workplace—see Chapter 1, where we outlined Dickens' (1999) three strategies for equality action: the business case, the legislative case and the joint regulation case. We believe that our research indicates strong support for Dickens' assertion that these three strategies working together provide a much stronger basis for action on equality and diversity issues than either of them alone. PSO is a good case example here, in demonstrating the mediating interaction between all three strategies in ensuring that diversity issues remained a determining force on the restructuring process (see detailed discussion in Chapter 4 and Greene and Kirton 2008). While Dickens' definition of joint regulation deals specifically with union involvement, we would amend and extend the definition slightly to encompass the involvement of a wide group of organizational stakeholders, including in particular line-managers and non-management employees. However, for this to be achieved, organizations have to grapple with the thorny issue of how to involve the widest group of stakeholders possible. This is going to require action such as strategic and coherent thinking about existing representational and communication structures, and the development of performance management techniques that take diversity issues seriously. Perhaps the most important key theme of our research is that we do not believe that DM is simply something that can be 'done' to employees, and we do believe that organizations can benefit from the active involvement of all stakeholders. If organizations are going to address the worst excesses of inequality at the 'sticky floor', then the need to generate employee understanding and buy-in and the need to involve them has to be addressed.

Notes

NOTES TO CHAPTER 4

1. The first public sector duty was introduced in the Race Relations (Amendment) Act in 2002. The Disability duty was in force from December 2006 and the Gender duty from April 2007.
2. Sir Michael Lyons, Director of the Institute of Local Government Studies at the University of Birmingham , was asked to conduct an independent study into the scope for relocating a substantial number of public sector activities from London and the South East of England to other parts of the United Kingdom. The report 'Well Placed to Deliver?—Shaping the Pattern of Government Service' was published on 15 March 2004.
3. This refers to Sir Peter Gershon's review of public sector efficiency 'Releasing resources for the frontline: Independent Review of Public Sector Efficiency', published in July 2004. This document set out the scope for efficiencies identified within the public sector's back office, procurement, transaction service and policy-making functions. In addition, it identified opportunities for increasing the productive time of professionals working in schools, hospitals and other frontline public services, and makes a series of cross-cutting recommendations to further embed efficiency across the public sector.

NOTES TO CHAPTER 7

1. Hales (2005: 475) usefully cites Dunkerley (1975) and Kerr et al (1986) as summarising the supervisory role as "planning, scheduling and allocating work; monitoring output and conduct of work; checking equipment, safety and cleanliness; overseeing the introduction of new equipment and production problems; maintaining discipline; handling disputes; training; counselling; record-keeping and assisting with operational work".
2. Here autonomy is looked at in terms of their freedom to make decisions and the extent of monitoring from the centre. Managers in branch sites were asked, first, about issues relating to the scope for autonomous decision making, i.e. whether they had to follow policies set by managers elsewhere in the organization and whether they had to consult managers elsewhere before making a decision; and then, second, about issues relating to the extent of monitoring on their action, i.e. whether they regularly reported to managers elsewhere on these issues (Kersley at al 2006: 54–5).

Bibliography

ACAS (2005) Evidence to the Women and Work Commission. Available at: http://www.acas.org.uk/CHttpHandler.ashx?id=183&p=0] Accessed 29th July 2008.

Acker, J. (1990). 'Hierarchies, jobs, bodies: a theory of gendered organizations', *Gender and Society*, 4(2), 139–158.

Acker, J. (2000). 'Revisiting class: thinking from gender, race and organisations', *Social Politics*, 7(2), 192–243.

Adams, L., and Carter, K. (2007). *Black and Asian Women in the Workplace: The Employer Perspective*. Manchester: Equal Opportunities Commission.

Allen, R. S., Dawson, G., Wheatley, K., and White, C. S. (2008). 'Perceived diversity and organizational performance', *Employee Relations*, 200(1), 20–33.

Ashton, C. (2003). 'The importance of diversity in innovation', in M. Davidson and S. Fielden (eds.), *Individual Diversity and Psychology in Organizations*. Chichester: John Wiley, 19–40.

Aston, J., Hill, D., et al. (2006). 'The experience of claimants in race discrimination employment tribunal cases', in *Employment Relations Research Series ERRS55*, London: DTI.

Aston, J., Clegg, M., et al. (2004). *Interim update of key indicators of women's position in Britain*. London: Women and Equality Unit/Department for Trade and Industry.

Avery, D., McKay., Wilson, P. F., and Tonidandel, S. (2007). 'Unequal attendance: the relationships between race, organizational diversity cues and absenteeism', *Personnel Psychology*, 60(4), 875–902.

Bach, S., and Winchester, D. (2003). 'Industrial relations in the public sector', in P. Edwards (ed.), *Industrial Relations: Theory and Practice*, Second Edition. Oxford, UK: Blackwell, 285–312.

Bacharach, S., Bamberger, P., et al. (2005). 'Diversity and homphily at work: supportive relations among white and African-American peers', *Academy of Management Journal*, 48(4), 619–644.

Bajawa, A., and Woodall, J. (2006), 'Equal opportunity and diversity management meet downsizing: a case study in the UK airline industry', *Employee Relations*, 28(1), 46–61.

Bassett-Jones, N. (2005). 'The paradox of diversity management, creativity and innovation', *Creativity and Innovation Management*, 14(2), 169–175.

Bassett-Jones, N., Berman Brown, R., and Cornelius, N. (2007). Delivering effective diversity management through effective structures', *Systems Research and Behavioral Science*, 24, 59–67.

BBC. (2004). 'At a glance: spending review', Available at http://news.bbc.co.uk/1/hi/uk_politics/3887909.stm. Accessed September 1, 2008.

Bellard, E., and Rüling, C.-C. (2001). 'Importing diversity management: corporate discourses in France and Germany', Paper 2001.13, Ecole des Hautes Etudes

Commerciales, Universite de Geneve. Available at http://www.hec.unige.ch/recherches_publications/cahiers/2001/2001.13.pdf

Benschop, Y. (2001). 'Pride, prejudice and performance: relations between HRM, diversity and performance', *International Journal of Human Resource Management*, 12(7), 1166–1181.

Bergen, C. W., Soper, B., and Foster, T. (2002). 'Unintended negative effects of diversity management', *Public Personnel Management*, 31(2), 239–251.

Berthoud, R. (2008). 'Disability employment penalties in Britain', *Work, Employment & Society*, 22(1), 129–148.

Besen, Y., and Kimmel, M. S. (2006). 'At Sam's Club, no girls allowed: the lived experience of sex discrimination', *Equal Opportunities International*, 25(3), 172–187.

Blackett, A., and Sheppard, C. (2003). 'Collective bargaining and equality: making connections'. *International Labour Review*, 142(4), 419–457.

Blyton, P., and Turnbull, P. (2004). 'Employee relations and the state', in *The Dynamics of Employee Relations*, Third Edition. Macmillan: London, 170–216.

Bogg, J., Gibbons, C., Pontin., E., and Sartain, S. (2006). 'Occupational therapists' perceptions of equality, diversity and career progression in the National Health Service', *British Journal of Occupational Therapy*, 69(12), 540–547.

Boxall, P., and Purcell, J. (2000). 'Strategic human resource management: where have we come from and where should we be going?', *International Journal of Management Reviews*, 2(2), 183–203.

Bradley, H., (1999) *Gender and Power in the Workplace*, Basingstoke, Macmillan.

Brandling, J., and Mistral, W. (2007). *Equal Opportunities or Diversity Management in a Meritocratic Society? Accounts of Positive Action Trainees from Black and Minority Ethnic groups.* Unpublished.

Branine, M. (2004). 'Job sharing and equal opportunities under the new public management in local authorities', *International Journal of Public Sector Management*, 17(2), 136–152.

Brewster, C. (2007). 'Comparative HRM: European views and perspectives', *The International Journal of Human Resource Management*, 18(5), 769–787.

Brief, A., Umphress, E., et al. (2005). 'Community matters: realistic group conflict theory and the impact of diversity', *Academy of Management Journal*, 48(5), 830–844.

Briskin, L. (2002). The equity project in Canadian unions: confronting the challenge of restructuring and globalisation', in F. Colgan and S. Ledwith (eds.), *Gender, Diversity and Trade Unions*, London: Routledge, 28–47.

Bryson, A. (2001, April). 'The foundation of 'partnership'? Union effects on employee trust in management', *National Institute Economic Review*, 176, 91–104.

Bureau of Labor Statistics. (2007). *Charting the US Labor Market in 2006*, Washington, DC: US Department of Labor.

Business in the Community. (2007). Available at http://www.bitc.org.uk/what_we_do/where_we_work/wales/get_involved/workplace/diversity_2.html

Business in the Community, Doughty Centre for Corporate Responsibility and the Kennedy School of Government, Harvard. Available at http://www.bitc.org.uk/resources/publications/business_led.html. Accessed May 12, 2008.

Butler, P. (2005). 'Non-union employee representation: exploring the efficacy of the voice process', *Employee Relations*, 27(3), 272–288.

Cabinet Office. (2001). *Equality and Diversity: The Way Ahead*. London: Cabinet Office.

Campbell, J. L. and Pedersen, O. K. (2007) Institutional competitiveness in the global economy: Denmark, the United States, and the varieties of capitalism, *Regulation & Governance* 1, 230–246.

Carley, M. (2008). 'Danone signs international diversity agreement', *European Employment Review*, 409. Available at http://www.xperthr.co.uk/viewarticle.a spx?id=82700&searchwords=%22danone%22

CBI. (2008). *Talent Not Tokenism: The Business Benefits of Workforce Diversity.* London: Confederation of British Industry.

Chao, E. and Rones, P.L. (2007) Women in the Labor Force: A Databook. Washington: Bureau of Labor Statistics. Available at: http://www.bls.gov/cps/wlf-databook-2007.pdf Accessed 6th July 2008.

CIPD. (2003). *Age Discrimination at Work.* London: Chartered Institute for Personnel and Development (CIPD).

CIPD. (2006). *Diversity in Business: How Much Progress Have Employers Made? First Findings, Survey Report.* London: Chartered Institute of Personnel and Development (CIPD).

CIPD. (2007). *Diversity in Business: A Focus for Progress.* London: Chartered Institute of Personnel and Development (CIPD).

Clark, T., C. Maybey, D. Skinner (1998). Experiencing HRM: the importance of the inside story. *Experiencing Human Resource Management.* C. Mabey, D. Skinner and T. Clark. London, Sage: 1–13.

Cobble, D., and Bielski Michal, M. (2002). 'On the edge of equality? Working women and the US labour movement', in F. Colgan and S. Ledwith *(eds.), Gender, Diversity and Trade Unions*, London: Routledge, 232–256.

Cockburn, C. (1983) *Brothers: Male Dominance and Technological Change*, London: Pluto Press.

Cockburn, C. (1989). 'Equal opportunities: the short and long agenda', *Industrial Relations Journal*, 20, 213–225.

Cockburn, C. (1991). *In the Way of Women: Men's Resistance to Sex Equality in Organisations*, Basingstoke: Macmillan.

Colgan, F., and S. Ledwith, Eds. (2002). *Gender, Diversity and Trade Unions*, London: Routledge.

Colling, T., and Dickens, L. (1998). 'Selling the case for gender equality: deregulation and equality bargaining', *British Journal of Industrial Relations*, 36(3), 389–411.

Colling, T., and Dickens, L. (2001). 'Gender equality and trade unions: a new basis for mobilisation?', in M. Noon and E. Ogbonna (eds.), *Equality, Diversity and Disadvantage in Employment,.* Basingstoke: Palgrave.

Collinson, D., Knights, D., and Collinson, M. (1990). *Managing to Discriminate*, London: Routledge.

Committee of Economic and Social Affairs. (2003). *Aspects of the Economics of an Ageing Population*, London: House of Lords.

Cornelius, N., Gooch, L., and Todd, S. (2001). 'Managing difference fairly: an integrated 'partnership' approach', in M. Noon and E. Ogbonna (eds.), *Equality, Diversity and Disadvantage in Employment*, Basingstoke: Palgrave

Cornelius, N., Gooch, L., et al. (2000). 'Managers leading diversity for business excellence', *Journal of General Management*, 25(3), 67–78.

Cox, T. (1994). 'A comment on the language of diversity', *Organization*, 1(1), 51–58.

Cox, T., and Blake, S. (1991). 'Managing cultural diversity: implications for organizational competitiveness', *Academy of Management Review.* 5 (3), 45–56.

Creegan, C., and Robinson, C. (2008). 'Prejudice and the workplace', in A. Park, J. Curtice, K. Thomson, M. Phillips, M. Johnson, and E. Clery (eds.), *British Social Attitudes Survey: The 24th Report*, London: Sage.

Creegan, C., Colgan, F., Charlesworth, R., and Robinson, G. (2003). 'Race equality policies at work: employee perceptions of the 'implementation gap' in a UK local authority', *Work, Employment and Society*, 17(4), 617–640.

Crown Copyright. (2005). *Delivering a Diverse Civil Service: A 10-Point Plan.* London: Crown Copyright.

Cully, M., Woodland, S., O'Reilly, A., and Dix, S. (1999). *Britain at Work*, London: Routledge.

Cunningham, R. (2000). 'From great expectations to hard times? Managing equal opportunities under new public management', *Public Administration*, 78(3), 699–714.

Currie, G., and Proctor, S. (2001). 'Exploring the relationship between HR and middle managers', *Human Resource Management Journal*, 11(3), 53–69.

Danieli, A. (2006). 'Gender: the missing link in industrial relations', *Industrial Relations Journal*, 37(4), 329–343.

Dass, P., and Parker, B. (1999). 'Strategies for managing human resource diversity: from resistance to learning', *Academy of Management Executive*, 13(2), 68–80.

De los Reyes, P. (2000). 'Diversity at work: paradoxes, possibilities and problems in the Swedish discourse on diversity', *Economic and Industrial Democracy*, 21, 253–266.

Deeg, R., and Jackson, G. (2007). 'State of the art: towards a more dynamic theory of capitalist variety', *Socio-Economic Review*, 5, 149–179.

Deem, R., and Morely, L. (2006). 'Diversity in the academy? Staff perceptions of equality policies in six contemporary higher education institutions', *Policy Futures in Education*, 4(2), 185–202.

den Dulk, L. and de Ruijter, J. (2008) Managing work-life policies: disruption versus dependency arguments. Explaining managerial attitudes towards employee utilization of work-life policies', *The International Journal of Human Resource Management*, 19:7, 1222–1236

Devine, F., Baum, T., Hearns, N., and Devine, A. (2007). 'Cultural diversity in hospitality work: the Northern Ireland experience', *International Journal of Human Resource Management*, 18(2), 333–344.

Dickens, L. (1994). 'Wasted resources? Equal opportunities in employment', in P. Sissons (ed.), *Personnel Management..* Oxford: Blackwell, 253–295.

Dickens, L. (1997). 'Gender, race and employment equality in Britain: inadequate strategies and the role of industrial relations actors', *Industrial Relations Journal*, 28(4), 282–289.

Dickens L. (1999). 'Beyond the business case: a three-pronged approach to equality action', *Human Resource Management Journal*, 9(1), 9–19.

Dickens, L. (2000). 'Still wasting resources? Equality in employment', in S. Bach and K. Sisson (eds.), *Personnel Management*, Third Edition, Oxford: Blackwell, 137–169.

Dickens, L. (2006). 'Equality and work-life balance: what's happening at the workplace', *Industrial Law Journal*, 35(4), 445–449.

Dickens, L. (2007). 'The road is long: thirty years of equality legislation in Britain', *British Journal of Industrial Relations*, 45(3), 463–494.

Dickens, L. (1999). What Human Resource Management means to Gender Equality in M Poole (ed.) Human Resource Management: Critical Perspectives, London, Routledge.

Dickens, L., Townley, B., et al. (1988). *Tackling Sex Discrimination through Collective Bargaining*, Manchester: Equal Opportunities Commission.

DiMaggio, P. and Powell, W.W. (1983). The iron cage revisited: Institutional isomorphism and collective rationality in organizational fields American Sociological Review, 48 (2), 147–160

DRC (2006) Disability briefing March 2006. Stratford upon Avon: Disability Rights Commission.

DTI. (2007). 'Trade union density by industry 1995–2006', p18. Available at http://www.berr.gov.uk/files/file39006.pdf

Due Billing, Y., and Sundin, E. (2006). 'From managing equality to managing diversity: a critical Scandinavian perspective on gender and workplace diversity', in P. Prasad, J. Pringle, and A. Konrad (eds.), *Handbook of Workplace Diversity*, London: Sage 95–120.

Dunkerley, D. (1975). *The Foreman: Aspects of Task and Structure*, London: Routledge and Kegan-Paul.

Duxbury, N. (2008). *Golden Rule Reasoning, Moral Judgement and Law*. Paper 47, The John M. Olin Program in Law and Economics Working Paper Series, University of Virginia Law School. Available at http://law.bepress.com/uval-wps/olin/art47

Edwards, P. Ed. (2003). *Industrial Relations: Theory and Practice in Britain*, Third Edition. Blackwell: Oxford.

Edwards, P.K. (2003) The Employment Relationship. In P.K. Edwards (ed.), *Industrial Relations: Theory and Practice*. Oxford: Blackwell.

Edwards, P. K., Bélanger, J., and Wright, M. (2006). 'The bases of compromise in the workplace: a theoretical framework', *British Journal of Industrial Relations*, 44(1), 125–145.

Ellis, V. (1988). 'Current trade union attempts to remove occupational segregation in the employment of women', in S. Walby (ed.), *Gender Segregation at Work*, Berkshire, UK: Open University Press. Milton Keynes 55–7.

Ely, R. (2004). 'A field study of group diversity, participation in diversity education programs and performance', *Journal of Organizational Behavior*, 25, 75–780.

EOC. (2004). *Facts About Women and Men in Great Britain 2004*, Manchester: Equal Opportunities Commission.

EOC. (2007). *Enter the Timelords—Transforming Work to Meet the Future*, Manchester: Equal Opportunities Commission.

Equalities Review Panel (2007). Fairness and Freedom: the Final Report of the Equalities Review. London, Equalities Review Panel.

European Commission. (2005). *The Business Case for Diversity—Good Practices in the Workplace*, Luxembourg: Office for Official Publications of the European Communities.

European Commission. (2006). 'Flexibility and security in the EU labour markets: the effects of labour market policies and 'Flexicurity' regimes', Employment in Europe Report, Luxembourg: Office for Official Publications of the European Communities.

European Commission. (2007). *Developing Anti-Discrimination Law in Europe—The 25 EU Member States Compared*, Luxembourg: Office for Official Publications of the European Communities.

European Industrial Relations Review. (2006). 'PSA Peugeot Citroën signs CSR/ global council agreement', *European Industrial Relations Review*, Issue 388, 1/5/2006. Available at http://www.xperthr.co.uk/article/65260/inter-national—psa-peugeot-citro-0xeb-n-signs-csr-global-council-agreement.aspx?searchwords=peugeot

Fagan, C., and Burchell, B. (2002). *Gender, Jobs and Working Conditions in the European Union*, Dublin: European Foundation for the Improvement of Living and Working Conditions.

Fairbrother, P., and Hammer, N. (2005). 'Global unions: past efforts and future prospects', *Relations Industrielles/Industrial Relations*, 60(3), 405–431.

Fairclough, N. (1992). *Discourse and Social Change*, New York: Polity Press.

Fairclough, N. (2003). *Analysing Discourse: Textual Analysis for Social Research*, London: Routledge.

Fee, R. (2002). 'Contract compliance: subnational and European influences in Northern Ireland', *Journal of European Social Policy*, 12(2), 107–121.

Fleetwood, S. (2007) Why work-life balance now? *International Journal of Human Resource Management*, 18 (3), 387–400.

Forrest, A. (1993). 'A view from outside the whale: The treatment of women and unions in industrial relations', in L. Briskin and P. McDermott (eds.), *Women Challenging Unions: Feminism, Democracy and Militancy*, Toronto, London: University of Toronto Press.

Foster, C., and Harris, L. (2005). 'Easy to say, difficult to do: diversity management in retail', *Human Resource Management Journal*, 15(3), 4–17.

Franco, A. (2007) The concentration of men and women in sectors of activity. Statistics in Focus: Population and Social Conditions, Luxembourg: Eurostat.

Fredman, S. (2002). 'The Future of Equality in Britain', *Working Paper Series*. Manchester: Equal Opportunities Commission.

Friedman R. A., and McDaniel, D. C. (1998). 'In the eye of the beholder: ethnography in the study of work', in K. Whitfield and G. Strauss (eds.), *Researching the World of Work: Strategies and Methods in Studying Industrial Relations*, Ithaca, NY: Cornell University Press, 113–127.

Geertz, C. (1973). *The Interpretation of Cultures: Selected Essays*, New York: Fontana Press.

Gennard J., and Emmott, M. (2003, July 1). 'Employee relations: what is the employee relations agenda in high-performing organizations?', *CIPD Professional Standards Conference*, Stoke-on-Trent, England: University of Keele.

Gilbert, J., and Ivancevich, J. (2000). 'Valuing diversity: a tale of two organizations', *Academy of Management Executive*, 14(1), 93–105.

Gilbert, J. A., Stead, B. A., and Ivancevich, J. M. (1999). 'Diversity management: a new organizational paradigm', *Journal of Business Ethics*, 21, 61–76.

GLEA. (2000). *The Organisational and Managerial Implications of Devolved Personnel Assessment Procedures*, London: IES.

Glover, J., and Kirton, G. (2006). *Women, Employment and Organizations*, Abingdon: Routledge.

Glover, L., and Noon, M. (2005). 'Shopfloor workers responses to quality management initiatives: broadening the disciplined worker thesis', *Work, Employment and Society*, 19(4), 727–746.

Goldthorpe, J. H., Lockwood, J., Bechhofer, F., and Platt, J. (1968). *The Affluent Worker: Industrial Attitudes and Behaviour*, London: Cambridge University Press.

Gooch, L., and Blackburn, A. (2002). 'Managing people-equality, diversity and human resource management: issues for line managers', in N. Cornelius (ed.), *Building Workplace Equality: Ethics, Diversity and Inclusion*, London: Thomson.

Grainger, H. (2005). 'Trade union membership', in *Employment Market Analysis and Research*, London: Department for Trade and Industry.

Grayson, D. (2007). Business-Led Corporate Responsibility Coalitions: Learning from the example of Business in the Community in the UK. An Insider's Perspective. Business in the Community, Doughty Centre for Corporate Responsibility and the Kennedy School of Government, Harvard. Available at: http://www.bitc.org.uk/resources/publications/business_led.html. Accessed 12th May 2008.

Greene, A. M. (2001). *Voices from the Shop Floor: Dramas of the Employment Relationship*, Ashgate: Aldershot.

Greene, A. M. (2002). Industrial relations and women. *Reworking Industrial Relations: New Perspectives on Employment and Society*. P. Ackers, and Wilkinson, A.

Greene, A. M. (2003). 'Industrial relations and women', in P. Ackers and A. Wilkinson (eds.), *Reworking Industrial Relations: New Perspectives on Employment and Society*, Oxford, UK: University Press, 305–315.

Greene, A. M. (forthcoming). 'Equal opportunities and HRM', in A. Wilkinson, T. Redman, S. Snell, and N. Bacon (eds.), *Handbook of Human Resource Management*, Thousand Oaks, CA: Sage.

Greene, A. M., and Kirton, G. (2006). 'Trade Unions and equality and diversity', in A. Konrad, P. Prasad, and J. Pringle (eds.), *Handbook of Workplace Diversity*. London: Sage, 489–510.

Greene, A. M., and Kirton, G. (2008, June 26–28). 'Diversity management meets downsizing: the case of a government department', paper presented to British Universities Industrial Relations Association (BUIRA) Conference, Bristol.

Greene, A. M., Kirton, G., and Dean, D. (2007, Spring). 'Exploring the involvement of stakeholders in diversity management', *Industrial Relations Research Unit Briefing*, 14, 4–6.

Greene, A. M., Kirton, G., and Wrench, J. (2005). 'Trade Union perspectives on diversity management: a comparison of the UK and Denmark', *European Journal of Industrial Relations*, 11(2), 179–196.

Greenhouse, S., and Hays, C. L. (2004, June 23rd), 'Wal-Mart Sex-Bias Suit Given Class-Action Status', *New York Times*. Available at http://query.nytimes.com/gst/fullpage.html?res=9405E1D71039F930A15755C0A9629C8B63 Accessed 2nd July 2008.

Grimshaw, D., and Rubery, J. (2007). 'Undervaluing Women's Work', *Working Paper Series*, Manchester: Equal Opportunities Commission.

Guardian/The Observer. (2004, October 19th). *Report on the Conference Diversity in Action: The Winning Formula for Successful Implementation*. London: The Guardian/The Observer.

Guest, D. (1987). 'Human resource management and industrial relations', *Journal of Management Studies*, 24(5), 503–521.

Guest, D., and Peccei, M. (1998), '*The Partnership Company*', Involvement and Participation Association.

Gutek, B. (1985). *Sex and the Workplace: Impact of Sexual Behaviour and Harassment on Women, Men and Organizations*, San Francisco: Jossey-Bass.

Hakim, C. (2000). *Work-Lifestyle Choices in the 21st Century*, Oxford: Oxford University Press.

Hales, C. (2005). 'Rooted in supervision, branching into management: continuity and change in the role of first-line manager', *Journal of Management Studies*, 42(3), 471–506.

Hamilton, P. (2001). 'Rhetoric and employment relations', *British Journal of Industrial Relations*, 39(3), 433–449.

Hansen, L. L. (2002). 'Rethinking the industrial relations tradition from a gender perspective: an invitation to integration,' *Employee Relations*, 24(2), 190–210.

Healy, G., Hansen, L. L., and Ledwith, S. (2006), 'Editorial: still uncovering gender in industrial relations', *Industrial Relations Journal*, 37(4), 290–298.

Heath, A., and Cheung, S. (2006). *Ethnic Penalties in the Labour Market: Employers and Discrimination*, Leeds: Department for Work and Pensions.

Heath, A., J. Roberts, and D. McMahon (2001). Ethnic Minorities in the Labour Market. London, Cabinet Office.

Heer, G., and Atherton, S. (2008). '(In)visible barriers: the experience of Asian Employees in the probation service', *Howard Journal of Criminal Justice*, 47(1), 1–17.

Holgate, J., Hebson, A. and McBride, A. (2006). 'Why gender and 'difference' matters: a critical appraisal of industrial relations research', *Industrial Relations Journal*, 37(4), 310–328.

Holvino, E. (2003). Complicating gender: the simultaneity of race, gender, and class in organization change(ing), in R. J. Ely, E. G. Foldy, and M. A. Scully (eds.), *Reader in Gender, Work, and Organization*, Malden, MA: Blackwell, 87–98, 258–265.

Hope-Hailey, V., Gratton. L., McGovern, P., Stiles, P., and Truss, C. (1997). 'A charmeleon function? HRM in the 90s', *Human Resource Management Journal*, 7(3), 5–18.

Hoque, K., and Noon, M. (2001). 'Counting angels: a comparison of personnel and HR specialists', *Human Resource Management Journal*, 11(3), 5–22.

Hoque, K., and Noon, M. (2004). 'Equal opportunities policy and practice in Britain: evaluating the 'empty shell' hypothesis', *Work, Employment & Society*, 18(3), 481–506.

Howard, M., & Tibballs, S. (2003). *Talking Inequality: What Men and Women Think About Equality in Britain Today*, Manchester: The Future Foundation for the Equal Opportunities Commission.

Howard, M., and Tibballs, S. (2003). *Talking Equality: What Men and Women Think About Equality in Britain Today*, London/Manchester: Future Foundation/Equal Opportunities Commission.

Human Resource International Management Digest. (2003). 'Barclays pioneers a job-share register: . . . that helps to boost part-time working and work-life balance', *Human Resource Management International Digest*, 11(2), 14–16.

Human Resource International Management Digest. (2005). 'Diversity is about more than observing the letter of the law: a climate of inclusion benefits business performance', *Human Resource Management International Digest*, 13(4), 37–40.

Humphries, M., and Grice, S. (1995). 'Equal employment opportunity and the management of diversity', *Journal of Organizational Change Management*, 8(5), 17–32.

Hunt, B. (2007). 'Managing equality and cultural diversity in the health workforce', *Journal of Clinical Nursing*, 16(2), 2252–2259.

Hunter, L. (2003). 'Research developments in employment relations and diversity: a British perspective', *Asia Pacific Journal of Human Resources*, 41(1), 88–100.

Hurrell, K. (2006). Facts About Women and Men in Great Britain 2006. Manchester: Equal Opportunities Commission.

Hutchinson, S., and Purcell, J. (2003). *Bringing Policies to Life: The Vital Role of Front Line Managers*, London: Chartered Institute of Personnel and Development (CIPD).

Iles, P. (1995). 'Learning to work with difference', *Personnel Review*, 24(6), 44–60.

Jacoby, S. M. (2005). 'Corporate governance in comparative perspective: prospects for convergence', *Comparative Labor Law and Policy Journal*, 22(5), 5–32.

Jamieson, D., and O'Mara, J. (1991). *Managing Workforce 2000: Gaining the Diversity Advantage*, San Francisco: Jossey-Bass.

Janssens, M., and Zanoni, P. (2005). 'Many diversities for many services: theorizing diversity (management) in service companies', *Human Relations*, 58(3), 311–340.

Jehn, K., Northcraft, G., et al. (1999). 'Why differences make a difference: a field study of diversity, conflict and performance in workgroups', *Administrative Science Quarterly*, 44, 741–763.

Jenkins, R. (2004). *Social Identity*, Abingdon: Routledge.

Jewson, N., and Mason, D. (1986). 'The theory and practice of equal opportunity policies: liberal and radical approaches', *Sociological Review*, 34(2), 307–334.

Jewson, N., and Mason, D. (1987). 'Monitoring equal opportunities policies', in R. Jenkins and J. Solomos (eds.), *Racism and Equal Opportunity Policies in the 1980s*, Cambridge: Cambridge University Press, 218–234.

Johns, N. (2005). 'Positive action and the problem of merit: employment policies in the National Health Service', *Critical Social Policy*, 25(2), 139–163.

Johnson, L., and Johnstone, S. (2005). 'The legal framework for diversity', in G. Kirton and A. M. Greene (eds.), *The Dynamics of Managing Diversity: A Critical Approach*, Oxford: Elsevier, 143–168.

Johnston, W., and Packer, A. (1987). Workforce 2000: Work and workers for the 21st century. Indianapolis, IN, Hudson Institute.

Johnstone, S., Ed. (2002). *Managing Diversity in the Workplace*, London: Eclipse/ IRS.

Jones, D. (2004). 'Screwing diversity out of the workers? Reading diversity', *Journal of Organizational Change Management*, 17(3), 281–291.

Jones, D., and Stablein, R. (2006). 'Diversity as resistance and recuperation: critical theory, post structuralist perspectives and workplace diversity', in A. Konrad, P. Prasad, and J. Pringle (eds.), *Handbook of Workplace Diversity*, London: Sage, 145–166.

Jones, D., Pringle, J., et al. (2000). ' 'Managing diversity' meets Aotearoa/New Zealand', *Personnel Review*, 29(3), 364–380.

Kaler, J. (2001). 'Diversity, equality, morality', in M. Noon and E. Ogbonna (eds.), *Equality, Diversity and Disadvantage in Employment*, Basingstoke: Palgrave.

Kalev, A., Dobbin, F., and Kelly, E. (2006). 'Best practices or best guesses? Assessing the efficacy of corporate affirmative action and diversity policies', *American Sociological Review*, 71, 589–617.

Kamenou, N., and Fearfull, A. (2006). 'Ethnic minority women: a lost voice in HRM', *Human Resource Management Journal*, 16(2), 154–172.

Kamp, A., and Hagedorn-Rasmussen P. (2004). 'Diversity management in a Danish context: towards a multicultural or segregated working life?', *Economic and Industrial Democracy*, 25(4), 525–554.

Kandola, B., and Fullerton, J. (1994). *Managing the Mosaic: Diversity in Action*, London: IPD.

Kandola, R., and Fullerton, J. (1998). *Managing the Mosaic: Diversity in Action*, Second Edition, London: Chartered Institute of Personnel and Development.

Kelly, E., and Dobbin, F. (1998). 'How affirmative action became diversity management: employer response to antidiscrimination law, 1961 to1996', *The American Behavioral Scientist*, 41(7), 960–984.

Kelly, J. (1994, July). 'Does the field of industrial relations have a future?', paper presented to the *British Universities Industrial Relations Association Conference*, Oxford.

Kelly, J. (1998). *Rethinking Industrial Relations: Mobilisation, Collectivism and Long Waves*, London: Routledge.

Kerr, S., Hill, K. D., and Broedling, L. (1986). 'The first-line supervisor: phasing out or here to stay?', *Academy of Management Review*, 11(1), 103–117.

Kersley, B., Alpin, C., Forth, J., Bryson, A., Bewley, H., Dix, G., and Oxenbridge, S. (2006). *First Findings from the 2004 Workplace Employment Relations Survey*, London: Department of Trade and Industry.

Kersten, A. (2000). 'Diversity management: dialogue, dialectics and diverstion', *Journal of Occupational Change Management*, 13(3), 235–248.

Keter, V. (2005). 'Equality bill', in *Research Paper*, London: House of Commons Library.

Kim, M. (2002). 'Has the race penalty for black women disappeared in the United States?', *Feminist Economics*, 8(2), 115–124.

Kirton, G. (2002). 'What is diversity?', in S. Johnstone (ed.), *Managing Diversity in the Workplace*, London: LexisNexis, 1–23.

Kirton, G. (2006). *The Making of Women Trade Unionists*, Aldershot: Ashgate.

Kirton, G. (2007). 'Proposed new equality framework triggers mixed reaction', *European Industrial Relations Observatory*. http://www.eurofound.europa.eu/ eiro/2007/06/articles/uk0706029i.htm.

Kirton, G. (2008). 'Managing multi-culturally in organizations in a diverse society', in S. Clegg and C. Cooper (eds.), *Handbook of Macro Organizational Behaviour*, Thousand Oaks, CA: Sage.

Kirton, G., and Greene, A. M. (2002). 'The dynamics of positive action in UK trade unions: the case of women and black members', *Industrial Relations Journal*, 33(2), 157–172.

Kirton, G., and Greene, A. M. (2005a). *The Dynamics of Managing Diversity: A Critical Approach*, Second Edition, Oxford: Butterworth Heinemann.

Kirton, G., and Greene, A. M. (2005b). 'Gender, equality and industrial relations in the 'New Europe': an introduction', *European Journal of Industrial Relations*, 11(2), 141–149.

Kirton, G., and Greene, A. M. (2006). 'The discourse of diversity in unionised contexts: views from trade union equality officers', *Personnel Review*, 34, 431–448.

Kirton, G., and Greene, A. M. (2007, June 27–29). 'What does diversity management mean for the gender equality project? Views and experiences of multiple organizational actors in the UK', paper presented at the *Gender, Work and Organization Conference*, Keele University.

Kirton, G., and Greene, A. M. (2009). 'The costs and opportunities of doing diversity work in mainstream organisations', *Human Resource Management Journal*, 19, 2.

Kirton, G., Greene, A. M., and Dean, D. (2006, August 31–September 2). 'The multi-dimensional nature of work in the 'diversity industry', paper presented at the *Industrial Relations in Europe Conference, IREC* , Workshop on 'Industrial Relations and Diversity', Ljubljana, Slovenia.

Kirton, G., Greene, A. M., and Dean, D. (2007). 'British diversity professionals as change agents—radicals, tempered radicals or liberal reformers?', *International Journal of Human Resource Management*, 18(11), 1979–1994.

Kirton, G., and Healy, G. (1999). 'Transforming union women: the role of women trade union officials in union renewal', *Industrial Relations Journal*, 30(1), 31–45.

Kochan, T., Bezrukova, K., Ely, R., Jackson, S., Joshi, A., Jehn, K., Leonard, J., Levine, D., and Thomas, D. (2003). 'The effects of diversity on business performance: report of the diversity research network', *Human Resource Management*, 42(1), 3–21.

Konrad, A. (2003). 'Special issue introduction: defining the domain of workplace diversity scholarship', *Group & Organization Management*, 28(1), 4–17.

Konrad, A., and Linnehan, F. (1995). 'Race and sex differences in line managers: reactions to equal employment opportunity and affirmative action interventions', *Group and Organization Management*, 20(4), 409–439.

Konrad, A., Prasad, P., and Pringle, J., Eds. (2006). *Handbook of Workplace Diversity*, London: Sage.

Konrad, A., J Pringle and A Greene (2008). Implementing EEO in Gendered Organizations for Gendered Lives in Clegg, S. and Cooper, C (ed.) Handbook of Macro Organizational Behaviour, Sage

Korczynski, M. (2002). *Human Resource Management in Service Work*, Basingstoke: Palgrave/Macmillan.

Kossek, E., Lobel, S. A., and Brown, J. (2006). 'Human resource strategies to manage workforce diversity: examining the business case', in A. Konrad, P. Prasad, and J. Pringle (eds.), *Handbook of Workplace Diversity*, London: Sage, 53–74.

Kossek, E., Markel, K., et al. (2003). 'Increasing diversity as an HRM change strategy', *Journal of Organizational Change Management*, 16(3), 328–352.

Kulik, C., and Bainbridge, C. (2006). 'Psychological perspectives on workplace diversity', in A. Konrad, P. Prasad, and J. Pringle (eds.), *Handbook of workplace diversity*, London: Sage, 53–74.

Larsen, H. H., and Brewster, C. (2003). 'Line management responsibility for HRM: what is happening in Europe?', *Employee Relations*, 25(3), 228–244.

Lawrence, E. (2000). 'Equal opportunities officers and managing equality changes', *Personnel Review*, 29(3), 381–401.

Leach, J. (1995). 'Letting go or holding on: the devolution of operational personnel activities', *Human Resource Management Journal*, 41–55.

Ledwith, S. and Colgan, F. (eds.), (1996) *Women in Organisations: Challenging Gender Politics*, Macmillan: London.

Legge, K. (1995). *Human Resource Management: Rhetoric and Realities*, Basingstoke: Macmillan Press.

Liff, S. (1997). 'Two routes to managing diversity: individual differences or social group characteristics', *Employee Relations*, 19(1), 11–26.

Liff, S. (1999). 'Diversity and equal opportunities: room for a constructive compromise?', *Human Resource Management Journal*, 9(1), 65–75.

Liff, S., and Cameron, I. (1997). 'Changing equality cultures to move beyond 'women's problems', *Gender, Work and Organization*, 4(1), 35–46.

Liff, S., and Dickens, L. (2000). 'Ethics and equality: reconciling false dilemmas',in D. Winstanley and J. Woodall (eds.), *Ethical Issues in Contemporary Human Resource Management*, Basingstoke: Macmillan, 85–101.

Liff, S., and Ward, K. (2001). 'Distorted views through the glass ceiling: the construction of women's understandings of promotion and senior management positions', *Gender, Work and Organization*, 8(1), 19–36.

Lindley, J., Dale, A., et al. (2004, April). 'Ethnic differences in women's demographic, family characteristics and economic activity profiles, 1992–2002', *Labour Market Trends*, 153–165.

Linnehan, F., Chrobot-Mason, D., and Konrad, A. M. (2006). 'Diversity attitudes and norms: the role of ethnic identity and relational demography', *Journal of Organizational Behaviour*, 27(4), 419–442.

Litvin, D. (2002). 'The business case for diversity and the 'iron cage'', in B. Czarniawska and H. Hopfl (eds.), *Casting the Other*, London: Routledge, 160–184.

Litvin, D. (2006). "Diversity: making space for a better case', in P. Prasad, J. Pringle, and A. Konrad (eds.), *Handbook of Workplace Diversity*, London: Sage, 75–94.

Lorbiecki, A. (2001). *Openings and Burdens for Women and Minority Ethnics Being Diversity Vanguards in Britain*, Gender, Work and Organization, Keele University, UK.

Lorbiecki, A., and Jack, G. (2000). 'Critical turns in the evolution of diversity management', *British Journal of Management*, 11(Special Issue), S17–S31.

Luijters, K., van der Zee, K. I., and Otten, S. (2008). 'Cultural diversity in organizations: enhancing identification by valuing differences', *International Journal of Intercultural Relations*, 32(2), 154–163.

Mahon, R. (2002). Sweden's LO: learning to embrace the differences within?, in F. Colgan and S. Ledwith (eds.), *Gender, Diversity and Trade Unions*, London: Routledge, 48–72.

Marchington, M., and Wilkinson, A. (2005). 'Direct participation and involvement', in S. Bach (ed.), *Managing Human Resources*, Oxford: Blackwell.

Marchington, M., et al. (2001). *Management Choice and Employee Voice*, London: Chartered Institute of Personnel and Development (CIPD).

Marginson, P., Edwards, P., Edwards, T., Ferner, A. and Tregaskis, O. (2007). Channels and coverage of employee voice in multinational companies operating in Britain. Paper to the IIRA European Congress, Manchester, September 3rd–6th.

Maxwell, G. (2004). 'Minority report: taking the initiative in managing diversity in BBC Scotland', *Employee Relations*, 26(2), 182–202.

Maxwell, G., Blair, S., and McDougall, M. (2001). 'Edging towards managing diversity in practice', *Employee Relations*, 23(5), 468–482.

Maxwell, G., McDougall, M., and Blair, S. (2000). 'Managing diversity in the hotel sector: the emergence of a service quality opportunity', *Managing Service Quality*, 10(6), 367–373.

McBride, A. (2003). Reconciling Competing Pressures for Working-time Flexibility: An Impossible Task in the National Health Service (NHS)? *Work, Employment & Society*, 17 (1), 159–170.

McConville, T., and Holden, L. (1999). 'The filling in the sandwich: HRM and middle managers in the health sector', *Personnel Review*, 28(5/6), 406–424.

McCrudden, C. (1986). 'Rethinking positive action', *Industrial Law Journal*, 15(1), 219–243.

McDougall, M. (1996). 'Equal opportunities versus managing diversity: another challenge for public sector management?', *International Journal of Public Sector Management*, 9(5/6), 62–72.

McDougall, M. (1998). 'Devolving gender management in the public sector: opportunity or opt-out?', *International Journal of Public Sector Management*, 11(1), 71–80.

McGovern, P., Gratton, L., Hope-Hailey, V., Stiles, P., and Truss, C. (1997). 'Human resource management on the line?', *Human Resource Management Journal*, 7(4), 12–29.

McKay, P. F., Avery, D. R., Tonidandel, S., Morris, M. A., Hernandez, M., and Hebl, M. R. (2007). 'Racial differences in employee retention: are diversity climate perceptions the key?', *Personnel Psychology*, 60(1), 35–62.

McOrmond, T. (2004, January). 'Changes in working trends over the past decade', *Labour Market Trends*, 25–35.

Metzler, C. (2003, Spring). 'Selecting the diversity consultant: ensuring the emperor has clothes', *Workforce Diversity Reader*, 1–8.

Miller, D. (1996). "Equality Management: Towards a Materialist Approach." *Gender, Work and Organization* 3(4):202–214.

Miller, G. and J. Rowney (1999) "Workplace diversity management in a multicultural society." *Women in Management Review* 14(8): 307–315.

Mir, R., Mir, A., et al. (2006). 'Diversity: the cultural logic of global capital?', in P. Prasad, J. Pringle, and A. Konrad (eds.), *Handbook of Workplace Diversity*, London: Sage, 167–188.

Morgan, D. (1981). 'Men, masculinity and the process of sociological enquiry', in H. Roberts (ed.), *Doing Feminist Research*, London: Routledge and Kegan Paul.

Mullany, L. (2004). 'Gender, politeness and institutional power roles: humour as a tactic to gain compliance in workplace business meetings', *Multilingua*, 23, 13–37.

National Audit Office. (2006, July 25) *Achieving innovation in central government organisations: Detailed research findings*, Report by the Controller and Auditor General, HC 1447-II Session 2005–2006.

Ng, E., and Tung, R. (1998). 'Ethno-cultural diversity and organizational effectiveness: a field study', *The International Journal of Human Resource Management*, 9(6), 980–995.

Noon, M. (2007). 'The fatal flaws of diversity and the business case for ethnic minorities', *Work, Employment and Society*, 21(4), 773–785.

Noon, M., and Ogbonna, E. (2001). *Equality, Diversity and Disadvantage in Employment*, Basingstoke: Palgrave.

OECD (2001) Employment Outlook, Paris: OECD

Ogbonna, E., and Harris, L. C. (2006). 'The dynamics of employee relationships in an ethnically diverse workforce', *Human Relations*, 59(3), 379–407.

Ogden, S. M., McTavish, D., and McKean, L. (2006). 'Clearing the way for gender balance in the management of the UK financial services industry: enablers and barriers', *Women in Management Review*, 21(1), 40–53.

ONS. (2003). Regional distribution of the minority ethnic population. Available at http://www.statistics.gov.uk/CCI/nugget.asp?ID=263&Pos=1&ColRank=2 &Rank=448 Accessed June 21, 2008.

ONS (2007). Social Trends 33, London: Office for National Statistics.

ONS. (2008a). Labour Market Overview: June 2008. Available at http://www.statistics.gov.uk/downloads/theme_labour/LMS_QandA.pdf. Accessed 1st July 2008.

ONS. (2008). Public Sector Employment Increases: April 2008. Available at http://www.statistics.gov.uk/cci/nugget.asp?id=407

ONS (2008b) Labour Market Statistics December 2008. Available at: http://www.statistics.gov.uk/pdfdir/lmsuk1208.pdf . Accessed 3rd January 2009.

Opportunity Now. (2005). *Line Managers and Diversity: Making It Real*, London: Opportunity Now.

Orton, M., and Ratcliffe, P. (2005). 'New labour ambiguity, or neo-liberal consistency? The debate about racial inequality in employment and the use of contract compliance', *Journal of Social Policy*, 34(2), 255–272.

Pelled, L., Eisenhardt, K., et al. (1999). 'Exploring the black box: an analysis of work group diversity, conflict, and performance', *Administrative Science Quarterly*, 44. 1–28.

Pendleton, A., and Winterton, J., Eds. (1993). *Public Enterprise in Transition: Industrial Relations in State and Privatized Corporations*, London: Routledge.

Perotin, V., and Robinson, A. (2000). 'Employee participation and equal opportunities practices: productivity effect and potential complementarities', *British Journal of Industrial Relations*, 38(4), 557–583.

Peters, E. C. (2006). 'Making it to the brochure but not to partnership, *Washburn Law Journal*, 45.

Platt, L. (2006) Pay Gaps: The position of ethnic minority women and men. Manchester: Equal Opportunities Commission.

Pocock, B. (2000). 'Analysing work: arguments for closer links between the study of labour relations and gender', *Journal of Interdisciplinary Gender Studies*, 5(2), 10–25.

Point, S., and Singh, V. (2003). 'Defining and dimensionalising diversity: evidence from corporate websites across Europe', *European Management Journal*, 21(6), 750–761.

Prasad, A. (2006). 'The jewel in the crown: postcolonial theory and workplace diversity', in A. Konrad, P. Prasad, and J. Pringle (eds.), *Handbook of Workplace Diversity*, London: Sage, 95–120.

Prasad, P., and Mills, A. (1997). 'From showcase to shadow: understanding the dilemmas of managing workplace diversity', in P. Prasad, A. Mills, M. Elmes, and A. Prasad (eds.), *Managing the Organizational Melting Pot,*. Thousand Oaks: Sage, 3–30.

Prasad, P., Mills, A., et al. (1997). *Managing the Organizational Melting Pot*, London: Sage.

Prasad, P., Pringle, J., and Konrad, A. (2006). 'Examining the contours of workplace diversity: concepts, contexts and challenges', *The Handbook of Workplace Diversity*, London: Sage, 1–22.

Pringle, J., Konrad, A., and Prasad, P. (2006). 'Conclusion: reflection and future direction', in A. Konrad, P. Prasad, and J. Pringle (eds.), *Handbook of Workplace Diversity*, London: Sage, 531–539.

Purcell, J., and Hutchinson, S. (2007). 'Front line managers as agents in the HRM-performance causal chain: theory, analysis and evidence', *Human Resource Management Journal*, 17(1), 3–20.

Purcell, J., Kinnie, N., Hutchinson, S., Rayton, B., and Swart, J. (2003). *Understanding the People and Performance Link: Unlocking the Black Box*, London: Chartered Institute of Personnel and Development (CIPD).

Purcell, K. (2000). 'Gendered employment insecurity?', in E. A. S. Heery and J. London (eds.), *The Insecure Workforce*, London: Routledge.

Purcell, K. (2002). *Qualifications and Careers: Equal Opportunities and Earnings among Graduates*. Manchester: Equal Opportunities Commission.

Rasmussen, E., Lind, J. and Visser, J. (2004) Divergence in Part-Time Work in New Zealand, the Netherlands and Denmark, British Journal of Industrial Relations, 42 (4), 637–658.

Rees, T. (1992). *Women and the Labour Market*. London: Routledge.

Richards, W. (2001). 'Evaluating equal opportunities initiatives: the case for a 'transformative' agenda', in M. Noon and E. Ogbonna (eds.), *Equality, Diversity and Disadvantage in Employment*, pp. 15–31. Basingstoke: Palgrave.

Riisgaard, L. (2005). 'International framework agreements: a new model for securing workers rights?, *Industrial Relations*, 44(4), 707–737.

Riley, S. (2002). 'Constructions of equality and discrimination in professional men's talk', *British Journal of Social Psychology*, 41, 443–461.

Roberson, L., Kulik, C. T., and Pepper, M. B. (2003). 'Using needs assessment to resolve controversies in training design', *Group & Organization Management*, 28(1), 148–174.

Robson, P., Dex, S., et al. (1999). 'Low pay, labour market institutions, gender and part-time work: cross-national comparisons', *European Journal of Industrial Relations*, 5(2): 187–207.

Ross, R., and Schneider, R. (1992). *From Equality to Diversity*, London: Pitman.

Roulstone, A. and Warren, J. (2006) Applying a barriers approach to monitoring disabled people's employment: implications for the Disability Discrimination Act 2005, *Disability & Society*, 21(2), 115–131.

Rubery, J. and Fagan, C. (1995), 'Comparative industrial relations research: Towards reversing the gender bias', *British Journal of Industrial Relations*, 33: 2, pp 209–237.

Rubery, J., Smith, M. and Fagan, C. (1999) *Women's Employment in Europe: Trends and Prospects*. London: Routledge.

Rubery, J., Grimshaw, D., et al. (2005). 'How to close the gender pay gap in Europe: towards the gender mainstreaming of pay policy', *Industrial Relations Journal*, 36(3), 184–213.

Schein, V. (2007). 'Women in management: reflections and projections', *Women in Management Review*, 22(1), 6–18.

Schneider, R. (2001). 'Diversity now the ultimate test of management capacity', *Equal Opportunities Review*, 96, 11–17.

Schneider, S., and Northcraft, G. (1999). 'Three social dilemmas of workforce diversity in organizations: a social identity perspective', *Human Relations*, 52(11), 1445–1467.

Sefton, T., Baker, M. and Praat, A. (2005.) Ethnic minorities, disability and the labour market: A review of the data. London: Royal National Institute for the Blind.

Select Committee on Economic Affairs (2003). Select Committee On Economic Affairs 2nd Report, Session 2003–04: Government Response To Aspects Of The Economics Of An Ageing Population Report *House of Lords Papers*. London, Parliament. House of Lords.

Sinclair, A. (2000). 'Women within diversity: risks and possibilities', *Women in Management Review*, 15(5/6), 237–245.

Sinclair, A. (2006) Critical Diversity Management practice in Australia: romanced or co-opted? *Handbook of Workplace Diversity*. P. Prasad, J. Pringle and A. Konrad. London, Sage: 511–530.

Singh, V., and Point, S. (2006). '(Re)presentations of gender and ethnicity in diversity statements on European company websites', *Journal of Business Ethics*, 68(4), 363–379.

Singh, V., and Vinnicombe, S. (2006). *The Female FTSE Report 2006*. Bedford: Cranfield School of Management.

Sisson, K. (2001). Human Resource Management and the Personnel Function—a case of partial impact? *Human Resource Management*. J. Storey. London, Thomson: 78–95.

Sisson, K., and Marginson, P. (2003). 'Management: systems, structure and strategy', in P. K. Edwards (ed.), *Industrial Relations: Theory and Practice in Britain*, Oxford: Blackwell.

Soskice, D. (2005). 'Varieties of capitalism and cross-national gender differences', *Social Politics: International Studies in Gender, State & Society*, 12(2), 170–179.

Storey, J. (1992). *Developments in the Management of Human Resources*, Blackwell: Oxford.

Storey, J. (1995). 'Human resource management: still marching on, or marching out?', in J. Storey (ed.), *Human Resource Management: A Critical Text*, London: Routledge.

Subeliani, D., and Tsogas, G. (2005). 'Managing diversity in the Netherlands: a case study of Rabobank', *International Journal of Human Resource Management*, 16(5), 831–851.

Taylor, R. (2002). 'Diversity in Britain's Labour Market', in *ESRC Future of Work Programme Commentary Series Report*, Swindon, UK: ESRC.

Teicher, J., and Spearitt, K. (1996). 'From equal employment opportunity to diversity management: the Australian experience', *International Journal of Manpower*, 17(4/5), 109–133.

Thomas, D. (2004, September). 'Diversity as strategy', *Harvard Business Review*, 98–108.

Thompson, P., and Ackroyd, S. (1999). *Organizational Misbehaviour*, London: Sage Publications.

Treven, S., and Mulej, M. (2007). 'The systemic approach to the encouragement of innovativeness through employee diversity management', *Kybernetes* 36(2), 144–156.

TUC. (2007a). *Closing the Gender Pay Gap. Report for the TUC Women's Conference 2008*. London: TUC.

TUC. (2007b). *Ten Years After: Black Workers in Employment 1997–2007*. London: TUC.

Wacjman, J. (2000). 'Feminism facing industrial relations in Britain', *British Journal of Industrial Relations*, 38(2), 183–201.

Walby, S. (1990). *Theorising Patriarchy*, Oxford: Blackwells.

Walsh, J. (2007). 'Equality and diversity in British workplaces: the 2004 Workplace Employment Relations Survey', *Industrial Relations Journal*, 38(4), 303–319.

Watson, S., Maxwell, G., and Farquharson, L. (2007), 'Line managers' views on adopting human resource roles: The case of Hilton (UK) hotels', *Employee Relations*, 29: 1, 30–49.

Webb, J. (1997). 'The politics of equal opportunity', *Gender, Work and Organization*, 4(3), 159–167.

Wentling, R. M., and Palma-Rivas, N. (2000). 'Current status of diversity initiatives in selected multinational corporations', *Human Resource Development Quarterly*, 11(1), 35–59.

Wentling, R. M. (2004). 'Factors that assist and barriers that hinder the success of diversity initiatives in multinational corporations', *Human Resource Development International*, 7(2), 165–180.

Wheeler, M. (2003). 'Managing diversity: developing a strategy for measuring organizational effectiveness', in M. Davidson and S. Fielden (eds.), *Individual Diversity and Psychology in Organizations*, Chichester: John Wiley, 57–78.

Whitfield, K., and Strauss, G., Eds. (1998). *Researching the world of work: Strategies and methods in studying industrial relations*, Ithaca, NY: Cornell University Press.

Whittaker, S., and Marchington, M. (2003). 'Devolving HR responsibility to the line: threat, opportunity or partnership?', *Employee Relations*, 36(3), 245–261.

Wilkinson, A., Redman, T., Snape, E., and Marchinton, M. (1998). *Managing with Total Quality Management*, London: Macmillan Business.

Williams, M. (2000). 'In defence of affirmative action: North American discourses for the European context?', in E. Appelt and M. Jarosch (eds.), *Combating Racial Discrimination*, Oxford: Berg, 61–79.

Wilson, E. (1997). 'A woman's place? A study of a National Health Service Trust', in C. Armistead and J. Kiely (eds.), *Effective Orgnizations: Looking to the Future*, London: Cassell, 246–249.

Wilson, E., and Iles, P. (1999). 'Managing diversity-an employment and service delivery challenge', *The International Journal of Public Service Management*, 12(1), 27–48.

Women and Work Commission (2006). Shaping a Fairer Future. London: Department of Trade and Industry.

Woodall, J., Edwards, C., and Welchman, R. (1997). 'Organizational restructuring and the achievement of an equal opportunity culture', *Gender, Work and Organization*, 4(1), 2–12.

Woodhams, C., and Danieli, A. (2000). 'Disability and diversity—a difference too far?', *Personnel Review*, 29(3), 402–416.

Wrench, J. (2001). 'Diversity management—the new way of combating ethnic discrimination in Europe?', in *Ethnic Minority Workers and the European Employment Strategy*, Brussels: European Trade Union Institute.

Wrench, J. (2004). 'Trade union responses to immigrants and ethnic inequality in Denmark and the UK: the context of consensus and conflict', *European Journal of Industrial Relations*, 10(1), 7–30.

Wrench, J. (2005a). 'Diversity management can be bad for you', *Race and Class*, 46(3), 73–84.

Wrench, J. (2005b). 'Diversity management and unions in Europe: a comparison between the UK and Denmark', in L. Thisted and S. Nour (eds.), *Moving the Frontiers of Diversity Management*, Copenhagen: Borsens Forlag.

Wrench, J. (2007, July 9–13). 'The development of diversity management in Europe: convergence or constraints?', paper to the First International Diversity Summer School, University of Vienna.

Yakura, E. (1996). 'EEO law and managing diversity', in E. Kossek and S. Lobel (eds.), *Managing Diversity: Human Resource Strategies for Transforming the Workplace*, Cambridge, MA: Oxford, Blackwell, 25–50.

Young, I. M. (1990). *Justice and the Politics of Difference*. Princeton: Princeton University Press.

Young, K. (1987). 'The space between words: local authorities and the concept of equal opportunities', in R. Jenkins and J. Solomos (eds.), *Racism and Equal Opportunity Policies in the 1980s*, Cambridge: Cambridge University Press, 252–269.

Young, K. (1992). 'Approaches to policy development in the field of equal opportunities', in P. Braham, A. Rattansi, and R. Skellington (eds.), *Racism and Antiracism: Inequalities, Opportunities and Policies*, London: Sage.

Zanoni, P., and Janssens, M. (2007). 'Minority employees engaging with (diversity) management: an analysis of control, agency, and micro-emancipation', *Journal of Management Studies*, 44(8), 1371–1397.

Zanoni, P., and Janssens, M. (2004). 'Deconstructing difference: the rhetoric of human resource managers' diversity discourses', *Organization Studies*, 25(1), 55–74.

About the Authors and Contributors

AUTHORS

Anne-marie Greene is Reader in Industrial Relations in the Industrial Relations and Organisational Behaviour Group at Warwick Business School, University of Warwick, UK. She is a committed trade union activist and has been a member of the national executive of the Universities and Colleges Union (UCU). Research focuses on stakeholder involvement in equality and diversity management, equality and diversity in trade unions and the implications of information and communications technologies for collective action. She is author of *Voices from the Shopfloor: Dramas of the Employment Relationship* (2001) and co-author of *The Dynamics of Managing Diversity: A Critical Approach* 2nd Edition (2005). Recent work has been published in journals such as *Work, Employment and Society, International Journal of Human Resource Management* and *Industrial Relations Journal.*

Gill Kirton is Reader in Employment Relations at the Centre for Research in Equality and Diversity, School of Business and Management, Queen Mary, University of London, UK. Her research interests include equality and diversity theory, policy and practice; gender, 'race' and trade unionism; and 'minority' employee experiences of employment and organizations. Her recent work is published in journals such as *Work, Employment and Society, Industrial Relations Journal* and *International Journal of HRM.* She is the co-author (with Anne-marie Greene) of a leading diversity textbook, *The Dynamics of Managing Diversity* (2005) (Elsevier), and (with Judith Glover) of *Women, Employment and Organizations* (2006) (Routledge). She is also the author of a research monograph, *The Making of Women Trade Unionists* (2006) (Ashgate).

CONTRIBUTORS

Deborah Dean, is Senior Lecturer in Industrial Relations and Personnel Management in the Industrial Relations and Organisational Behaviour

Group at Warwick Business School, University of Warwick, UK. She was previously Research Fellow in the Industrial Relations Research Unit, University of Warwick. Her research interests include gender and equality issues, legal and social regulation of employment, non-standard work and the entertainment industry. Recent work is published in journals and books including *Work, Employment and Society, Gender, Work and Organisation, Industrial Relations Journal* and the forthcoming third edition of *Industrial Relations: Theory and Practice*.

Chris Creegan is Deputy Director of the Qualitative Research Unit at the National Centre for Social Research. He leads research and evaluation programmes for government departments and other bodies on a wide range of issues in the areas of equality and social inclusion. Chris has written and researched extensively on equality and diversity issues. His work is published in journals and books including *Work, Employment and Society and Union Recognition: Organising and Bargaining Outcomes* (Gregor Gall, Routledge). He was previously Deputy Director of Equal Opportunities for the public service trade union Unison.

Index

A

'Accelerated Development Plan' 75
'accommodating differences' approach
    34–5
accountability 87; line-managers 144–5,
    153–6
active participants, employees as 166–7,
    183
activists 115, 121, 136
affirmative action (AA) 26–9
age 75, 99
ageing populations 48–9
Amicus 17, 55, 194
appraisal 161, 207
assimilationist ideal 5–7
Atherton, S. 168
Australia 29, 116
AUT 194
awareness of DM: employees 174–7;
    raising at ServiceCo 106, 113

B

Bach, S. 65, 66–7, 70, 76
Bainbridge, C. 8
Bajawa, A. 87, 96
banking sector 198–9, 201–2, 205,
    210
Bassett-Jones, N. 96, 105
Bellard, E. 93
benchmark targets 79, 215
Bergen, C.W. 149
Blackburn, A. 156
Blyton, P. 66
Bogg, J. 168
bonus distribution 75
Brandling, J. 167
Brewster, C. 96
Brief, A. 42
budget cuts 76

business case 28, 58, 90, 213, 226;
    continuity of generic business
    case 218–20; critique of 37–9;
    discourse on 9; diversity practi-
    tioners' perspectives 124, 131–2,
    136–7; and employees 41, 220;
    for equality 11–12, 36–7; key
    aspect of DM 35–7; Labour
    government and 31; line-manag-
    ers and 144–5, 159–60; public
    sector 71–2; rhetoric-reality gap
    in private sector 95–6; ServiceCo
    case study 101, 103–4, 112–13,
    114; three-pronged approach
    11–12, 114, 198, 208–9, 230;
    trade unions and 40, 191
Business, Enterprise and Regulatory
    Reform Department (BERR) 54
Business in the Community (BITC) 94
business opportunities, creating 36

C

Cabinet Office 35
Cameron, I. 95
campaign organizations 19, 25
campaigners, diversity 21, 118, 119,
    130–6
case studies 15–19; see also PSO (Public
    Sector Organization) case study,
    ServiceCo case study
champions, diversity 21, 118, 121–2,
    122–30, 207
Chartered Institute for Personnel and
    Development (CIPD) 49, 95–6,
    111, 154
chief executive officers (CEOs) 126; see
    also senior management
children, number of 49–50
Civil Rights Act 1964 (USA) 26, 50

civil service 86–9, 172–3; Gershon
    Review 76, 233; gradism 172–3;
    Lyons Review 76, 233; public
    sector reform programme 76;
    10-Point Plan 84, 85–6, 150–1;
    see also PSO (Public Sector
    Organization) case study
Civil Service Management Board 77
Clark, 164, 183
class action suit 95
Coca-Cola 38
Cockburn, C. 30, 115–16
collective bargaining 3, 39–40, 187–90;
    see also trade unions
Colling, T. 56, 187, 189
Collinson, D. 61
Commission for Racial Equality (CRE)
    54
composition of workforce 47–8; PSO
    73–4; ServiceCo 98–9
Comprehensive Spending Review 76
Confederation of British Industry (CBI)
    54–5
conflict 42; between DM paradigm and
    context 222–3; policy conflicts
    156–7
Connect 194
Conservative government 30, 65–6, 189
consultants, diversity 21, 118–19,
    130–6
consultation 52, 127–8
contexts 13, 22, 45–64, 160; changing
    perceptions and discourses of
    equality and diversity 57–8; con-
    flict between DM paradigm and
    222–3; economic context and
    labour market 46–9; industrial
    relations 55–7; key equality and
    diversity issues and challenges
    58–64; legal and policy context
    50–5; line-managers' role and
    139–41; private sector 90–3;
    public sector 65–70; social con-
    text 49–50; variation in 39
contract compliance 106, 155
coordinated market economies 92
Cornelius, N. 141
corporate social responsibility (CSR)
    117, 125, 132
Cox, T. 26
creativity, enhancing 36
Creegan, C. 69, 71, 160, 165, 168, 169
critical discourse analysis 9
critical theory perspective 9–10

cross-border/cross-culture managing 36
culture 167; organizational *see* organi-
    zational culture
culture change 33, 44, 113–14, 125,
    151, 213
Cunningham, R. 67, 69, 88
Currie, G. 142
customers, public sector 71
CWU 194

D
Danieli, A. 221
Danone 94
Dass, P. 13, 145, 146, 160
Deeg, R. 92
Deem, R. 169
Delivering a Diverse Civil Service: A
    10-Point Plan 84, 85–6, 150–1
Denmark 40–1, 96, 193
devolution to line-managers 43, 141–4,
    160; difficulties of 143–4
Dickens, L. 11–12, 36–7, 39–40, 56,
    71, 90, 95, 96, 113, 114, 158,
    160, 187, 189, 198, 208, 230
difference: broadening awareness of
    multiple dimensions of 113;
    perspectives on 4–8
disability equality duties (DED) 53
Disability Discrimination Act 1995 103
Disability Discrimination Act 2005 103
Disability Rights Commission (DRC)
    54
disabled people 79, 91; composition of
    PSO workforce 73–4
discourses 12–13; changing discourses
    on equality and diversity 57–8;
    diversity practitioners' perspec-
    tives on diversity discourse
    122–4, 130–2
discretion of line-managers 43, 144–5,
    159, 161–2, 179
discrimination 5, 59–60, 195; allega-
    tions against Wal-Mart 95
'dissolving differences' approach 34–5,
    165, 177
distributive justice 6
diversity: changing perceptions and
    discourses 57–8; diversity practi-
    tioners' perspectives on diversity
    discourse 122–4, 130–2; key
    issues and challenges 58–64;
    PSO context 73–6; in the public
    sector 70; ServiceCo context
    98–100

diversity campaigners 21, 118, 119,
    130–6
diversity champions 21, 118, 121–2,
    122–30, 207
diversity consultants 21, 118–19, 130–6
Diversity Impact Assessment 85–6, 161
diversity management (DM) 4–5, 22,
    24, 25–44, 211–31; challenges
    of 37–43; fault lines in 184–5;
    going global 29–32; key aspects
    of 32–7; operationalization of
    DM paradigm 221–4; perspec-
    tives on 8–10; in the private
    sector 93–7; prospects for
    advancing the equality agenda
    224–6; state of DM practice
    in the UK 211–21; towards an
    industrial relations perspective
    on 10–13; USA experience 26–9;
    value of a stakeholder approach
    226–30
diversity management industry 149
diversity objectives, in performance
    reviews 79–81
diversity practitioners 23, 115–37,
    214, 216, 227–8; categoriza-
    tion 21, 117–19; demographic
    characteristics 21, 118, 119–20;
    interviews with 19–22; personal
    qualities and work background
    120–2; perspectives on diver-
    sity discourse 122–4, 130–2;
    perspectives on policy and
    practice 124–6, 132–4; perspec-
    tives on stakeholder involvement
    126–30, 134–6; ServiceCo case
    study 100–1; views from inside
    organizations 122–30; views
    from outside organizations
    130–6
'Diversity Season' 79, 82
diversity specialists 21, 117–18,
    122–30, 132
diversity training *see* training
Dobbin, F. 28, 29
documentation 16
downsizing 76, 83–4, 85–6, 87–8

E

economic context 46–9
economic hardship 72, 76
efficacy of DM 165, 180–2
employee attitudes and behaviours
    research 167

employee diversity groups 82, 161–2,
    175, 178, 181–2, 199–200, 217
employee network groups 129
employee performance and motivation
    research 167
employees 10, 23, 164–85, 192, 226,
    229–30; benefits of DM 41–2;
    and the business case 41, 220;
    diversity practitioners' perspec-
    tives on employee involvement
    127–8, 136; experiences at the
    sticky floor 183–5; maximiz-
    ing potential of 36; perceptions
    of efficacy of DM 165, 180–2;
    perceptions of implementation
    of DM 165, 168, 177–80, 184;
    perceptions of organizational
    culture 165, 169–74; percep-
    tions of ownership of DM 165,
    174–7; PSO 82, 161–2, 172–4,
    174–5, 178–9, 180–2, 199–200,
    217, 220; ServiceCo 109–10,
    170–2, 175–6, 179–80, 182,
    217, 220
Employers Forum on Age 25
Employers Forum on Disability 25
Employment Act 2002 51
Employment Tribunal system 52–3, 59
equal employment opportunity (EEO)
    26–9
Equal Employment Opportunity Com-
    mission (EEOC) 27
equal opportunities (EO) 1, 30, 40, 57,
    115, 219, 223; continuity of
    practice with 212–15; differences
    from DM 32, 33; diversity prac-
    titioners' perspectives 122–4,
    125, 130–1; key dimensions to
    EO policies 165; line-managers
    142–3, 163; private sector 92;
    PSO case study 86; public sector
    68; ServiceCo case study 102–3;
    trade unions and 190, 191, 192,
    196–7
Equal Opportunities Commmission
    (EOC) 54, 63
equal outcomes 57
Equal Pay Act 1970 51
Equalities Review 54–5, 57–8, 59
equality 105; business case for 11–12,
    36–7; changing perceptions and
    discourses 57–8; DM paradigm
    and prospects for advancing
    the equality agenda 224–6; key

issues and challenges 58–64; PSO context 73–6; in the public sector 70; ServiceCo context 98–100; trade unions and bargaining for 39–40, 187–90
Equality and Diversity: The way ahead 52
equality duties 53, 69–70, 103
Equality and Human Rights Commission (EHRC) 54
equality officers 115–16
equality professionals 177
ethnicity *see* race and ethnicity
ethnographically-informed methods 14
Europe 31–2, 93
European Social Fund (ESF) project 1–2, 15–22; case studies 15–19; interviews with DM practitioners 19–22
European Union (EU) 52, 97; social agenda 189; Social Charter 51
events 16

F
family 49–50
fast-track leadership programme 107, 182
fault lines in DM 184–5
First Division Association (FDA) 18
Fleetwood, S. 97
flexibility 46–7, 63–4, 81, 97, 157, 178–9, 207
focus of policy 169
Foster, C. 96, 145, 156, 163, 166, 222
France 93
Friedman, R.A. 14
Fullerton, J. 31, 36, 141, 152, 213, 223
Future Foundation, The 177

G
gender 202; composition of PSO workforce 73–4; composition of ServiceCo workforce 98–9; discrimination by 95, 172; gendered humour 109–10; labour market segregation 60–1, 100; policy initiatives in PSO 78–9
gender equality duties (GED) 53
generic business case 218–20
Germany 93
Gershon Review 76, 233
GMB 194
goals 27
Gooch, L. 156

GPMU 194
gradism 172–3, 181
'Great Debate' 109
Greene, A.M. 193, 225, 230
Grice, S. 116
group-conscious policies 7
groups: employee diversity groups 82, 161–2, 175, 178, 181–2, 199–200, 217; social groups 6–8, 222; work groups and teams 42, 43, 155
Guest, D. 139–40
Gutek, B. 172

H
Hakim, C. 45
Hales, C. 138, 141
Harris, L. 96, 145, 156, 163, 166, 222
health and safety 179–80
Healy, G. 4
Heer, G. 168
Holden, L. 138–9, 158, 163, 228
holding pool 203
Holgate, J. 4
Hope-Hailey, V. 142, 144
Hoque, K. 94–5, 100, 142, 169–70
horizontal segregation 91
households 49–50
Howard, M. 57
human resource management (HRM) 117, 121, 132, 164–5, 189; institutional reinforcement of HR practices 148–9, 153–4; line-managers 139–41, 143; location of DM in HR departments 117, 125, 215; perspective 8–9
humour, gendered 109–10
Humphries, M. 116
Hunter, L. 186
Hutchinson, S. 140–1

I
Iles, P. 66, 72
impact assessments 125–6
implementation of DM: diversity practitioners' perspectives 124–6, 132–4; employee perceptions 165, 168, 177–80, 184; ServiceCo 110–12; trade union perceptions 205–8; vacuum of responsibility 223–4
implementation gap 177–80, 184
in-depth interviews 14

individuals, focus on 5–6, 35, 213, 226; diversity practitioners' perspectives 123–4; employees and 41; trade unions and 40, 191–2, 195–6
induction programme 150
industrial relations 2–4, 199–201; changing context of DM 55–7; perspective on DM 10–13; public sector 65–70
information dissemination 129–30
institutional racism 70
institutional reinforcement of HR practices 148–9, 153–4
institutions 3
intensification of work 46
international framework agreements 94
International Labour Organization (ILO) Declaration on Fundamental Principles and Rights at Work 188
intersectionality 54
interviews 14, 16, 19; with DM practitioners 19–22
IUF 94

J
Jackson, G. 92
Janssens, M. 13, 39, 160, 166
Jenkins, R. 6
Jewson, N. 165
Johnston, W. 28
joint regulation (social regulation) 11–12, 114, 198–201, 230–1; *see also* trade unions
Jones, D. 9, 10, 41, 193

K
Kalev, A. 96, 97
Kandola, B. 36, 141, 152, 213, 223
Kandola, R. 31
Kelly, E. 28, 29
Kelly, J. 12
Kersley, B. 142
Kirton, G. 37, 38, 116, 160, 193, 225, 230
Kochan, T. 42
Konrad, A. 8, 9, 140, 149, 160
Kossek, E. 8, 9, 42
Kulik, C. 8

L
Labour government 31, 66–7, 187, 189

labour market: changing 46–9; segregation 48, 60–1, 91, 158–9; taking advantage of diversity in 36
Larsen, H.H. 96
Lawrence, E. 116, 119, 168–9
Lawrence, S. 70
leadership fast-track programme 107, 182
legal compliance 33, 89, 212, 214–15; line-managers 144–5, 151–2; ServiceCo case study 101, 103–4, 107, 110–11
legal context 50–5
legal regulation 11–12, 91–2, 114, 230
length of service 99
liberal market economies 92
liberal reformer 105
Liff, S. 33–5, 95, 145, 165
line-managers 23, 42–3, 96, 138–63, 213; accountability for DM 144–5, 153–6; devolution of responsibility for DM to 43, 141–4, 160; discretion 43, 144–5, 159, 161–2, 179; diversity practitioners' perspectives 126–7, 135–6, 137; employees and 166, 168–9, 178–9; involvement in DM 152–3, 162–3; perceived as obstacle to success of DM 216–17, 228; PSO case study 87–8, 146–7, 150–1, 153, 154–5, 156–8, 161–2, 162, 220; public sector 69; relative place of DM within priorities of 156–62; role in a context of DM 139–41; ServiceCo case study 107–8, 110–12, 114, 147–8, 151–2, 153, 155–6, 158–9, 162, 220; trade unions' perception of role 205–8; training 148–52, 157; understandings of DM 96–7, 114, 144–8
Linnehan, F. 140, 149, 160
Litvin, D. 9, 116, 131
long hours culture 81, 125, 157
Lorbiecki, A. 116, 119
Lyons Review 76, 233

M
MacPherson Inquiry 70
mainstreaming of DM 125, 133, 134, 168–9
'malestream' industrial relations 2–4
Marchington, M. 156

marginalization 5, 188
Mason, D. 165
Maxwell, G. 107, 143
McConville, T. 138–9, 158, 163, 228
McDaniel, D.C. 14
McGovern, P. 141, 148–9, 153–4,
    160–1
Mistral, W. 167
Modernising Government agenda 44,
    66–7, 68–9, 77
monitoring 133, 135–6, 207–8; private
    sector 92–3, 98–100
Morely, L. 169
MSF 189
multi-dimensional model for flexible
    working 63

N

national trade union equality officers
    194, 194–5, 198, 205, 209
natural wastage 48
neo-liberalism 37
Netherlands, the 96, 143
New Public Management (NPM) 44,
    66–9
New Zealand 116, 193
NHS 189
non-management employees *see*
    employees
non-standard work 46
Noon, M. 45, 94–5, 100, 142, 169–70,
    174
Northcraft, G. 156
Northern Ireland 106

O

observation 14, 16
occupational segregation 48, 60–1, 91,
    158–9
Ogbonna, E. 45
'old boys' network 202
operationalization of DM paradigm
    221–4
Opportunity Now (formerly Opportu-
    nity 2000) 19, 25, 68, 143, 150,
    154, 157, 219
oppression 5
Organization for Economic Co-operation
    and Development (OECD) 49
organizational culture 42, 95; culture
    change 33, 44, 113–14, 125,
    151, 213; employee percep-
    tions 165, 169–74; trade union
    perceptions 201–5

organizational performance 39, 167
outsourcing 171
ownership of DM 215–18; employee
    perceptions 165, 174–7; line-
    manager perceptions 152–3

P

Packer, A. 28
Palma-Rivas, N. 153
Parker, B. 13, 145, 146, 160
part-time work 61, 74–5, 91
passive recipients, employees as 166–7,
    183
pay gaps 62, 91, 201
peer trainers 105
performance management 153–4;
    appraisal 161, 207; diversity
    objectives 79–81
Point, S. 31, 93
policy context 50–5
policy development: line-managers'
    involvement in 152–3; ServiceCo
    100–2
policy-making, within a 'difference'
    paradigm 72–3
policy reviews 83
politics of difference 5–7
positive action 29–30, 134, 182, 192,
    213
positive discrimination 182
post-colonial theory 9–10
post-structuralist perspective 9–10
Prasad, A. 9
Prasad, P. 5
primary care trusts 103–4
Pringle, J. 8, 229
private-public partnerships 67
private sector 15, 19, 22–3, 90–114;
    case study *see* ServiceCo case
    study; diversity management
    93–7; UK context 90–3
procedural justice 160–1
Proctor, S. 142
*Promoting Equality, Valuing Diversity: A
    Strategy for the Civil Service* 85
promotions 75, 180–1, 182, 202
Prospect 18
PSO (Public Sector Organization) case
    study 15, 18–19, 23, 73–89,
    213–14, 222, 227, 229–30; civil
    service and PSO policy context
    76; employees 82, 161–2, 172–4,
    174–5, 178–9, 180–2, 199–200,
    217, 220; equality and diversity

context 73–6; future directions
83–6; key policy initiatives 78–81;
line-managers 87–8, 146–7,
150–1, 153, 154–5, 156–8,
161–2, 162, 220; policy reviews
83; restructuring 76, 83–4, 85–6,
87–8, 157–8, 162; stakeholder
involvement 81–2, 88–9; strategy
and policy 77–8; trade unions
18, 81–2, 194, 196–7, 199–200,
202–4, 205–8, 209–10
psychological perspective 8
Public and Commercial Services Union
(PCS) 18, 194, 196
public-private partnerships 67
public sector 15, 22–3, 44, 65–89;
case study *see* PSO (Public Sector Organization) case study;
context and industrial relations
65–70; emergence of DM 70–3;
equality and diversity 70; legal
context 53; reform 66–7
Purcell, J. 140–1
Purcell, K. 46–7

Q
qualitative research methods 4
quality of policy delivery 168
quantitative research methods 4
quotas 27

R
race equality duties (RED) 53
race and ethnicity 47–8, 202–4; availability of monitoring data 75–6;
composition of PSO workforce
73–4; composition of ServiceCo
workforce 98–9; family and
employment 50; labour market segregation 48, 60–1, 100;
policy initiatives in the PSO case
study 78–9
Race for Opportunity 19, 25, 68
Race Relations Act 1976 30
Rasmussen, E. 96
rationalization 61, 76
Reagan, R. 27
recruitment 99–100, 182
reproduction 61
research methods 13–15
resistance 61
responsibility for DM: devolution to
line-managers 43, 141–4, 160;
vacuum 223–4

restructuring 76, 83–4, 85–6, 87–8,
157–8, 162
reverse discrimination 27
rhetoric-reality gap 37–9, 94–7, 183–5
RMT 17
Rüling, C.-C. 93

S
'same treatment' principle 145
sameness approach 5–7
Scandinavia 193
Schneider, S. 156
segregation, labour market 48, 60–1,
91, 158–9
Select Committee on Economic Affairs
48–9
senior management 41–2, 79, 213,
215–16, 227; diversity practitioners' perspectives 126, 134–5;
DM as top-down managerial
activity 40, 192; training at
ServiceCo 151, 152
service sector 46
ServiceCo case study 15, 16–18, 23,
97–114, 213–14, 222, 229–30;
DM policy 102–5; employ-
ees 109–10, 170–2, 175–6,
179–80, 182, 217, 220; equality
and diversity context 98–100;
generic business case 219,
220; impetus for and development of DM 100–2; key policy
initiatives 105–7; line-managers
107–8, 110–12, 114, 147–8,
151–2, 153, 155–6, 158–9, 162,
220; policy implementation
110–12; stakeholder involvement 107–10; trade unions 17,
107, 108–9, 194, 197–8, 200–1,
204–5, 208
sex discrimination 95, 172
Sex Discrimination Act 1975 30
sex-role spillover 172
shareholder capitalism 90
short-termism 156–8
Sinclair, A. 116
Singh, V. 31, 93
Single Equality Act 54
social context 49–50
social groups 6–8, 222
social identity 6
social issues 188
social justice 101, 104, 136–7
social partnership 97

social processes 3
social regulation *see* joint regulation, trade unions
Spearitt, K. 29
'special contribution' perspective 34–5
specialists, diversity 21, 117–18, 122–30, 132
Stablein, R. 9, 10
staff forums 109, 151
staff surveys 129
stakeholder perspective 2, 10–13, 14–15, 24, 211–31; continuity of limited stakeholder involvement 215–18; diversity practitioners' perspectives on stakeholder involvement 126–30, 134–6; private sector and stakeholder involvement 95, 96–7; PSO case study 81–2, 88–9; ServiceCo case study 107–10; understanding of DM 95, 96–7; value of this approach 226–30
stand-alone diversity units 117
sticky floor 11; employee experiences at 183–5
Stonewall 25
Storey, J. 142, 144
sub-contractor compliance 106, 155
Sweden 193
systemic transformation of the organization 33, 72

T
target benchmarks 79, 215
teams 42, 43, 155
Teicher, J. 29
TGWU 17
Thatcher government 30, 66
three-pronged approach 11–12, 114, 198, 208–9, 230
'Three Rs' 61
Tibballs, S. 57
tokenism 183
top-down, managerial activity 40, 192
trade unions 11, 17, 21, 23–4, 186–210, 217, 226; bargaining for equality 39–40, 187–90; challenges of DM 39–41; Conservative government reform 66; context of DM 55–7; diversity practitioners' perspectives 128–9, 136; engagement with critiques of DM 194–8; experiences of DM in the UK 194–208;

input into DM development and implementation 209–10; joint regulation of equality and diversity 198–201; membership rates 55–6, 186–7; perceptions of DM implementation 205–8; perceptions of organizational culture 201–5; private sector 93; problems with DM 40, 190–2; PSO case study 18, 194, 196–7, 199–200, 202–4, 205–8, 209–10; public sector 67–8; responses to DM 192–4; ServiceCo case study 17, 107, 108–9, 194, 197–8, 200–1, 204–5, 208
Trades Union Congress (TUC) 189, 194; Black Workers Conference 193
training 217; diversity and equality training at ServiceCo 105–6, 110–11; diversity practitioners' perspectives 127, 133–4; line-managers 148–52, 157; PSO 84–5; trade unions 204–5, 208
Turnbull, P. 66

U
understanding of DM: employees 174–7; line-managers 96–7, 114, 144–8
undervaluation 62
UNIFI 194, 198–9, 201–2, 205, 210
Unison 17, 194
United States of America (USA) 42, 45, 50–1, 97, 116, 143, 149; Civil Rights Act 1964 26, 50; definition of DM 32; EEO, AA and DM 26–9; trade unions 55–6, 186–7; *Workforce 2000* report 28, 47
'utilizing differences' approach 34–5

V
'valuing differences' approach 34–5, 165, 177
vertical segregation 91

W
Wal-Mart 38, 95
Watson, S. 140
Wentling, R.M. 102, 146, 153
Whittaker, S. 156
Wilson, E. 66, 72
Winchester, D. 65, 66–7, 70, 76

women: employment participation rates 47; *see also* gender
Woodall, J. 87, 96
Woodhams, C. 221
work groups and teams 42, 43, 155
work-life balance 63–4; PSO policy initiatives 81
workforce audits 125
Workforce 2000 report 28, 47
Workplace Employment Relations Surveys (WERS) 92, 209

workplace trade union representatives 194, 196–8, 199–201, 202–5, 205–8, 209
Wrench, J. 193

Y
Young, I.M. 5–7, 10
Young, K. 169, 172

Z
Zanoni, P. 13, 39, 160, 166

For Product Safety Concerns and Information please contact our EU
representative GPSR@taylorandfrancis.com
Taylor & Francis Verlag GmbH, Kaufingerstraße 24, 80331 München, Germany

www.ingramcontent.com/pod-product-compliance
Ingram Content Group UK Ltd.
Pitfield, Milton Keynes, MK11 3LW, UK
UKHW021607240425
457818UK00018B/422

* 9 7 8 1 1 3 8 8 7 9 4 3 0 *